ROUND BRITAIN WINDSURF

The Royal National Lifeboat Institution will receive 20 per cent
of the royalties from this book

ROUND BRITAIN WINDSURF

1800 miles on a 12ft board

Tim Batstone

Photography by Chris Darwin

DAVID & CHARLES
Newton Abbot   London   North Pomfret (Vt)

British Library Cataloguing in Publication Data

Batstone, Tim
  Round Britain windsurf : 1800 miles on a 12ft
  board.
  1. Windsurfing – Great Britain   2. Great Britain
  – Description and travel
  I. Title
  914.1'04858   DA632

  ISBN 0-7153-8753-7

Phototypeset by Typesetters (Birmingham) Ltd,
Smethwick, West Midlands
and printed in Great Britain
by Butler & Tanner Ltd, Frome
for David & Charles (Publishers) Limited
Brunel House   Newton Abbot   Devon

Published in the United States of America
by David & Charles Inc
North Pomfret   Vermont 05053   USA

CONTENTS

All photographs in this book are the work of Chris Darwin except: *The Standard* (page 53 above), Tim Batstone (page 72 below), Liz Bindon (page 161 above right), Alice Lumsden (page 161 above left), *Southend Evening Echo* (page 192 above), *Yellow Advertiser Newspaper Group* (page 192 below).

TO HENRY

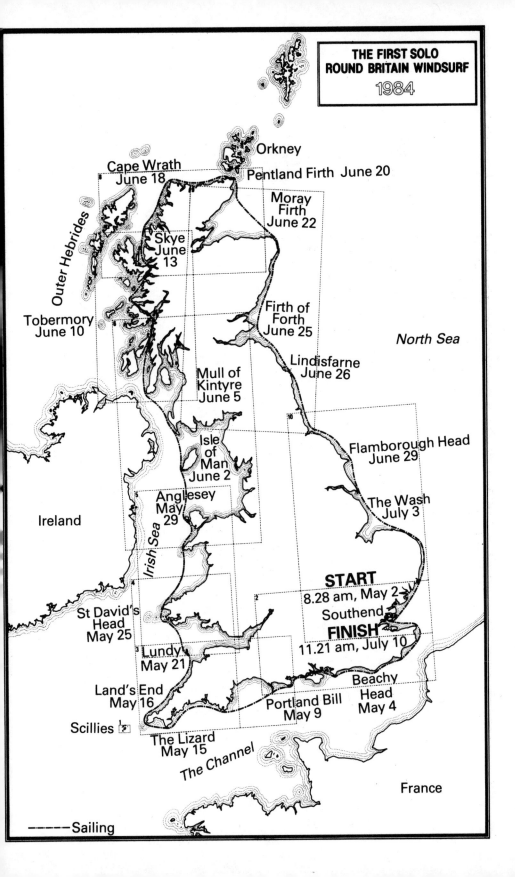

THE FIRST SOLO
ROUND BRITAIN WINDSURF
1984

Orkney

Cape Wrath
June 18

Pentland Firth June 20

Moray
Firth
June 22

Skye
June
13

Outer Hebrides

Firth of
Forth
June 25

North Sea

Tobermory
June 10

Lindisfarne
June 26

Mull of
Kintyre
June 5

Flamborough Head
June 29

Isle
of
Man
June 2

The Wash
July 3

Anglesey
May
29

Ireland

Irish Sea

START
8.28 am, May 2

St David's
Head
May 25

Southend
FINISH
11.21 am, July 10

Lundy
May 21

Land's End
May 16

Beachy
Head
May 4

Portland Bill
May 9

Scillies

The Lizard
May 15

The Channel

France

——— Sailing

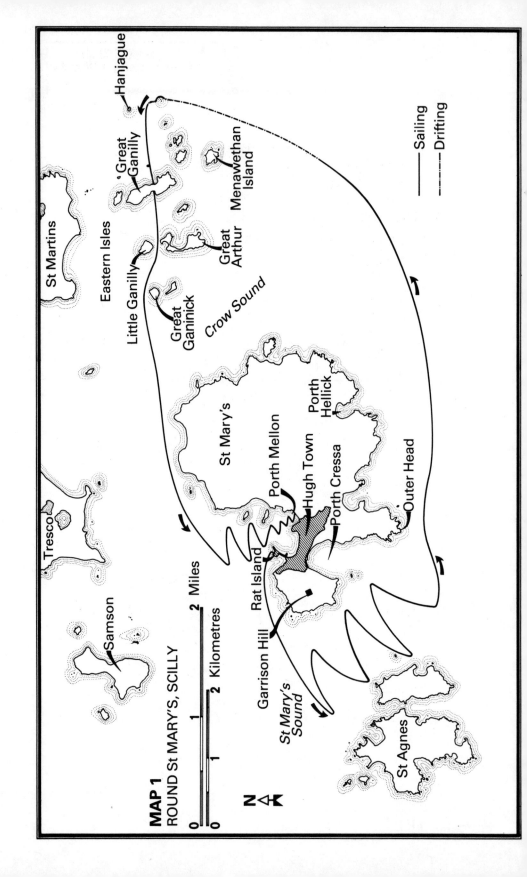

MAP 1
ROUND St MARY'S, SCILLY

N

Samson

Tresco

St Martins

Eastern Isles

Hanjague

Great Ganilly

Little Ganilly

Great Ganinick

Menawethan Island

Great Arthur

Crow Sound

St Mary's

Porth Mellon

Hugh Town

Porth Hellick

Garrison Hill

Rat Island

Porth Cressa

Outer Head

St Mary's Sound

St Agnes

——— Sailing
------- Drifting

0   1   2 Miles

0   1   2 Kilometres

1 ROUND ST MARY'S, ISLES OF SCILLY

A huge, angry sea was running. The wind ripped the shred of sail from my grasp again and again. Following a series of catapult falls I caught the edge of the board on my way into the sea, smashing my left shoulder. The next time the wind felled me I flung myself away to avoid another bruising and lost my board, having to swim frantically after it as it surfed away from me. Catching up at last I scrambled onto the deck and lay there coughing up sea water, my heart pounding with the effort. I was exhausted and could no longer cope with the conditions; the wind and sea had taken over completely. I had strayed from the route round St Mary's and, unable to sail, was lost in the open Atlantic.

I had no flares or other means of attracting attention and no one could possibly know where I was. In such poor visibility not even a lifeboat would have any hope of finding me. The wind howled ever stronger and monstrous waves threatened to tip me off my board. I straddled the board tightly, then, bobbing up and down in the confused sea, felt wretchedly sick and vomited over the side. Shivering from the cold, which now penetrated my whole body, I pulled my numb feet out of the sea as if this could warm them.

A miserable blob on the wild ocean, I thought about my chances of survival. Any ideas of drifting out the storm and eventually being picked up were soon dispelled – in the cold, with no food or fresh water, I could not hope to last long. I searched the sky for some indication of an improvement in the weather but found none: galleon clouds cruised overhead, the horizon darkening as I watched. I swore at the wind and then, half crying with exasperation, punched the water and cursed my own stupidity. Having ignored a clear warning not to set out in the first place, I had only myself to blame and, thinking of Keith's warm sail loft, I longed to be back on dry land. Looking round at these watery prison walls, I wondered whether I would ever escape, ever see anyone again.

I had arrived in the Scilly Isles two days earlier, catching the helicopter from Penzance. It had been blowing a near gale that day and the sea beneath us was a mass of white-capped breakers. As we flew over Land's End I had been preoccupied with how to pass this awesome stretch of coast on my way round Britain next year, little realising that within two days I would be out and lost in the same expanse of ocean.

The Scilly archipelago, lying some twenty-five miles south-west of Land's End, is an ideal venue for windsurfing. My intention was to spend a week there practising as much as possible before returning to London for a winter of working to raise money for the Round Britain Windsurf project. I was staying with Neville Wakefield, a long-time windsurfing friend, and his parents, Humphrey and Helena, who run the pottery on St Mary's, the main island in Scilly.

It was late September and the day of my sail round St Mary's was typical for early autumn – fresh and blustery. After lunch, Neville and I went down to the harbour to see Keith Buchanan, a friend of Neville's, who, as well as being a chandler, is the local windsurfing instructor. Out of the biting wind in his cosy sail loft we discussed our plans for the afternoon, and that was when I first had the idea of sailing round St Mary's. Keith had done the trip once before but began to counsel me against it. 'I sailed round on a perfect summer's day. On a day like this the sea could be very rough on the south side of the island. Anyway, are you sure you're experienced enough to handle it?'

In my heart I suppose I knew that I was not good enough but refused to admit it. If I could not cope with a fifteen-mile jaunt like this how could I even contemplate windsurfing two thousand miles round Britain next summer. In my mind, Keith's words became a challenge rather than a warning and reinforced my own impatience.

With the smallest sail, $3.4m^2$, on the mast I launched from a rocky outcrop known as Rat Island just west of Hugh Town harbour. Neville's last words were that I ought to consider just going round the corner to Porth Cressa (about three miles) and beaching the board there. I nodded at him but knew that by now it was all the way or bust – I was committed.

Leaving the safety of the harbour area I headed west towards St Mary's Sound. The wind was gusty in the lee of Garrison Hill and I had to jig around a little before picking up the breeze proper. Then I was away and going at a fine lick towards the open water of the sound. It was good to be out on the sea and I felt fresh and confident.

Ahead of me I could see white horses and, once beyond the Barrel of Butter headland, a blast of wind hit me. The power took me aback for a moment, but immediately the adrenalin began to flow into my veins and, instead of turning back, I leant out to take the strain, flying forward across the sound. The swell was eight feet or more, rolling rhythmically down the mile-wide channel between St Mary's and St Agnes islands.

Points of sailing:

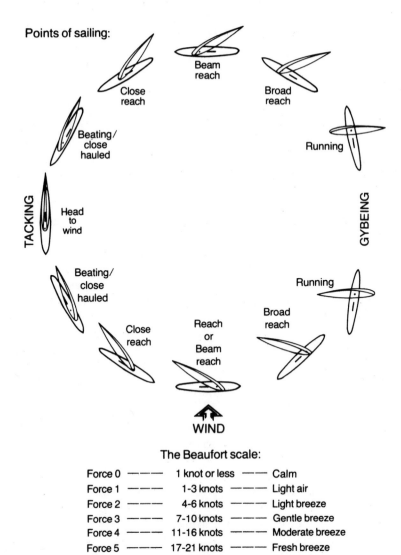

TACKING

Close reach

Beam reach

Broad reach

Beating/ close hauled

Running

GYBEING

Head to wind

Beating/ close hauled

Running

Close reach

Reach or Beam reach

Broad reach

WIND

The Beaufort scale:

Force 0	1 knot or less	Calm
Force 1	1-3 knots	Light air
Force 2	4-6 knots	Light breeze
Force 3	7-10 knots	Gentle breeze
Force 4	11-16 knots	Moderate breeze
Force 5	17-21 knots	Fresh breeze
Force 6	22-27 knots	Strong breeze
Force 7	28-33 knots	Near gale
Force 8	34-40 knots	Gale
Force 9	41-47 knots	Strong gale

The wind was blowing from dead ahead, making the passage up the sound a hard beat. I held each tack for as long as possible because the sea knocked me in each time I went about. Uphauling was impossible, again because of the waves, and to begin sailing I had to waterstart. Out of necessity, for the first time I mastered this manoeuvre which involves lying in the water and pushing up the sail so that it catches the wind and shoehorns you out the of sea. In this strenuous manner of waterstarting and falling in, falling in and waterstarting, I proceeded south. On about the fifth tack I was opposite the little cove of Porth Cressa where Neville had suggested I stop. From my vantage point about two hundred yards from the mouth, all that could be seen was spray from waves crashing onto the reefs in the middle of the cove. The beach was not even visible. It would be impossible to land there; my alternatives were to turn back now or carry on. I was flushed with excitement at being out in the stiff conditions and so far mastering them. Ahead lay a dangerous ten-mile circuit round St Mary's, but I disregarded this, thinking that my success so far proved me capable of the whole trip.

As I pressed on, the wind freshened and my speed increased in proportion. For the last half-mile down the sound, the board took off momentarily on each wave, lifting several feet off the sea. With my feet locked into the footstraps I worked hard to keep control. Never had I sailed in such extreme conditions on the open sea. 'This is just the practice I've been looking for,' I said to myself, thoroughly exhilarated. On the next tack I was able to point directly past Outer Head, the southernmost point of the island. My speed picked up even more as I bore away onto a reach and I careered up and down through the waves, eating up the miles for twenty minutes or more. While I was sailing along the granite southern shore of the island it dawned on me that if my equipment failed now I would be blown onto the rocks in a matter of minutes. I tried not to let this thought disturb me unduly and pointed further off the coast so that I was a good half-mile clear. But the edge had been taken off my enjoyment and from this point on things gradually got out of hand.

As the wind rose my spirits fell. I was going too fast for comfort. The board began to spin sideways for no reason and throw me off. Several times big waves simply piled up and buffeted me in. The sea had changed from an exciting companion to an aggressive adversary.

At the same time I was having problems with my sense of direction. I could not decide when it was safe to change course and head north up the east coast of St Mary's. I had to be sure of being well past the island itself, otherwise I risked being smashed to pieces on the rocks. I could only glimpse St Mary's when perched briefly on the top of a wave and even then the outline was blurred. Stopping, I sat on my board – standing was out of the question by now – and strained my eyes. There was what looked like a channel off to port. Was it Crow Sound or could it be the cove of Porth Hellick? Before setting out I had memorised the route from an Ordnance Survey map of the Scillies. But at this moment my memory and geography failed. Hard though it was to believe afterwards, I could not recall the scale of Porth Hellick cove and dared not risk this channel being a dead end. I decided to carry on further, just to make sure.

For the next half-hour the conditions deteriorated and I grew more and more worried, but by the time I realised that I had definitely missed the turning it was too late to do anything. I could no longer control my board.

I drifted at the whim of the elements for what seemed like hours before hearing the drone of an engine faintly above the roar of the wind. It sounded like a helicopter and for a brief moment my misery lifted. I scanned the grey sky above me urgently, but once again my hopes sagged. The helicopter was no more than a black shape in the distance and moving rapidly away. It must be the Scillies passenger helicopter – perhaps even the one I had flown in – but it was not looking for me. Even if it were, how could it possibly find me? I knew what I would look like from that helicopter: a speck among acres of mountainous sea. The whirr of the helicopter blended into the background of the storm.

Suddenly, above the smoking waves, I saw land close in front. It was an inhospitable sight – three or four fists of granite poking out of the sea in a black clump. The rocks did at least give me a clue as to my whereabouts. I remembered that some islands called the Eastern Isles lay to the north-east of St Mary's and took these rocks for them. That meant I must have strayed a long way off course into the Menawethan tide-race, a strong tidal pull that sweeps past the Scillies to Land's End. Only this pile of rocks and the Seven Stones lighthouse lay between me and Cornwall. The rocks loomed ever closer and I realised to my horror that I was going to be washed onto them. The enormous rise and fall of the sea meant that, poised up on the crest of each wave, it seemed that I hung right over the storm-battered outcrop. The dark glistening pile of boulders exploded into white fury on the impact of each wave and, hypnotised with fear, I clung to my board watching as I was sucked nearer.

I told myself that it was crazy to die like this; I had to put up a fight and sprang out of the trance in a panic of self-preservation. I considered abandoning the rig and paddling my board, but did not think that would get me out of the way fast enough. I had given up trying to sail over an hour ago but the only chance was to try again. I tried waterstarting, but no sooner had I lurched out of the water than I was catapulted over the other side of the board. On the third try, by which time I could all but feel the rough kiss of the granite ahead, I lingered in the waterstart position, keeping the sail well down over the sea so that the wind could not catch it. To my surprise and relief, the board moved forward slowly but effectively under this unlikely propulsion. Spluttering from the waves that washed continually over my head, I hung on for a good twenty yards before a swingeing gust of wind prised its way under the sail and tore it from my straining fingers. I tried the same manoeuvre again, and again it worked. Moments later I was lying thankfully on my board as I swept unharmed past the rocks.

Dusk was approaching but this little victory had given me some confidence. If only I could work out a sensible direction to travel in, I could surely inch my way home by this new-found technique. I drifted on for a further half-mile or so and was then in sight of a larger slice of granite off to the left. Peering into the gloom I saw with a surge of hope what looked like a yellowish strip against the rock. It could be a beach. Summoning my remaining energy, I began to work my way towards it. As I got closer it became more and more distinct – it was definitely a beach. My spirits lifted – I was saved if I could just get there. I prayed that nothing would go wrong and crabbed erratically towards this haven. At last I was in the lee of some outlying rocks and able to substitute normal sailing for the immersion method. Coasting the last few hundred yards to the beach I was ecstatic with relief.

In the shallows a flock of birds flew up to greet me and I flopped into the water, swimming my board the last few feet till I could touch the sand. I let out a whoop of delight as soon as I felt solid ground beneath my feet. Dragging the board a little way up the beach I fell forward and hugged the ground – never had the earth felt so wonderful. A hundred yards away the sea still raged, but it had been cheated of a victim – it could not touch me any more. I could stay on this mean little island forever if necessary!

Once I had rested for a few minutes, thoughts began to crowd my head. It would soon be dark and my friends on St Mary's would be worried and probably out looking for me. I set out to reconnoitre the island – perhaps it was inhabited, perhaps even had a telephone. A three-minute run to the highest point dispelled these ideas. It was a tiny island and, bar a few birds, totally uninhabited. From my vantage point I could see some of the rest of the archipelago of Scilly. I was on the easternmost of the Eastern Isles, Great Ganilly, as I later found out. To the west I could see St Mary's in the distance across Crow Sound and to the north St Martin's with Tresco beyond. I knew now what had to be done.

Sprinting back down to the beach, I carried the board and sail two hundred yards across the narrow neck of the island and put it in the water on the western side of Great Ganilly. Then I set off to pilot my craft through the other Eastern Isles – Great Arthur, Little Ganilly and Little Gannick – and across Crow Sound to St Mary's. The islands protected me from the worst of the weather and the going was easy compared with before. Crossing Crow Sound, I met the full force of the elements again and had to throw all my remaining energies into the effort to stay on top of the board. But I knew where I was going now and the fear of returning to my former abject state lent wings to my flight and I eventually reached the shelter of the island of St Mary's itself.

I sailed down St Mary's Road and one by one familiar landmarks came into view: the Garrison, Newman House and finally Hugh Town harbour. It was dark and I was cold and wet but I was home except for a twenty-minute beat into the beach at Porth Mellon. I was so happy that I began to sing, my nightmare forgotten.

The board ground on to Porth Mellon beach at 7.45pm, nearly five hours after the voyage had begun. A short fifteen-mile jaunt had turned into a harrowing struggle for survival. Walking home up the hill I bumped into two figures in orange oilskins carrying torches – Helena Wakefield and a local lifeboatman. They had been all over the island looking for me and were so glad to find me in one piece that tears of relief pricked my eyes.

Neville and Humphrey were still out searching and returned half an hour later. They had been checking the coves on the south side of the island, half expecting to find a battered body. Apologising profusely, I explained to them what had gone wrong. But explanations could not remove my guilt. I knew what a fool I had been to set out in the first place. Humphrey was reassuringly philosophical and insisted on opening a bottle of champagne to celebrate my safe return.

This experience did not frighten me into giving up the round Britain journey, but it made me rethink my cavalier attitude. If there was to be any chance of success, safety must be a primary concern, and back-up was needed the whole way. There was also a lot more work to be done on the windsurfing front!

2 TARIFA TO TOWER BRIDGE

My first brush with windsurfing was on holiday in France in 1978. After a week of wrestling with the wind, losing my balance and falling in, I lost interest. Three years later it was rekindled with a vengeance.

This time I was at the beach in Spain on an afternoon windy enough to blow a sand-spattered ice-cream right out of your hand and for an hour or more I watched a display of such exciting windsurfing that it quite took my breath away. Out among the crashing breakers a young local danced back and forth, leaping off the tops of the waves on his way out to sea and returning with the surf to execute masterful pirouette turns on the wave faces. I was hooked; it looked such fun – one day I just had to be that good.

The next summer, 1982, I bought a board of my own and headed off to Europe to learn to windsurf. Our first port of call was Biarritz, the French Atlantic resort noted for its big surf, where I was over-eager to get amongst the action. Within moments of taking to the water I was back on the beach somewhat cut and bruised, with a broken mast and boom to boot. I spent the rest of that holiday on the gentler Mediterranean and after a few weeks' practice was thoroughly enjoying myself on the water – able to sail up and down quite effectively.

On the way home while crossing the Pyrenees and gazing out of the car window, I hit upon the idea to windsurf round Britain. 'I'd have to be mad,' was my first reaction, but over the rest of the journey I could not put the thought out of my mind. The more I thought, the more the idea caught my imagination; a unique challenge which would surely be a great adventure. Since my earliest schooldays I had always enjoyed outdoor sports – especially if endurance was demanded – and this project seemed like the ultimate marathon. I was entering my last year at university with nothing definite planned for the future. Windsurfing round Britain could be the perfect springboard away from a conventional career.

And so it was that with hardly a backward glance and with little more than a month's windsurfing experience behind me I began to plan a sea journey right round Britain's coast. For the rest of the vacation I worked as a reporter on a local Oxford paper, snatching time to windsurf in windy lunch hours and travelling to the coast at weekends. I mastered the harness, a device which takes weight off the arms, thereby conserving strength and enabling one to stay out on the water much longer. As my technique improved so my enjoyment of windsurfing increased and my commitment to the trip.

One weekend in late September remains a particularly strong memory. I was returning to Oxford from the Westcountry and had just joined the M5 when I saw from the surrounding trees that a healthy breeze had sprung up. I turned off at the exit to Weston-super-Mare and, sure enough, there was a firm wind blowing in from the sea. Within minutes I was splashing wetsuit-clad into the muddy, foam-flecked waters of the Bristol Channel. It was a wonderful evening's sail. For two hours I frolicked in the sea, the board surging beneath me, the wind beating freshly against my face and the whole ocean seemingly my oyster. When I returned to the beach the tide had gone out, leaving a half-mile trudge through knee-deep mud to the car, but not even this could disturb my contentment. After such effortless sailing, I thought, what could be better than several thousand miles of the same round Britain!

Over the next few months I plotted and planned sporadically while working for Finals. A firm pencil line appeared on my wall map of Britain, cutting a swashbuckling line across great stretches of water such as the Irish Sea and the Moray Firth and forging through notorious tide-races like Portland Bill and the Pentland Firth. With a length of string I estimated the circuit at close on two thousand miles and, after further rough calculations, concluded that it would take me about two months to sail around Britain. Assuming summer to bring the kindest weather, the original plan was to set off in July 1983 as soon as I left Oxford. But as I delved deeper into the project it dawned on me that this was not the casual operation I had first imagined. Departure was thus postponed until summer 1984, giving me a year to get ready.

I began the year in haphazard fashion, knowing there was a great deal to do but uncertain how to set about doing it. My first-hand knowledge of boats and the sea was negligible – my most significant sailing memory being a painful trip in a Mirror dinghy up the narrow, willow-lined River Cherwell. I needed professional advice. Unfortunately, all the yachtsmen and seadogs I managed to contact thought, in common with my family and friends, that I was mad even to contemplate such a scheme. Their advice, consequently, tended to be counter-productive!

One morning I got an unexpected lead from *The Times*. I came across a reference to someone who had supposedly windsurfed around Britain two years previously. With my heart in my mouth I followed up the story and found to my relief that he had been part of an eight-man relay – not a solo effort. Furthermore, the team had passed through the Caledonian Canal, so missing out the northern coast of Scotland. Fright over, this was a highly promising lead and I duly tracked down Ken Way, one of the team, in Nottingham.

He greeted me with a mixture of amusement and astonishment. 'Are you really serious? Frankly, I doubt if it's possible for one man – certainly not within an acceptable time . . . you'll mostly find the winds either too light for comfortable sailing or too strong to sail at all . . . the physical strain is severe – several of our team have still got back pain two years on.' But I had grown too attached to the project to be put off now, even by such a weighty warning. Ken's words exaggerated my determination to prove the voyage possible, and he nonetheless gave me some valuable advice.

The possibility of being plagued by light winds worried me and I realised that outsize sails would be vital to the armoury of equipment. As a further measure I decided, using old weather reports from *The Times* as a meteorological data base, to set off a couple of months earlier – at the beginning of May – in the hope of stronger winds. At the same time I determined to work hard at my windsurfing and fitness so that I could be sure of coping with the testing conditions.

In early July after my Finals I made an approach to the RNLI. I had decided that the proposed circumnavigation of Britain lent itself so well to raising money for charity that it would be criminal to waste the opportunity. Because of the growing number of windsurf rescues the lifeboats were making every year, the Royal National Lifeboat Institution seemed a natural choice of charity.

At first I was nervous about contacting their Head Office, thinking they would scoff at my idea and probably dismiss it out of hand as too risky. Then I met Marie Rydin, a highly enthusiastic local branch secretary. During a long evening in The Six Bells, Kidlington, we convinced ourselves that the trip was the best thing ever to have happened to the RNLI, so how could they refuse my offer?!

Head Office reaction to my proposal was cautious and it was several months before I could arrange a meeting. But waiting did not dampen my enthusiasm and eventually the RNLI agreed to go along with the scheme, on condition that safety was the number one priority. The director himself commented, 'Windsurfing is obviously here to stay and we might as well learn to live with it.' From then on I worked closely with the RNLI on the fund-raising, and their involvement was an invaluable support to the whole project, even if not completely whole-hearted in the odd case. On one visit to HQ in Poole I was taken aside by the naval commander in charge of

The Sailboard:

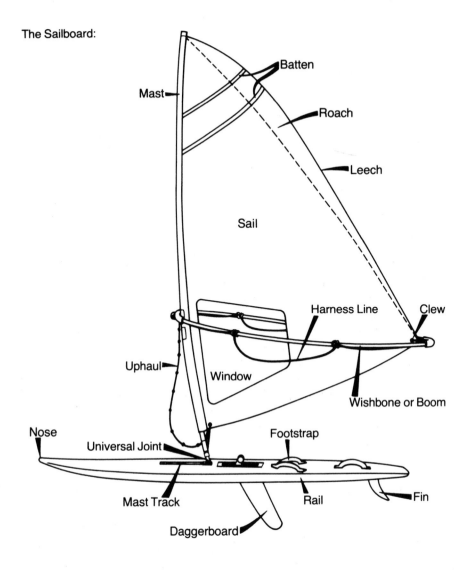

operations and informed, with some reproach, of his nightmares about my sailing through the Pentland Firth; 'the whole scheme is a damn-fool idea,' he finished. On occasions I had to agree.

Throughout the summer I concentrated on windsurfing. Completing an instructor's course in the Lake District gave me some proof of my competence and this was followed by a breakthrough on the sponsorship front. I managed to talk my way into some free equipment (a Klepper board and three sails) from the London Windsurfing Centre. Delighted with this tangible evidence that I was at last going somewhere, I went to Tarifa for two months. This town on the southernmost tip of Spain is a European Mecca for windsurfing with strong breezes – the Levante from the Sahara or the Poniente from the Atlantic – almost guaranteed. I camped on the beach and practised hard, learning some of the skills that I should perhaps have made sure of before ever conceiving the ocean marathon: gybing, or turning downwind, running before the wind and, in particular, waterstarting. I was pleased with my progress and returned to England in high spirits. Shortly afterwards my visit to the Scilly Isles taught me the difference between full-blooded British weather and Spanish summer sea breezes.

Returning from the Scillies in October I was left with seven months to departure and it seemed like a horribly short time. I still had to find a support boat and a team of about six people. Most essential, I had to find a sponsor to pay for it all.

I put together a package consisting of a budget of £20,000, an outline of my plans, a map of my proposed route and a curriculum vitae – carefully worded to make me sound as intrepid as possible. With a letter enthusing about 'media coverage' and the value of my sail as a billboard, I sent the package out to various companies which I hoped would be interested. £20,000 was a great deal of money and the companies I approached had reputations for heavy advertising spending and usually a history of sport sponsorship. I was sure one of them would jump at the idea but the response from this first wave of fifty letters was not encouraging. About half turned me down flat on the grounds of 'committed budgets' or 'not their area'; the others did not even reply.

Then I had a lucky break – a centre-page article in *The Standard* which was the first press coverage for the project. One or two companies pricked up their ears. The first approach was from Walt Disney UK which sounded promising but, though I had a subsequent meeting with the marketing director, we never progressed beyond a proposal to kit me out as Mickey Mouse for the launch. Lee Cooper Jeans then telephoned and said they had been 'just waiting for some idiot to try and windsurf round Britain'. Clad in my best denims and trying to look as macho and hardwearing as possible, I went to a meeting where they appeared so enthusiastic that I came away in a mood of celebration. Evidently their keenness did not last, as a week or so later they lost interest and, every time I telephoned, my contact was either 'out of the office', 'in a meeting', or if I was really lucky 'on the other line'. I gave up and went back to the grind, sending out another forty letters to likely companies.

For nine weeks I worked almost full-time on the sponsorship drive. My day began at 7.30 with an hour's training in Cannon's Gymnasium in the City – weights, running, swimming – followed by a morning of telephoning and an afternoon of letters, more calls

Rigs:

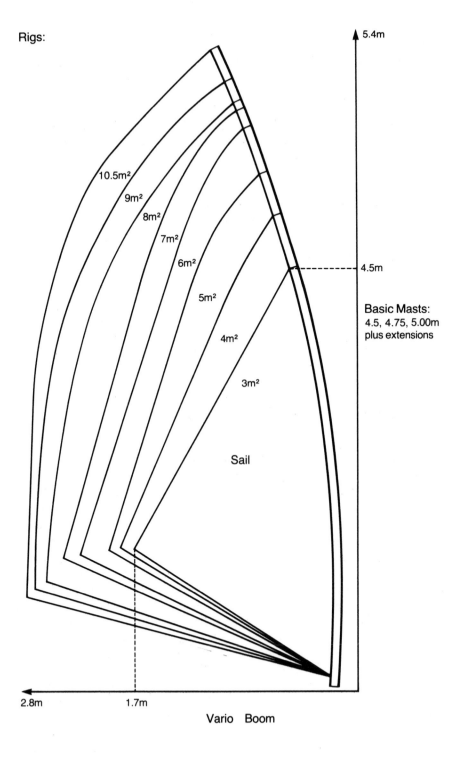

5.4m

10.5m²
9m²
8m²
7m²
6m²
5m²
4m²
3m²

Sail

4.5m

Basic Masts:
4.5, 4.75, 5.00m
plus extensions

2.8m   1.7m

Vario   Boom

and perhaps a meeting. The tiny flat I shared with a friend doubled as my office and gradually became overrun with paperwork and other expedition trappings.

My success was strictly limited. To add to my Klepper boards I was given sails, plus £2,000, by Neil Pryde Sails in Hong Kong, and obtained some food vouchers from Sainsbury's. But as to a major backer, I had drawn blanks with most of my hopes: Coca-Cola, Kellogg's, Old Spice, Mars, Beefeater, Debenhams and Cadbury's. I had tried the big sponsorship agencies, IMG and West Nally, who were not interested, and had even broken a resolution by approaching cigarette companies – also in vain. I was running out of companies and with little over four months to go began to despair of ever finding this vital commodity – a sponsor.

During this period I found time to windsurf at weekends. As it was winter, the conditions were mostly cold and windy and by mid-December several unpleasant experiences had reinforced the Scilly Isles disaster: trying to sail the fifteen miles round Hayling Island, off the Hampshire coast, I was reduced to clinging to a buoy in the middle of a tide-torn channel before fighting back to land; on another occasion in Portland harbour I nearly drowned, trapped under my sail by force 8 gusts; on a third occasion my board was dumped on the beach by large waves at Deal, Kent, and cheese-wired in half by one of the harness lines. Still more disconcerting, Robin Brockway, a friend of mine attempting to race the Channel ferry across to France, nearly perished mid-way when his rescue boat got into difficulties in a gale. And I had yet to find a rescue boat!

Despite the setbacks, one positive feature emerged from this time – a team started to assemble. Out of the blue I was telephoned by Chris Darwin, a twenty-two-year-old photography and psychology graduate from Oxford Polytechnic, who announced that he, too, wanted to windsurf round Britain. Chris had an entrepreneurial history (not only having Charles Darwin as a great-great-grandfather, but having started a bicycle rickshaw service in London in the summer); when we met later, however, Chris decided that I was nearer to the goal than he (albeit marginally) and that he would join me instead as photographer. The second recruit was a cook. My girlfriend, Alice, whom I met at Oxford, had long been debating whether or not to come along and now, on an 'if you can't beat 'em, join 'em' impulse, decided to handle all the food. So we were three.

In the week before Christmas 1983 three more favoured companies, Carlsberg, Black & White Whisky and Long Life, turned down my proposal. I was down to the last one or two and pinned my diminishing hopes on a champagne company, Charles Heidsieck. A friend, Henry Farrer, who sells their champagne in the Midlands, having heard me interviewed on the radio, had recommended the scheme to them. They were reviewing the idea and making a decision after Christmas at a meeting in Paris. I expected the by now familiar 'no' and went for long runs to try and take my mind off the grisly prospect of starting all over again in the New Year.

On 30 December, Henry came to lunch bringing the incredible news that Charles Heidsieck were going to back the project lock, stock and barrel, putting up as much as £30,000. I was almost speechless with joy and relief. At last the event was really going to happen. Charles Heidsieck have a successful history of sailing sponsorship though with large boats until now, their yacht *Charles Heidsieck III* having come a close second in the 1981/82 Whitbread Round-the-world Race. With their weight behind us we could now press ahead with confidence.

On New Year's night I was still celebrating and, standing on a windy hill with champagne glass in hand, I shouted the absurdly rash challenge to the elements: 'Nothing can stop me now!' The very next day proved me quite wrong.

On 2 January 1984 Chris, Alice and I drove down to the Hampshire coast for our first sea trial of a possible support boat. The boat in question was a powerful twin-engined Princess 41 cabin cruiser and fulfilled two of our criteria, being both fast and capable of sleeping at least six. However, we needed to see it in action.

The owner and skipper greeted us at Beaulieu marina with the news that gales were forecast. It seemed that the weather would be ideal for our purposes and as we motored into the Solent a blustery wind was rising. All went smoothly for a couple of hours while I sped back and forth across the Solent with the Princess bumping along behind. By the time I came to a stop the wind had freshened to about force 7, the seas were steep and the visibility very poor. Our problems began.

A line was thrown and with some difficulty I attached it to the board which was then hauled in. The Princess made several unsuccessful passes with a rope for me and I felt more and more vulnerable wallowing in the waves. I waited expectantly as they bore down once again, engines revving. With seconds to spare, it dawned on me that I was out of their view and the boat was coming straight at me. I scrabbled against the hull, praying that I would not feel the propellers chomping into my legs. Once the noise had passed I opened my eyes and swore after the receding boat. Twenty tense minutes later and after much gesticulation a safe pick-up was negotiated well to the stern of the boat. The unfortunate incident somewhat altered my views on the suitability of motor boats!

Three days later we were at Earl's Court for the London Boat

Show and our first contact with the public. We were joined by David Barraclough, a friend who ran the local delicatessen in Oxford. We had long chatted about the scheme over the taramasalata and baked beans and now, having sold his shop, David started to work on our public relations and fund-raising.

At the show we had a corner of a stand thanks to *On Board* magazine and from there, with a special printed brochure, we launched our sponsorship drive for the RNLI. The reaction from the public was mixed. Some were evidently cynical: one chap said it was 'like trying to walk to the moon' and another that 'people like you bring the sport into disrepute and ruin the enjoyment for everyone!' But on the whole the response was encouraging. One fellow, Alan Griffin, came down from the Midlands on the first day of the show, took a sponsorship form and came back a week later with £200. By the end of ten days we had taken promises of over £4,500 for the RNLI if I made it round the coast. It seemed that I had to now!

The show seemed the ideal place for finding a support boat, but ten days of enquiries came to nothing. I wanted a boat capable of fifteen knots (anticipating at least these speeds on my board) but, as recent experience had shown, fast motor boats generally have planing hulls, not designed for rough seas. I looked at everything from pilot boats to motor catamarans and even naval patrol boats but there was always a stumbling block. In early February I was about to travel to Hull to look for an out-of-work trawler when I got a phone call from Rodney Hill. He had learnt of the project from HM Coastguard (whom I told of my need for a support boat) and he offered us a choice of three boats for charter: a 115ft ferry, a 46ft ketch and a 40ft pilot boat, as well as his paid services as skipper.

Eagerly, Alice and I set off to meet Rodney at his home in West Mersea, Essex. We found a stocky fifty-year-old with grey hair and a weather-beaten face. Conversation over lunch removed any doubts about his qualifications for the job: he had years of sailing experience including Atlantic crossings and was credited with saving a number of lives in the tragic 1979 Fastnet Race. He also turned out to be Honorary Secretary of the West Mersea lifeboat! The only question that remained was the choice of boat. In the end I was persuaded against the pilot boat on the grounds of comfort and practicality and settled for the 46ft ketch, *Morningtown*. Compared to the pilot boat with its one gas ring, portaloo and cold tap, *Morningtown* was luxurious as well as being more seaworthy and cheaper to run. The drawback was that she could only make ten knots, but we compensated for this by deciding on a fast, 16ft inflatable as close support. I considered an inflatable of some description vital as a stepping stone between mother ship and board.

Morningtown

Oyster 46

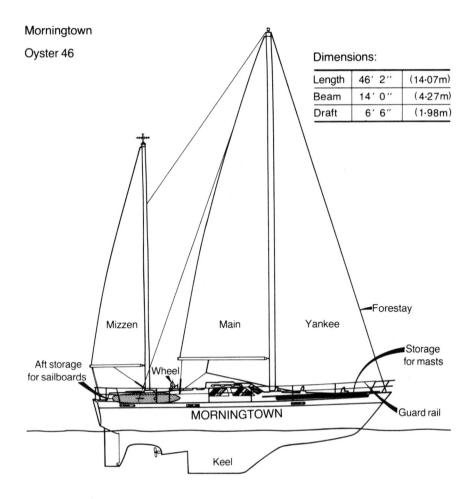

Dimensions:

Length	46′ 2″	(14·07m)
Beam	14′ 0″	(4·27m)
Draft	6′ 6″	(1·98m)

Forestay

Mizzen

Main

Yankee

Aft storage
for sailboards

Wheel

Storage
for masts

MORNINGTOWN

Guard rail

Keel

Morningtown section:

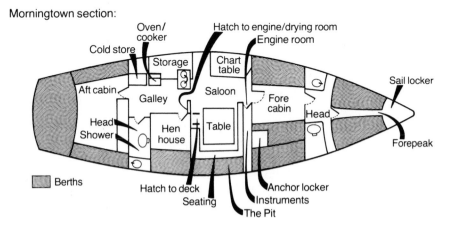

Oven/
cooker

Hatch to engine/drying room

Engine room

Cold store

Storage

Chart
table

Aft cabin

Galley

Saloon

Fore
cabin

Sail locker

Head
Shower

Hen
house

Table

Head

Head

Berths

Hatch to deck

Seating

Anchor locker

Instruments

The Pit

Forepeak

It was a great step forward to have a support boat and an experienced sailor on hand for advice and soon West Mersea became a focus for expedition preparations. We grew used to the Mersea mud, the marsh birds and the oyster beds, going down on weekends for preliminary forays out to sea to test radios and other equipment. We commissioned a 5m inflatable dinghy to be built by Blagg Boats and found someone to drive it – Charlie Williamson, a cousin of mine who was a part-time chef and waterski instructor.

With two months to go I was training at my hardest. Progress was supervised by John McFadyen of Southampton University, the Olympic yachting trainer, and he tested me every two months on a series of ten special exercises. We concentrated on the vital areas – stomach, back and arms – and by the end of six months my overall performance had improved by a third, which was a great boost to my confidence. I was still training at Cannon's Gym and used to feel closest to the impending trip when swimming lengths in the darkened pool – imagining myself in a hostile sea, I would grit my teeth and swim for the shore!

Arguably more important than my fitness, my windsurfing was at last developing. I had joined a club just outside London, Queen Mary Reservoir, and, with the days growing longer, was able to spend the morning working and still make it onto the water for an afternoon's sail. For a number of weeks I averaged three or four outings on the reservoir and supplemented this with trips on weekends to the coast. The aggression of the wind at sea still made me shiver with anticipation but the basics were knitting together.

Inevitably, my ideas on boards came at the last minute. With seven weeks to go I decided that a special long, thin board would give me vital extra speed. Since such a style was outside the range of Kleppers provided by the London Windsurfing Centre, two days later I was down in Cornwall in the converted chapel of Limited Edition near Redruth, watching my new idea being shaped from a foam 'blank' before glassing. 'Do you think it'll shift?' I asked rather nervously of Tris Cokes, the custom builder who had agreed to make the board. 'This'll be the fastest thing on the water,' he replied grinning, teeth matching the hair prematurely white from polystyrene dust.

Tris did not realise what he was letting himself in for. The four-metre-long fibreglass slither was finished three weeks later, but on its maiden sail I put a nasty dent in the flank and discovered (I'm not making excuses!) that, though fast in a straight line, the board was difficult to sail on other points: the tail was too narrow and insubstantial, the footstraps too far back, and I kept tripping over the compass, daggerboard and mast-track fittings that protruded from the deck. Tris kindly promised to have the Mark II, this time made out of strong epoxy instead of polyester, ready for the launch.

A board of character needed a name and we decided to call it *Pytheas* after the Greek from Marseilles, who made the first circumnavigation of Britain in 328BC. Pytheas sailed in search of tin and amber and was reputedly the first man to navigate by the stars and to understand the tides. He evidently encountered a storm of monumental proportions on his way across the top of Scotland as he reported waves 80 cubits (120ft) high in the Pentland Firth. Pytheas put to sea in a galley powered by fifty oarsmen and I hoped he would approve of his journey being attempted two thousand years later by a craft as basic as a sailboard!

As the start approached, media attention increased and we did everything we could to encourage this. My experiences on one particular day in early April taught me not always to expect great results. I had driven across London for an 'important' press conference at the Wind & Surf Show at Alexandra Palace to be followed by an interview with BBC's *60 Minutes*. Stuck in traffic for an hour I arrived a little late and hurried to the press room expecting to find it packed with 'important' journalists. There was a solitary reporter, who turned out to be from the *Bournemouth Herald*, quietly drinking his way through the free booze. The press co-ordinator carried it off bravely: 'Have you met everyone, Tim?' she trilled.

There was still the TV crew and, while waiting for them to arrive, I decided to acclimatise myself to the conditions on the duck pond at the back of the Palace, and launched the board. In the fickle breeze I was gradually driven onto a clump of bamboo in the middle of the pond and was still fighting to extricate myself half an hour later when David appeared and shouted the news that the BBC had changed their plans and were not coming after all!

In the first week of April we seemed to be faced with a conspiracy of problems: our Blagg inflatable ran into problems, all our waterproof radios were stolen from the hall of my flat, and David found himself unable to cope with all the appeal and publicity work. Replacement radios were subsequently found after an appeal on Capital Radio and a corresponding article in *The Standard* entitled 'Lifeboat marathon sunk!'. We put an advertisement in *The Times* and recruited Mark Hubbard, a twenty-three-year-old unemployed history graduate, to help David out. The Blagg problem was the most intractable.

Mariner, who were supplying and fitting the engines, had trouble mounting them and the managing director finally washed his hands of the whole project. To cut a long story short, we were left with no engines, no boat and no time to look for an alternative. Deep gloom descended on the camp for several days until Woody Blagg (of Blagg

Boats) proffered his demonstration boat as a substitute. The only apparent difference being that his boat had a single 85hp engine as opposed to the twin 40s we hoped to use, the offer was accepted eagerly. It was only later that we discovered what huge quantities of fuel had to be carried because the 85hp engine was so greedy and used four times as much petrol as a single 40hp (our other 40 was to be in reserve). This weight was eventually to scupper the Blagg.

The nucleus of the team – Alice, Chris, Charlie and myself – all moved down to Mersea for the last few weeks before departure, occupying the flat above the Yacht Club with a fine view over the little harbour. There were a 101 things to do. Rodney generously allowed us the use of his workshop and his garden to store all our equipment but relations started to become strained: he mistrusted the Blagg on sight and was having second thoughts about the wisdom of putting to sea with us at all.

Shortage of people was the next major problem to rear its head. Rodney had hired an out-of-work fisherman, Graham Knott, to skipper *Morningtown* in the event of his leaving us during the trip to attend to his marine engineering business. On the day of our first outing (which coincided with a day's filming for *Blue Peter*) Graham did not show up. Rodney had tried to track him down and described, in an imitated Mersea drawl, the conversation he had had with Graham's mother. 'Mrs Knott, Graham definitely knew about it – I told him to put the date in his diary,' said Rodney. 'But you see Mr Hill, Graham hasn't got a diary . . .!' Graham never did show up and we were left with two crew short as a navigator was also needed for Charlie in the Blagg.

With just a week to go we found someone. Rodney and I were involved in a minor row on the Yacht Club lawn, which might easily have developed into a major one had there not been the sudden boom of a maroon, an explosive flare signalling a call-out for the lifeboat. Rodney, as Honorary Secretary, was needed in the lifeboat house and he disappeared at a run in that direction, vaulting with surprising ease a low hedge on his way. The call-out turned out to be a false alarm, but the Blagg was roped into an offshore search all the same. When we got back to the shore a bespectacled young man with straight black hair stepped up, introducing himself as Haydn Cook. He had heard that we were looking for crew and wanted to volunteer. It turned out that he was married and both he and his wife had 'retired' to Mersea having made their fortunes in property. Haydn was still only thirty and I guess in the mood for an adventure.

All we lacked now was a skipper. Two days later Rodney came up trumps. He hired Paul Harrison, a local aged only twenty-four, who had great experience of sailing and, to my delight, also of windsurfing. His father was a boatbuilder and Paul had got his sea legs at the age of eight and been racing ever since. After leaving Cambridge University two years earlier he had sailed the Atlantic twice – on the second trip their yacht was dismasted and they covered the last thousand miles with a jury-rigged mast. Paul was an incredibly lucky find and played a key role throughout. His New Zealand girlfriend, Liz, also joined us as a valuable crew member.

The team now complete and looking strong for the first time, we entered the final few days of preparation. Everyone was busy: Rodney, Paul and Liz working on *Morningtown*; Haydn and Charlie on the Blagg; Alice in the local Cash & Carry counting corned beef, packet soups and biscuits; Chris assembling his cameras and miles of film; Mark fitting out a Bedford motor-home as land support vehicle, with trailer for petrol, radio and signwriting; David and all at Charles Heidsieck working on the press launch; and I was assembling my equipment – boards (four altogether), sails (ranging from 3 to 9m^2 in size), wetsuits, drysuits, harnesses, flares, charts, and so on.

In black comedy fashion the Blagg somehow continued to provide much of the excitement. One afternoon its hulls filled with water and the extra weight broke its trailer, so that it had to be anchored out for the night. The next morning we discovered that the specialised radio aerial had been pinched from the boat. Later that day Chris, Charlie and I were working on the boat when a man passed carrying an identical aerial. Charlie was as tactful as possible when asking where he had got it but obviously offended the man as he went away muttering and shaking his head. Chris was upset by the incident and eager to make amends for the mistake, but he must have had some sort of memory black-out since he approached the next stranger who came along with words of apology, 'Charlie didn't mean it. He wasn't really calling you a thief.' The man stared at him dumbfounded while Charlie and I, stifling our laughter, hid behind the boat!

The forty-eight hours before departure were a nightmare. The tensions that had been brewing between Rodney and the nucleus team erupted sporadically into heated confrontations and the atmosphere was appalling. It struck me as a sad way to start an expedition, but at last the moment came for us to sail to London.

It was Sunday 29 April and the day began with a surprise: a 16ft 'D' Class inflatable had arrived from RNLI headquarters in Poole. Rodney had organised the boat as a back-up for the Blagg – we had reason to be grateful for this later – and it was loaded onto *Morningtown* with the mountain of other gear. We were in a hurry to leave in order to cross the shallow 'spitway' channel, but there was

one last hitch. The wind was blowing at about force 6 from the
north-east and there was a nasty sea. Rodney refused to tow the
Blagg behind *Morningtown* and ordered that it travel round by land.
This was impossible as the truck, our only transport, had already left
Mersea for St Katherine's Dock. Paul, in what was to become
characteristic fashion, intervened diplomatically, and it was agreed
that the Blagg would follow us under its own steam for the first few
miles 'on approval'.

Finally we were away. The Blagg coped with the rough conditions
and was permitted to continue, Chris and Charlie seeming to relish,
in the first excitement of the voyage, the crashing and continual
soakings. I looked back at Mersea now receding into the horizon.
What a relief it was to be actually on the sea – to be away from the
telephones and the petty problems and hassles. In all the activity of
the last two weeks I had been unable to windsurf and had almost
forgotten what I had originally set out to do. I looked at the frothy
sea, felt the keen wind on my face, and remembered. I felt ready now.

The forty miles to Tower Bridge took us about seven hours. I
enjoyed the time on the yacht, taking a hand at the wheel and feeling
the slow pull of the sails against the weight of the boat – so different
from what I would be doing. Cutting across The Swatchways,
Morningtown's great keel struck the Whittaker Sands with a heavy
thump. The momentum allowed her to grind on for a few necessary
yards and then she slithered back into deep water. No damage done!

The brief excitement seemed to break the ice and the tensions of
the last hours began to evaporate. We sheltered in the cockpit, drank
coffee and ate pineapple chunks. Everyone was in better spirits. I
thought about the team in those first moments at sea: Rodney,
delighted to be at sea in his beloved boat, adjusting instruments and
studying charts; Paul, strong and confident, beginning to teach the
others about sailing; Haydn, intelligent, full of ideas and a willing
worker; Alice, excited to be at sea for the first time, already with the
galley under control; Liz, devoted to Paul, a competent sailor; and
the two in the Blagg – Charlie, tough and reliable, would not let us
down, Chris, high-spirited, the joker of the team.

As if reinforcing this last thought, the Blagg roared past and made
us laugh as Chris sat nonchalantly in a deck chair they had found
floating in the sea. 'The pensioner put up a hell of a fight!' he
shouted. We were approaching Southend and, the wind having
slackened, we took the Blagg in tow for the twenty-mile trip up the
river to Tower Bridge.

As darkness fell the banks of the Thames lit up with a myriad
welcoming lights. We arrived at Tower Pier at 1am or so and
moored for the night – our first on board. It was comforting to bed

down in the solid, friendly ship and exciting to wake up with the
berth gently rocking and the sound of the Thames lapping past.
Sunshine was streaming through the portholes. The press launch was
to take place the next morning and the Southend start the following
day. Originally, I had intended to sail down the Thames, but then
had discovered that craft under sail are forbidden to pass through the
barrier, so Tower Bridge was made the public start and Southend the
official beginning of the voyage.

I hoped the weather would hold. For the last ten days it had been
sunny with excellent north-easterly winds, ideal for the passage
down the Channel to Land's End, but now a depression was drifting
over from the Atlantic. This would eventually bring rain and, if it
deepened enough, might change the winds to westerly.

At midday we were able to motor through the lock into the yacht
basin of St Katherine's Dock and spent the afternoon tying up loose
ends: stowing boards, masts and booms on *Morningtown*, doing odd
jobs, buying a last few items at the chandler's. I had a couple of
interviews on the dockside with Keith Michelmore for *Waterlines* and
Garth Crookes for Capital Radio.

That evening I found myself gazing into a glass of beer and
thinking. Ahead lay the focus, the main event, a two-thousand-mile
windsurf, a leap into the unknown. Behind me was more than a year
of thinking, planning and hard work. I would always be glad to have
got this far even if something happened which prevented me from
getting much further.

I re-read a good luck card from Martin, the friend whose flat I
shared in London. In it were quoted a few lines from *Markings* by Dag
Hammarskjold: 'Never let success hide its emptiness from you,
achievement its nothingness, toil its desolation. And so keep alive the
incentive to push on further, that pain in the soul that drives us beyond
ourselves. Whither. That I don't know. That I don't ask to know.'

The next morning – Tuesday 1 May, the day of the launch – Alice,
Mark and I made a foray into the City to buy travellers cheques; we
thought this was the simplest way to pay for petrol for the Blagg and
truck. It was still sunny. *Morningtown* was a hive of activity –
everyone evidently keyed up. While rigging my sail I thought about
windsurfing off from Tower Bridge in front of a crowd of people
and felt a wave of nerves. By the time I had laid out my few items of
clothing – neoprene drysuit, rubber shoes and harness jacket – it was
a full-blooded attack of butterflies. My mind was a jumble of
thoughts – hopes of success and niggling doubts.

The launch was held at the nearby Warehouse restaurant and I
walked in to a welcome from Oliver Moore, the young director of
Charles Heidsieck assigned to the project. The party was in full

swing, hundreds of people had turned up. Not feeling hungry, I gulped down a couple of glasses of champagne. My memory of any conversation is hazy, but time flashed by and the moment came for the formal farewell. Jean Marc Heidsieck, over from France for the occasion, took the stage and declared how delighted Champagne Charles Heidsieck were to be sponsoring the event. He was followed by Vice Admiral Sir Peter Compston of the RNLI, who said a few words on their behalf, and Norris McWhirter, editor of the *Guinness Book of Records*, who read out a message from Prince Charles:

> I have recently heard of your delightfully rash proposal to windsurf your way around the British Isles. Having experienced the difficulties of trying to remain upright on a board for even a short distance, I am full of admiration for such a venture, coupled as it is with raising much needed funds for the RNLI. This brings my best wishes for a successful, and safe, surf.

With 'delightfully rash' echoing in my head, I muttered my thanks to everyone, assured them that I would 'give it a go' and headed out to change. Zipped up tight in my drysuit, I pushed slowly through the throng to the edge of the pontoon where *Pytheas* was waiting, soon to be officially named by Norris McWhirter. A cork popped and champagne cascaded over the board and then, inevitably, over me. There were no more formalities now – it was 2.40pm (almost perfect timing) and *Pytheas* was swung into the water.

Stepping onto the board I was very nervous but, as I began to pull the sail up and bent to the physical task of the windsurfing, my nerves left me. Within seconds I realised that something was horribly wrong. In one tack across the river from the pontoon I had made no ground downstream towards the sea; the tide was still flowing hard up the river. As I watched, bottles, rubbish and bits of driftwood streamed past me towards Tower Bridge. By my calculations the tide should have been slack, or just starting to ebb, but something had obviously gone wrong somewhere as there were still three knots against me. To make matters worse, the wind was gusty and blowing up-river, which made sailing down-river extremely difficult. To cap it all, I was on *Pytheas* Mark I (the Mark II having not yet arrived) which was unstable and fickle in these conditions.

I tacked at the far side of the river and tried desperately to make some headway. No sooner had I got going than I came under the lee of the north bank of the river and lost all way. I stood helplessly on my board, trying not to think about the crowd I was now drifting away from. One tack later and I was actually floating under the bridge on up towards HMS *Belfast*. It was too embarrassing for words. Not in my wildest dreams had I imagined a beginning like this. A gust of wind caught the back of the sail, flicked me in and left me choking on brown river water which did not mix well with champagne. I spluttered back onto the board to find a TV launch hovering nearby, its deck lined with amused faces. It was not until much later that I was able to see the funny side myself.

Before long the Blagg came alongside and Charlie and Chris offered to pick me up. 'Stay away! I've got to see this through,' I yelled, determined to sail down this stretch of the river even if I had to float back up to Oxford in the process. I sneaked back under the arch of the bridge and, before the tide carried me away again, snatched a glance at the pontoon: the crowd was sensibly returning to the party. I wondered what they thought of my chances round Britain now. A bookmaker would surely have given very long odds.

The tide, backed up by an easterly wind, turned half an hour late and, finally, I was able to make headway down-river. On reaching the bridge an American shouted down to me: 'You're doing a tremendous job!' I could not tell whether he was referring to the whole trip or to my getting off first base – either way it did not matter. I went under the bridge for what I reflected was the fourth time in less than an hour, taking care to avoid smashing my board on the stone supports. At last I was away and sailing. In a freshening wind I had a couple of healthy bursts and was round the corner towards Wapping. Easy! Once out of sight of Tower Bridge I could stop. The Blagg picked me up, I unrigged the sail and clambered onto *Morningtown*. I must have worn an expression combining relief with sheepishness, but everyone was sympathetic and seemed impressed that I had stuck it out. I was given a cup of steaming tea from the galley which removed the Thames-taste from my mouth and, warm and dry again, I was able to relax.

The incident made me more determined than ever to get things right on the trip itself, starting for real in just over twelve hours. I kicked myself for misjudging the tide and realised to my dismay that I had made the same mistake with the timing of the Southend launch. A yachting magazine was subsequently to comment: 'I hope Mr Batstone will learn to read a tide-table before he reaches some of the tide-torn headlands on his journey!'

Our passage down-river was uneventful. We were to anchor for the night in Ray Gut, near Leigh-on-Sea to the west of Southend, but we touched mud trying to find the channel and decided to tuck in just south-west of the pier. We turned in early after supper, but Alice and I were kept awake for a while by the rocking of the boat and a strange noise which sounded like a robot being spanked on deck. Paul told us in the morning that it was only the wire halyards flapping inside the mast. We would have to get used to that.

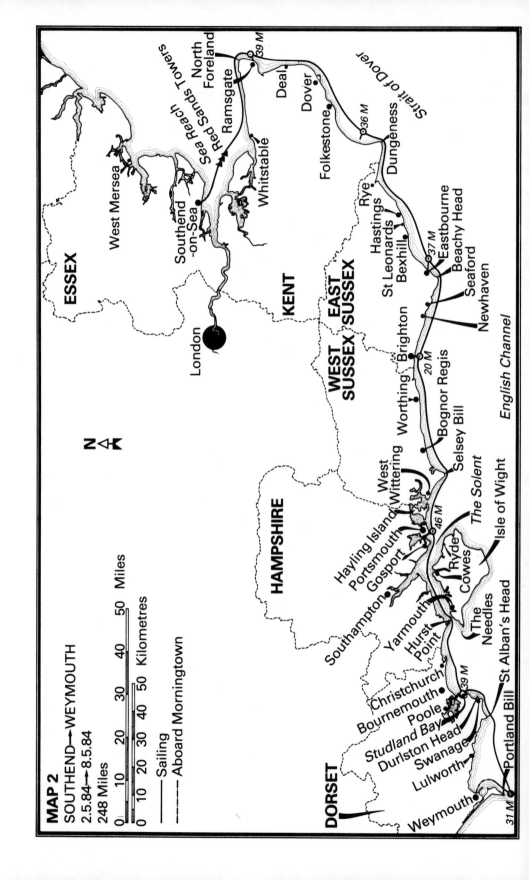

MAP 2

SOUTHEND→WEYMOUTH

2.5.84 → 8.5.84

248 Miles

Miles

Kilometres

—— Sailing
—— Aboard Morningtown

N

ESSEX

West Mersea

Southend
-on-Sea

London

Sea Reach Towers

Red Sands Towers

North
Foreland

Ramsgate

Whitstable

Deal

Dover

39 M

Strait of Dover

KENT

Folkestone

Dungeness

36 M

Rye

Hastings

St Leonards

Bexhill

Eastbourne

Beachy Head

Seaford

Newhaven

37 M

EAST SUSSEX

WEST SUSSEX

Brighton

Worthing

Bognor Regis

Selsey Bill

20 M

English Channel

HAMPSHIRE

West
Wittering

Hayling Island

Portsmouth

Gosport

Southampton

The Solent

Isle of Wight

Ryde

Cowes

46 M

Yarmouth

Hurst
Point

The Needles

Christchurch

Bournemouth

Poole

Studland Bay

Durlston Head

Swanage

Lulworth

St Alban's Head

Portland Bill

39 M

Weymouth

31 M

DORSET

3 SOUTHEND TO WEYMOUTH

Rodney woke the ship at 7am on Wednesday 2 May. This was the big day. I got up quickly and went out on deck to look at the weather. It was dull, misty and grey – rotten visibility – but at least the wind, northerly force 2–3, was in the right sort of direction for heading east. I had tea and toast followed by a quick look at the day's chart with Paul and Rodney. It was some forty miles across the Thames estuary to our destination, Ramsgate, and I was given a slip of paper with compass bearings by Rodney in case we were separated in the mist. I put on my gear, carefully checking the contents of my backpack: waterproof radio to talk to *Morningtown*; iron rations, rope and knife; smoke and flares in case I did get lost; a Locat distress beacon for dire emergencies; and a ten-pence piece for a call-box.

Coming up on deck I saw that there was a hitch. Charlie and Haydn were in the Blagg bailing like mad. During the night the boat had filled with water nearly to the top of the transom and the engines would not start.

A few moments later two lifeboats came roaring towards us out of the mist – the Sheerness boat from across the estuary and the other from Southend. It was 8am and time to go. On *Pytheas I* with a 6m sail I made my way towards the pier. It appeared to be deserted – perhaps no one was turning up. I was all set to head off when, rounding the end of the pier, I caught sight of people in the lifeboat shed at the top of the launching ramp. I beached on the mud and walked up, unable to stop myself smiling. Early on a cold, grey morning here were two dozen people standing around in a shed at the end of a one-and-a-half-mile-long pier drinking champagne! After shaking hands with the Mayor of Southend I took a hefty swig of champagne, said thanks to David, Mark and the others who had nobly got out of bed to see me off and walked back down to the board.

As I crossed the starting line, an imaginary one between the pier and the end of the slip, I heard a bang as a maroon went off. I was officially away. It was 8.18am; the voyage had begun at last.

I sailed down Sea Reach in a small flotilla consisting of *Morningtown*, the Blagg (engines now going), the two lifeboats and a police launch. Two windsurfers, locals from the Southend Club, had also appeared but they quite quickly turned for home. I was not sorry, enjoying the role of lone windsurfer in these early stages. One by one the escort boats dropped out with a blast of a horn or, in one lifeboat's case, the wave of an empty champagne bottle. I felt comfortable and contented; there was a pleasant breeze and, despite the adverse tide, I was making steady progress. Soon the pier and the land behind me had disappeared into the mist. I leant back in the harness, tweaked the sail and looked back with pleasure at the livid white trace of my wake stretching back across the brown water. 'At this rate, it'll be a doddle,' I reflected.

An hour or so had elapsed when our problems began – with the failure of the Blagg's engine. Charlie tried to resurrect it but in vain; the fuel tanks were contaminated with sea water. *Morningtown* and I were about a mile ahead when Charlie and Haydn radioed for assistance. 'The Blagg's sick!' Rodney shouted, and ordered me to turn and follow *Morningtown* back.

Once the stricken boat was in tow, I was able to resume progress in the right direction and, to my frustration, found myself sailing the same mile stretch for the third time. My frustration increased when the wind died off a short while later and my speed was cut almost to nothing by a strong foul tide. For what seemed like hours I was trapped next to a group of World War II anti-aircraft forts, Red Sands Towers. There was something mournful about these monstrous, decaying structures and the place was made still more dismal by a navigation buoy emitting an eerie wail nearby.

The little wind that was left now came on the nose so I changed to the Klepper Division II board (a flat-water special for sailing upwind) and the large 8m sail. No sooner had I changed than the wind mysteriously freshened and I was fighting hard even to keep hold of the sail. The board lurched violently from one rail to the other as I sailed first too close to, then too much off the wind. I was exhausting myself and making little headway. I dropped the rig and sat down to catch my breath. As I sat, my precious watch somehow came loose and slipped off my wrist. I thrust my hand after it in the silty brown water but the watch was gone, to lie forever in the mud of Oaze Deep.

This was the last straw. To cheer myself up I decided to halt for half an hour, eat some lunch and wait for the tide to slacken. I had been sailing for four and a half hours but was little more than a third of the way to Ramsgate. We marked our position on the chart using a 'fix' from the Decca – a radio navigation system accurate to within a hundred yards – a procedure which was followed throughout the journey.

At 1.40pm we motored back to the spot marked X and I resumed sailing, this time with *Pytheas I* and the 6m sail. I made enough ground upwind to clear Red Sands and then enjoyed a close reach across the Kentish flats towards the coast. I eventually hit the Kent coast in sight of the stark ruin of St Mary's Church at Reculver, a landmark that has guided sailors in the Thames estuary for over eight hundred years. Pleased to be near land again, I went ashore for five minutes. Sitting on the shingle I drank some orange squash from my backpack and took out the radio. '*Morningtown, Morningtown.* This is *Pytheas, Pytheas.* Do you read me? Over,' I called. 'Receiving you loud and clear *Pytheas.* Go ahead!' came the reply. I asked how far it was to North Foreland and on hearing 'round the next headland' thought, 'Great. Nearly there!'

Back on the board the wind was dead on the nose and I made a series of long tacks while *Morningtown* steamed straight ahead, keeping roughly level with me. I whooshed backwards and forwards past their stern, showing off to those on deck, before reaching what I took to be the chalk cliffs of North Foreland. To my dismay, there was another headland still some way further on – there always is. This was only the first of four false North Forelands.

By the time I reached the real one it was 5.30pm; I had been on the board for over eight hours and was tired and dispirited. I was tempted to stop now but decided to push on the last three miles to Ramsgate. This was a big mistake. Sailing down the Kent coast away from the wind I was on a run. I had never tried this point of sailing on *Pytheas I* and found it almost impossible. You have to stand well back on the board, but *Pytheas*'s stern was so narrow that I could barely place my feet side by side; it was like being on a tightrope and I was at the mercy of every wave that rolled under me. Falling in and struggling back on repeatedly I became so whacked that in the end I could not stand up. I lay, exhausted, on my board just off Ramsgate.

Despite my dejected state, a smile was forced out of me by the sight of Charlie and Haydn puttering over in *Morningtown*'s liferaft – more or less a rubber ring with a tiny engine. They had come to collect me. 'Is this Rodney's idea of a joke?' I asked them, crawling aboard and nearly capsizing the dinghy. 'I think it's our punishment for the Blagg episode this morning,' Haydn said, grinning.

It emerged that when the Blagg had flooded during the night, water had somehow penetrated the fuel breather pipes and hence the fuel tanks themselves. The boat had to be removed from the water, the leak located and the engine completely stripped down. This, on day one, was effectively the end for the jinxed boat. After all the effort we had put into the Blagg it was a maddening finale, but I knew that with it would go much of the tension that had infected the expedition.

Mark and David were waiting in Ramsgate with the truck and

they came on board for supper to swap news. It turned out that a group of windsurfers had been waiting to see me off Whitstable. Having missed us in the haze they had dubbed me the Invisible Man. I felt numb enough to be invisible at the time and retired to my bunk straight after supper.

It had been a bad day – nine and a half hours' sailing to cover thirty-nine miles. Forty miles was my intended daily average, but I seriously doubted my ability to repeat the day's efforts, let alone fifty times more. I felt as if I had just run a marathon and scaled a couple of mountains for good measure – weak as a baby, with stabbing pains in my lower back, and ankles which seemed sprained.

Lying on my bunk I reached for the pocket cassette machine and, turning my face to the panelled wall of the cabin, began recording the day's events. My voice came out so depressed that I dared not risk anyone else on the boat hearing and gave up. After that I never used the recorder but wrote everything down instead.

I slept deeply till 6.45am when Rodney roused the ship. On getting out of bed I stretched. Hell! I was so stiff that it seemed a herd of buffalo had trampled over me the day before.

There were two temporary additions to the crew since last night: Jill, Rodney's wife; and Jack Williams, an old sailing friend of theirs and future mayor of Colchester. Watching me force down tea and toast, Jack asked how I was feeling. 'Rotten,' I admitted. 'Never felt less like going windsurfing in my life!' But there was no let up. We were in a hurry to catch the tide down to Dover and at 7.30 we motored out of Ramsgate, with a final look at the Blagg, waterlogged next to the quay.

It was a cold, misty morning with a feeble wind from the north. It would be a slow run and this time I took my largest, most stable board (the Klepper 103) and a large 8.2m sail. The first half-hour was agonising because of the stiffness in my back and ankles. Searching for a more comfortable sailing angle than the run, I strayed off course towards the Sandwich flats and was almost out of sight of *Morningtown* before I noticed and corrected. We carried on down the coast inside of the Goodwin Sands, those notorious ship-swallowers, unable in the haze to see either them or the land.

The breeze was pitifully light and I was only making ground owing to a healthy tide of about two knots in my favour. This was not at all the fast, exciting sailing I had been expecting. I was limping along behind my escort yacht, being bumped helplessly by the waves and relying mostly on the tide. Far from having dramatic views of the coast I was surrounded by a sickly mist.

Reflecting on the absurdity of what I was doing, I swore loudly to myself. After less than fifty miles I felt like quitting. The impulse to stop kept attacking me, but I resisted and managed to postpone repeatedly the action of laying down the sail. I thought of all the effort of the last year and just had to continue. The alternative was not worth contemplating.

One hundred yards ahead of me was *Morningtown* and, looking towards her, I felt sure that those on board could have little idea of what I was going through. People wandered about on deck quite unconcerned as we crept towards Dover. Charlie even appeared to be fishing!

After what seemed an eternity, I came in sight of land: the green, chalky hills beyond Deal. I was just south-east of the Downs and only three or four miles from Dover. A large tug was lying close to the shore, looking somehow like a huge scavenger. Later I found out that it was waiting for salvage – lurking near the busiest shipping lane in the world, ready to be the first onto a 'kill'. I felt like giving myself up but accepted that I did not represent too attractive a salvage proposition.

Rodney had radioed in advance to Dover Harbour Control who were prepared for me to pass. I figured that there was just enough wind and set off towards the massive concrete hemisphere jutting out from the cliffs. As we approached I got a message from *Morningtown* that Harbour Control had redirected all shipping. A hovercraft was heard requesting permission to proceed and was instructed, 'On no account impede the passage of the windsurfer,' and I witnessed the curiously cheering sight of a hovercraft, like a huge red and white maybug, whirr out of my way. Next came a message from Harbour Control: 'You have our full admiration,' quickly followed by, 'but rather you than me!' This phrase became a favourite quip of coastguards and RNLI men alike that we came across.

When I was well past the harbour, a tug approached towing the most enormous object, later identified as a jack-up dredger. *Morningtown* made radio contact to see if the tug had spotted me, and a cheery northern voice came over: 'My tow is rather heavy. Don't worry if I go quite close to your windsurfer – I won't knock him over!'

At about midday off Folkestone the tide turned – too vigorously for there to be any point in continuing – and we anchored to wait it out. Now was a chance to relax – out of my clammy drysuit. After lunch I lay in the cockpit in the hazy sunshine and tried to sleep. I had turned two corners now and was heading westwards down the Channel to Land's End. The enormity of the distance in front staggered me; I still had to learn not to look ahead but just to concentrate on the present.

I resumed sailing at 5pm with the largest, 9.3m, sail for a three-hour run to the east side of Dungeness promontory. For a while I used the waterproof stereo which helped the time pass, but it was impossible to change tapes without letting water in and, after forty-five minutes of disco, I sailed on in silence. With *Morningtown* often several hundred yards away I felt quite lonely, especially as evening approached, and was relieved when we halted just off Dungeness. I had done thirty-six miles.

We were anchored for the night and too inaccessible for Mark and David to join us, but there were already ten of us on board anyway. It was incredible how *Morningtown* swallowed up so many bodies (not to mention all their gear!): Paul and Liz in the forepeak; Alice and I in the forward cabin; Haydn in 'the pit' in the main cabin; Chris and Charlie crammed in 'the hen-house' next to the engine-room; and Rodney, Jack and Jill in the aft state-room. It was crowded but jolly. After a good steak-and-kidney dinner we turned in for a fairly bumpy night.

The day dawned misty with the sea a mirror calm and we sat tight after breakfast, waiting for something to develop. I was glad of the reprieve and a chance to join in the activity on *Morningtown*. We took the opportunity to launch the RNLI 'D' Class inflatable – later to be christened *Bumble* – and fitted a 40hp engine on the back.

Jack was the first to spot a puff of wind and soon the fog began to clear. It was about 10am and I set off with the Klepper 103 and the 9m sail. The sun broke through, lighting up the water, and the spit of Dungeness began to take shape. Fishermen were starting the day, their tubby boats slithering like seals down the shingle. It was nice to see the rest of the world again. On such a beautiful morning even the grotesque power station of Dungeness looked somehow in place.

I reached the nose of the promontory and looked up the shingle at the enormous lighthouse, which dwarfed me completely. A fishing boat bobbed out to *Morningtown* and told them I was too close inshore – the stronger tide began in the deep water a hundred yards further off. I sailed out into the main stream and hitched a lift till I was round the corner and heading towards Rye.

Morningtown needed to pick up fresh water and went ahead to Rye while I continued with *Bumble*, manned by Haydn and Charlie. Curiously, the tide turned against me so I sailed inshore, hoping for a back-eddy close to the beach. The wind freshened and I clipped

(*opposite above*) The launch – Norris McWhirter, *Pytheas* and Jean-Marc Heidsieck; (*below*) Teething troubles on the Thames
(*overleaf*) Evening on the way to Lundy

along nicely with the monster sail, measuring my progress against the lines of groynes that I passed. The wind freshened further – now a solid south-easterly 3 – and Haydn recommended cutting right across Rye Bay. Following his advice I had a perfect five-mile reach, gliding effortlessly across the dappled, blue water – my first really enjoyable sailing of the trip. My mood brightened and as the aches of the first couple of days receded, I had a taste of what fun this journey could be.

Haydn and Charlie came roaring up in *Bumble* and flagged me down. Haydn was waving his Ordnance Survey map excitedly: 'It says there's a pub just here,' he called, adding, 'and we're hungry!' By now it was one o'clock so we stopped a few hundred yards further on at Cliff End and pulled our respective craft up the shingle. From the top of the bank we could see the pub, Smugglers Inn. When we walked in dripping, fresh from the sea, neither barman nor clientele batted an eyelid. They were used, perhaps, to more exciting visits by furtive customers peddling brandy and silk scarves from across the Channel. However, we all felt so pleased with ourselves, sneaking ashore like this for a pint, that we insisted all the same on telling everyone what we were up to.

Sailing again, we were joined by *Morningtown* and pushed on towards Eastbourne. I lost the wind, straying too close inshore to look at some cliffs called Lovers Leap and by the time we reached Hastings I was flagging. I was not sorry when Rodney shouted that I had been invited ashore to meet the lifeboat crew and to 'kiss babies', as he put it.

Hastings is a picturesque town nestling in a fold of the sandstone coast with dozens of fishing boats regimented on their hawsers along the shingle, well out of reach of the ocean, and rows of tall, wooden net-drying huts sheltering under the cliffs. As we touched the beach, Joe Martin, the local lifeboat coxswain, greeted us. He was an impressive-looking seadog accompanied by two balding alsatians that sniffed hungrily at my drysuit. Rodney, Alice, Charlie and Haydn all came ashore, too, and we sat in the lifeboat shed for a cup of tea. After some useful advice about Beachy Head from Joe, some disagreement over the weather forecast, and the kind gift of a lifeboat coffee mug, it was time to go.

I plugged on past St Leonards and Bexhill towards Eastbourne, unaware of the minor disaster behind me: somehow, getting on or off *Morningtown*, Alice, designated 'purser' because of her cool efficiency, had dropped her purse into the sea! With it went £1,500

(*above*) A near gale in the Solent on a day when a lifeboat was lost off Flamborough Head; (*below*) End of the day, Studland Bay

worth of travellers cheques, various credit cards and a wad of cash. Several phone calls on the ship's radio cancelled the cheques and cards and nothing more was heard. We hoped that the sudden influx of wealth did not disturb the marine ecology of Hastings too much!

The stretch to Eastbourne was gruelling. With a lively breeze on my back I was running at full stretch and had to concentrate hard to maintain balance. This continued for a solid three hours, but there was company for part of the way. A windsurfer appeared from nowhere and sailed along beside me for about a mile before wishing me luck and turning back. I reached Eastbourne pier at about 7pm, another thirty-seven miles under the belt. Progress over these first three days, though slow, had been remarkably consistent: thirty-nine, thirty-six and thirty-seven miles.

We anchored off the pier and Charlie drove ashore in *Bumble* to collect David and Mark for supper. The wind was blowing strongly from the north-east and quite a sea had built up in which *Morningtown* was rolling maliciously and several people had difficulty keeping down their food. I, who had shocked myself before the trip by getting seasick one night on a waterbed, had to eat on deck, while David and Mark both went very green and had to retreat to the truck in a hurry.

Just then we had a call from the Eastbourne Lifeboat House: 'We know you're there 'cos we can see you. Are you coming ashore for a swift one?' It would have been churlish to refuse and going ashore seemed an attractive prospect anyway. There was a stampede for *Bumble* and we had an exhilarating three-mile trip along the darkened shoreline towards the point of a searchlight which marked the lifeboat house. We arrived breathless to be met by all the crew and, after examining their spotless lifeboat, we repaired to the local drinking house, The Fisherman's Rest. Our shiny new yellow oilskins provoked some comment and one drinker at the bar remarked to his neighbour in a loud voice, 'Gawd, they look like a bunch of bananas!' Soon I was involved in a conversation with the coxswain who had numerous difficult questions up his sleeve. 'How are you going to get round ole Scotland?' he asked. 'Trial and error,' I suggested. 'Rather you than me ole son!' he said.

Even after the refreshment we had an uncomfortable night, for me largely sleepless, listening to the endless slap, slap of the anchor chain in its locker. We rose at 6am on Saturday 5 May to tackle the first major landmark of the journey, Beachy Head. The day was chill and overcast, the sun barely up. As usual for the first half an hour I struggled to readjust to the pattern of the wind and waves, falling in several times and getting into a temper. It was really too early for such strenuous activity, I concluded.

Beachy Head lived up to its name – beautiful headland – a majestic chalk buttress rising some five hundred feet sheer from the frothy sea. No one could continue sulking with such a view. My mood lifted in an instant as I sailed on, one moment glancing at the waves ahead and the next gazing up in awe at the cliffs above. I kept close in to avoid the worst of the tide-race – a feature of all headlands – and the wind steadily freshened from behind. By the time I reached Beachy Head lighthouse I was screaming along, perched on the back few inches of the board and straining with every sinew to control the 9m sail which was tugging and billowing like a line of washing in a gale. At any second I expected the board to fly. Before long I did. A bolt of wind flattened the sail with the force of a catapult and exploded me into the air. I landed eventually with a cold, breathless crunch that denuded me of shoes and harness jacket. The sail was evidently too big!

There were some tense faces as the 6m sail was rigged on *Morningtown*'s foredeck in what were the fiercest conditions so far. Rodney skilfully handled the ship while Paul masterminded the sail change. His knowledge of windsurfing was a godsend, enabling him to sift through the not-yet-ordered mound of equipment in my cabin and find any item in a hurry.

Armed with the new sail, I restarted and ran down past Beachy Head and Birling Gap towards the Seven Sisters. Then the sun came out lighting up in bright white splendour the undulating chalk cliffs, and I reached for a magical twelve miles past Seaford and Newhaven all the way to Brighton. Feet thrust in footstraps to gain purchase, I leant out in the harness, occasionally skimming the blue water with my back as I streaked along. Everyone was taken by surprise by my speed which at a steady twenty knots left *Morningtown* well behind and even outpaced *Bumble*. They nearly ran out of petrol trying to keep up. I arrived in Brighton in time for elevenses, glowing from the morning's work – twenty miles in no time at all. If only it could all be like that, I thought.

Brighton, perhaps England's best-known resort on the south coast, boasts a most extensive marina – a huge, luxury enclosure housing over two thousand boats. We were generously given a free berth, thanks to our RNLI flag, and most of the crew went straight off to make use of the excellent showers. Shortly after our arrival, Woody Blagg contacted us via the marina office, wanting to get his boat back into commission. This was not an attractive proposition now that *Bumble* was proving its worth. In fact, I was embarrassed at how much more suitable for us *Bumble* was proving to be: robust, economical on fuel and able to be easily beached. Plans to reinstate the Blagg were dropped but not before some grumbling from

Charlie who, after all his hours of effort in fitting out the boat, was reluctant to see it abandoned for good. Later Chris returned, also out of spirits. He had left *Morningtown* in Rye to take photos from the shore and had not only failed to see us as we passed down the coast but had missed rejoining us in Eastbourne.

All this emotional drama reminded me that I lacked sleep and I went below for a couple of hours. I came back on deck to find Oliver Moore (of Charles Heidsieck) sitting in the cockpit thoughtfully drinking red wine. I joined him for a glass and quizzed him on his sudden arrival. 'Just keeping tabs on you,' he assured me. 'The company want me to check that you really can windsurf!'

What a treat it was to sleep that night without the ketch rocking and rolling. I woke early and went to have a shower. While shaving I got talking to a 'yachtie' who seemed to be on intimate terms with the south coast of England. Since we were heading for the Solent, either Chichester or Gosport, and Selsey Bill looked like being the difficult part, I asked his advice. 'It's a rough spot, that,' said the yachtie, 'but you'll be all right in a decent sized boat. How big is yours?' 'Not big at all, about twelve feet, well, it's not really a boat at all . . . it's a sailboard,' I said. 'You've got to be joking!' he gasped.

Back at *Morningtown*, a good force 5–6 was blowing from the north-east with possible gales forecast later. Having popped out of the marina in *Bumble* to look at the sea conditions, we decided that *Bumble* and I should take advantage of the flatter water close inshore and operate as a separate unit from *Morningtown* for the day. Radio contact would be maintained either direct, or through the coastguard every two hours.

My new board, *Pytheas* Mark II, had arrived and looked just the job for the fast conditions. I chose the small 5m sail, taking the 4m wrapped on a mast in *Bumble* in case the gale came through. At 11am I set sail from outside the marina where I had finished the day before. The wind was disturbed near the harbour walls and I had trouble getting started, feeling embarrassed before an audience of three lifeboats, who were looking on like vultures, just waiting to rescue 'this joker'. We heard later that the Newhaven coxswain had asked his crew, 'Are you sure we've got the right guy?'

Finally, I managed an effective waterstart, lurching out of the sea and off along Brighton sea front and missing the end of Palace Pier by inches in the waves. It was not the reach I had hoped for. The coastline sloped away southwards just enough to make my course a run. It was going to be a grind.

A police launch, the *Norfolk*, presently came over to give me a wave. I overheard them on the radio asking *Morningtown*, 'Do we get extra points if he waves back and falls in?' This was an unnecessary bout of windsurfer-baiting as I was falling in frequently without any prompting. Every hour and a half or so I stopped for a cup of coffee and a chocolate biscuit in *Bumble*. The attraction of a chat with Haydn and Charlie over a hot drink considerably outweighed the joys of windsurfing on this occasion and it was tempting to linger over the stops but Haydn kept me moving with mutterings of gales and tides turning at Selsey Bill. I wanted to be in the Solent by tonight.

At Shoreham I flitted through a racing fleet of dinghies and then took part in my own little race against another itinerant windsurfer. Much to Charlie's and Haydn's amusement my opponent was just ahead when he turned back. There was a crowd of windsurfers off Bognor and several of them sailed over to wish me good luck. Then came a resounding three-gun salute from the lifeboat house. It was a timely tonic for waning energies as well as a warning of the approaching Selsey Bill.

We could see the white crests of the breakers from quite a distance; they came curling in from the Channel and met in an evil confusion at the tip of the bill. Charlie took a tortuous roundabout path through the jungle of waves to avoid *Bumble* being turned over. Lacking this manoeuvrability, I had little choice but to steam straight ahead. As I met each hunk of water I crouched with bent knees and then juddered from foot to foot while the board climbed the wave, teetered on the crest and slid down into the trough on the other side. By sheer luck I stayed upright and bobbed round the bill to find that the lifeboat house on the beach was full of people shouting and cheering. What a great reception! 'Please don't let me fall in now,' I prayed.

After Selsey the coast slopes more north and my course hardened onto a reach. What joy! I flew the next few miles to West Wittering. Here we found dozens of windsurfers racing, watched by a crowd on the beach. We went ashore to stretch our legs and several people gave us contributions for the lifeboat appeal. As we left, Channel 4, who were covering the racing, asked if they could film me disappearing towards Hayling Island. I was determined not to fall in until well out to sea but someone zoomed up and said, 'Hello!' It was Robin Brockway so I waved nonchalantly back – and fell in.

Hayling Island brought back memories and, passing over the East Winner Sands, I reflected on the hours and hours of sailing I had put in there during training, and how much more fun it was then! Interrupting my nostalgia, another windsurfer came up – it was a popular day for visitors – as if to greet me, but changed his mind and attempted to run me down. I kept my balance and gave him a deserving shove as we collided, which brought a cheer of appreciation from *Bumble*.

I was achingly tired but we only had a few miles to go. *Morningtown* was already in Gosport. Crossing the entrance to Portsmouth harbour we hit a slick of smooth purple water, several acres of it, that smelt suspiciously of sewage – I was glad not to fall in. At last we reached Southsea Castle and I could stop. I collapsed into *Bumble* and sank down against the rubber sponson; the muscles in my arms and back felt teased out like overstretched springs. But it had been the best day yet – forty-six miles. We were in the Solent and beginning to make a dent on that map of Britain.

Back on board *Morningtown* I peeled off my drysuit, hanging it up with my gloves to dry in the engine-room, and changed into some warm clothes. Chris and Charlie disappeared together in the direction of a pub and missed supper. When the rest of us had eaten, Alice and Mark took some sponsorship forms over to the *Samuel Whitbread*, a youth-training ship that was moored nearby. The 'youths', however, were more interested in finding out the night spots of Gosport than in the RNLI!

That night, the wind made a terrific noise, whistling in the rigging of the many boats sheltering in the harbour, and we rose at 5.30am on 7 May to a raw dawn. Chris and Charlie were slow to get up, emerging from the hen-house only when the smell of bacon from the galley became irresistible. They were still struggling into their drysuits and oilskins when we left at six o'clock to catch the tide through the Solent. On *Pytheas II* with the 5m sail I made excellent progress towards the Isle of Wight in a north-easterly wind, force 5. I was feeling surprisingly loose-limbed, but with the sun hardly risen it was bitterly cold and twice I had to stop and vigorously windmill my arms to thaw out fingers frozen even in dry gloves.

I passed Southampton Water where one or two big ships were plying seawards and found myself sailing, for a change, with land on both sides. To my left were the green wooded hills between Ryde and Cowes and to my right the Hampshire coast. The wind freshened as the morning aged and soon I reached the limit of control. After two spectacular bruising catapult falls I decided, in the interests of staying in one piece, to change sails. *Morningtown* was far away near the Isle of Wight but we were carrying the 4m sail in *Bumble* so I signalled to the boys to follow me onto Lymington flats. Chris had joined *Bumble*'s crew for the day and the two of us rerigged on the hard mud, watched by a flock of gulls as we wrestled to contain the flapping canvas.

From the flats I was forced to bear away onto a run to make the narrow channel between Fort Albert on the Isle of Wight and Hurst Point on the mainland. I was sailing gingerly to avoid more bad falls, standing well back on the board and raking down the sail each time I sensed a particularly vicious gust behind me. At Jack in the Basket buoy, feeling rather shell-shocked, I stopped for a coffee and a pep talk with the boys. Chris rose to the occasion: crawling onto *Bumble*'s nose to attach a line to my board, he went an inch too far and overbalanced, sliding slowly head first into the icy water with a cigarette dangling from his mouth. Charlie almost fell in after him because he was laughing so much, and the recollection of this incident kept me amused for the rest of that difficult stretch to the end of the Solent.

Reaching Hurst Narrows at last, I gulped at the monster waves funnelling through. Not possible, surely? But encouraged by the philosophical observation that 'it's only water', I reefed in the sail for an extra burst of speed, caught a wave and surfed all the way to the end. At the ruin of Hurst Castle (built by Henry VIII so that he could close the Solent at leisure) I turned sharp right and sailed up to *Morningtown* sheltering at anchor behind the thin curve of shingle.

Paul and Rodney both congratulated me on coming successfully through the near gale and, in contented mood, we all sat down to a hearty meal of celery soup and cheese. There was at least a five-hour wait before slack water and after lunch I went on deck to watch the strong spring tide bubbling past. Glancing aft, I suddenly noticed that *Pytheas II* had disappeared; the painter line was trailing empty behind *Morningtown* – it must have pulled free in the tide. I scanned the sea quickly but there was nothing – a white board would have no chance of being seen amongst all the breaking waves. It could have come loose half an hour earlier and be miles away by now. But where? I felt sick. Just when things were starting to go well, a moment's carelessness had lost my board. It might take a week to get a replacement, and I needed it this afternoon. Everyone was on deck now and I suggested a search in *Bumble*. Chris wanted to go. 'It was I who tied the knot,' he admitted bravely. 'I've been trying to perfect that bowline!'

In the end Paul and Charlie went. Our first thought was that the wind would have taken the board east towards The Needles and out into the Channel. Rodney reckoned, however, that the strong tide would have carried it back into the Solent against the wind. 'I bet it will end up on the beach near Yarmouth,' he concluded. No sooner had *Bumble* left than we were joined by the Mudeford lifeboat – a 'D' Class but smart and new compared to our old boat. The RNLI boys kindly gave us a bottle of rum and offered to help look for the board. Twenty minutes later both boats returned and reported that there was no sign of *Pytheas* but fantastic surf in the narrows. We notified the Solent coastguard of the loss and sat down for a tot of rum, gloomy about the prospects of the board turning up.

An hour or so later the coastguard radioed back to say that the board had been picked up on the beach at Yarmouth. By chance it had suffered only a minor nose fracture which we mended with epoxy filler. Scrawled on one side in green felt pen was, 'Found by ranger. To be picked up.' If that ranger could only have known how relieved I was. We did our best and arranged for him to be sent a bottle of champagne, by courtesy of Charles Heidsieck.

That day was a bank holiday and a number of big yachts sailed past us on their way down the coast, well heeled over and enjoying the full-blooded conditions. At 4pm we followed their path towards Poole. As in the morning, I took the 4m sail but was never comfortable in the variable breeze that had me galloping along one minute and floundering the next. It was a frustrating fifteen miles past Christchurch Bay, Hengistbury Head and Bournemouth. I was tired and fed up when we arrived at Poole harbour entrance two and a half hours later, smashing the last few hundred yards through the surf and beaching on the golden sands of Studland Bay. I lay down on my back, glad that that stretch was over.

Unknown to me, some distance away on the other side of the harbour entrance at Sandbanks were almost a hundred disappointed windsurfers. They had been waiting for us to arrive all afternoon, watching with binoculars as we got closer and closer. At the last minute we had veered away and sailed to a different beach, oblivious of the scores of people across the choppy sea. David and Mark were also at Sandbanks with the truck and trying desperately to reach us on the radio.

Bad communications seemed to be the story of the day: we arrived at Poole marina to hear of more disappointed people. The RNLI had been informed that we were arriving at about 3.30pm – at the time we were still anchored fifteen miles away – and a reception committee waited in vain for several hours. It appeared that, for once, the coastguard were the root of the faulty information. Throughout the rest of the voyage they efficiently monitored our progress, sending telexes of our exact position to the RNLI several times a day.

Crossed lines and lack of communication left us with a charged atmosphere which before long ignited into a full-scale row. David came on board *Morningtown* and, in a tetchy voice, began to ask Rodney for a detailed exposition of the day's radio communications. 'What business is it of yours?' snapped Rodney and, going red in the face, he barked, 'Off my ship . . . get off . . . out!' David retaliated in like tones as he retreated out of the cabin.

Trouble had been brewing between the two of them since the trip began. David was understandably irked by Rodney's outspoken

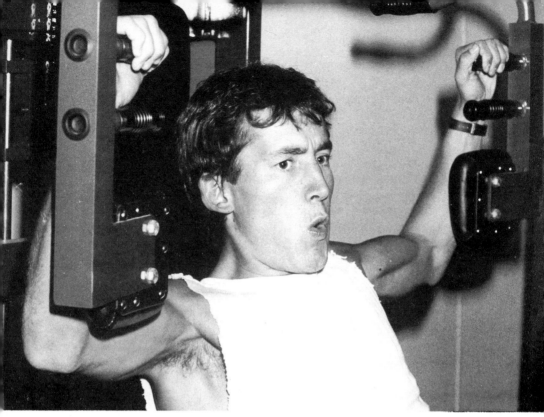

(*above*) 'Working out' at Cannon's Gymnasium, London; (*below*) With the team – Alice, Mark, Charlie, Chris, Paul, Liz and Haydn – and the right champagne!

(*above*) Loading up the Blagg at West Mersea; (*below*) Racing *Bumble* to Salcombe

contempt for all media and PR people whom he labelled 'reptiles', and now Rodney was confirming all David's worst expectations about 'tyrannical skippers'. Both were inflexible towards each other's jobs, and reconciling press engagements with tide-tables was a permanent problem.

The glaring confrontation left an embarrassed silence in the cabin which Jack broke by saying tactfully that he would go off and talk to David. Rodney said after Jack had left, 'He's done a lot of miles at sea with me; he understands how I work.' Later Jack returned from the pub having smoothed the troubled waters somewhat with shots of whisky, but the uneasiness simmered on the next day. David telephoned Charles Heidsieck with an ultimatum that either Rodney went or he did. Oliver Moore drove down to Poole and succeeded in calming things down temporarily. No one departed then, but ironically, in the end, both David and Rodney were to leave.

During our morning at Poole, Haydn demonstrated some of the business talent that led to his early retirement, persuading Mariner to loan us a 40hp engine as a spare for *Bumble*. It was carried thereafter on *Morningtown*'s aft deck. Before we moved on I spent some time calming relations with the RNLI and among other people talked to the coxswain of the Poole lifeboat. For once I found a lifeboatman dour and truculent even when I asked for his advice in an effort to make conversation. 'Give up windsurfing!' he suggested with a blank expression. I returned to *Morningtown* and met Nigel Fawkes, from the London Windsurfing centre, who was joining us for the day. We left with the tide at 3pm from Studland Bay in a north-easterly force 4. I took a 6m sail on the Klepper 103 and picked up the breeze nicely for a fast reach across Swanage Bay to Durlston and St Alban's Head. We passed Old Harry Rocks, Harry looking like a great crumbling molar, and his wife a slender front tooth. This whole coast is interspersed with gaps and shapes sculpted out of the chalk cliffs by the relentless sea. Two of the best examples – Lulworth Cove and Durdle Door – lay just ahead.

It was a crystal clear day and on rounding St Alban's Head I could see the whole Dorset coastline stretching towards Weymouth. Even the whale-shaped lump of Portland Bill was visible and from this distance appeared to be an island. I wondered what this great headland held in store for me. With up to eight-knot tides it has a reputation as the second most difficult stretch of water in Britain after the Pentland Firth. But conditions looked favourable today, with a following wind and tide.

The wind was gusting gently. At the top of the gusts my board lifted out of the water, planing happily on a broad reach, and in the lulls I hardened up the reach to stay on the plane. I made a series of gybes, tacking downwind for the first time and traversing wide arcs across *Morningtown*'s line – keeping level with them despite covering much greater distances. The swell from the previous day's strong winds was going my way and I caught rides on a series of large waves, surfing down wave after wave and building up tremendous speeds for long stretches at a time. With the sun reflecting brilliantly on the surface of the sea it seemed I was shooting down a great silvery polished staircase.

The noise of an engine interrupted my harmony and *Bumble* roared up. 'You're straying too close to Lulworth firing range. Head more out to sea!' shouted Hadyn. I had wanted to stay as close as possible to the coast between Kimmeridge and Ringstead, where we once used to enjoy family holidays, and reflected on how firing ranges have an annoying habit of being situated in the loveliest places. It sounded as if the boys were expecting shells to be bursting round us at any moment, but I waited in vain for the whiff of cordite and the whizz of shrapnel.

As we approached Portland Bill we saw several naval vessels coming from the base in Portland's massive man-made harbour. We would be heading back there tonight. By this time the hot sun had taken its toll and I had a headache – what a contrast to yesterday's frost-bitten fingers. I stopped for a minute and bobbed face down in the cool sea to ease the throbbing. The wail of a desolate navigational buoy announced the approach of Portland race. It was a spectacular prospect – sheer, grey cliffs bordering a boiling sea.

The white confusion of the tide-race ahead put me in mind of *The Sea Around Us* by Rachel Carson, a book I had read as part of my pre-trip diet. She imagines a time millions of years ago when the moon is much closer to the earth and exerts a far greater gravitational pull on the oceans:

> . . . The sweep of the tides must have been beyond all comprehension. Twice each day, the fury of the incoming waters would inundate all the margins of the continents . . . the waves would batter the crests of high cliffs and sweep inland to erode the land masses . . . No living thing could exist on the shores or pass beyond them!

With this awesome description in mind how could I be frightened by today's tides, now diminished out of all comparison? Except, a voice told me, this is Portland Bill where the tide is up to four times stronger than the average. I had to work hard to stay on the board. Steep walls of water rose, wobbled and crashed in all directions around me while here and there the turmoil was punctuated by a patch of suspiciously smooth water. These smooth patches are caused by water surging up from the depths to fill the gaps left by diverging currents, while the jumbled waves or overfalls arise from the clash of swirling tide and wind.

My instructions had been to stay close to *Morningtown* but I ignored them, deciding that the only chance of staying on my feet was to take my own line, maximising speed and hence stability through the race. The currents carried me through swiftly and, apart from some waves toppling onto the board and once onto my head, I was quickly into calmer waters, even feeling a little cheated of the blood-curdling excitement I had been anticipating. Nevertheless, all on *Morningtown* heralded my passage as a significant landmark and effusive congratulations were sent over the radio. The afternoon's four and a half hours had been worth thirty-one miles.

We planned to return to Weymouth for the night and a long-awaited rest day. It was too rough to tow *Bumble* back, but I managed to scramble aboard *Morningtown* for some hot soup and we set off in convoy towards Weymouth. For over an hour we barely made headway even at full throttle owing to a five-knot tide against us, which gave ample opportunity to re-examine the bill – noted for its cement quarries and a Borstal. It was freezing cold now. The evening had set in and we thought of the inmates in that exposed place.

We ate on the way back, passing Portland harbour. In the roly-poly conditions Alice needed the arms of an octopus to hold everything down in the galley. We motored up the River Wey following the green and red navigation lights marking the channel and found an excellent berth alongside the harbour wall in the heart of Weymouth. We were just in time for last orders at a quayside pub. Everyone was in good spirits as we turned in except Chris, who lost a camera in the muddy waters of the Wey as he jumped back on board *Morningtown*.

In the morning I wandered off alone into Weymouth. It was a joy to stretch my legs and relax knowing that today I did not have to sail. Paul and Charlie had proposed a windsurfing outing themselves, to which my reaction was, 'How could you?' I ended up on the sea front, a solid Georgian crescent, and sat down on a bench looking out over the bay. It was a moment to take stock of the seven days since leaving Southend. I had covered 250-odd miles, which was on target for a nine-week trip, but only at the expense of extra hours on my board. My average speed was five and a half knots, half what I had been hoping for. Longer hours meant greater physical strain and although I had only minor complaints so far – a wrenched shoulder and several numb fingers from the cold windy day in the Solent – I was very tired and wondered how long this charmed life would continue.

I decided that a more comfortable sailboard was an essential measure – a board designed for light winds and running – long, flat and wide. Later that day I telephoned Tris who rose to the occasion and promised he would meet us with such a monster in Penzance.

Sitting peacefully on the sea front it struck me how little time there was for thinking on the voyage. Somehow, I had expected long tranquil hours of being at one with the elements, but generally I had to concentrate too hard on the sailing itself, or on my comfort or lack of it, to think about much else. Even when my mind wandered off briefly in the evenings, it only took the sound of the wind in the rigging to anticipate tomorrow and yet another day on the sea.

Returning to the boat I attended to one or two minor but important jobs, glueing fresh Pro-grip on the booms, and fixing tugs, or handles, onto my sails to facilitate rigging. Pro-grip is a rubber sleeve designed to stop the hands from blistering. It had been recommended by Arnaud de Rosnay*, a colourful French baron famous for such daring windsurfing exploits as crossing the Bering Straits. I met him at the Weymouth speed trials the year before, 1983, and this tip of his proved a lifesaver. My hands were not suffering at all.

Later, we had a visit from the local RNLI honorary secretary who presented us with some lifeboat beermats. A representative from the local windsurfing club, Dave Hackford, also turned up and gave us a cheque for the RNLI appeal and a club tankard. At the time Dave was one of four hopefuls for the Olympic Boardsailing Team – the first ever – going to Los Angeles, and was in fact selected a month later ahead of the favourite, Dave Perks.

That evening Paul and I sorted out sails on *Morningtown*'s foredeck – how many we wanted ready-rolled on masts, and so on – while Haydn was plumbing the murky depths of the harbour trying to locate Chris's camera with a heavy-duty magnet he had bought in a local chandler's. He fished out a succession of dubious objects, the most exciting being a large rusty nail, earning our mockery in the process. A yelp of delight finally broke the quiet, however, when a muddy camera was produced dripping off the magnet. Haydn now plans to go into the salvage business!

---

*In December 1985, Baron de Rosnay tragically went missing while windsurfing from China to Taiwan.

4 PORTLAND BILL TO PENZANCE

Five o'clock the next morning, 9 May, found us motoring past Portland Bill once again to begin our first real open sea stretch, across Lyme Bay to Dartmouth. I stayed in bed until the last moment to get some extra sleep, a habit that got me into all sorts of trouble the following day. I was up, dressed and, although not raring to go, at least ready by 6am, but *Bumble* chose this moment to give us some problems. Charlie, pulling like crazy, was unable to start the engine – owing to a fuel blockage, we later found out – and the powerless boat drifted away from us back into the Portland race. The wind was freshening nicely by the time we went back to pick up the stranded boat and I was champing at the bit.

I set off on a fast reach into the gloom of Lyme Bay, wanting to get this leg over in as short a time as possible and hoping the weather would not turn foul when we were half-way across. For a couple of hours I made steady progress and as the wind picked up ever more I played tag with *Morningtown* and began to outstrip her. I was about a mile ahead when the wind became too much for my 9m sail, and reluctantly I waited for a smaller sail before continuing. Sitting on the board, radio in hand, I watched a huge ship approach fast out of the haze, apparently heading straight for me. I tried to sound unconcerned as I asked *Morningtown* if it would be possible to get me a sail and fast! *Bumble* was to be despatched with it, but the engine problems recurred and I had to sit helpless on my board while the huge mass of steel forged on towards me at about fifteen knots. 'They must be able to see me now,' I thought. 'They'll veer off any second.' At what seemed the last opportunity the boat passed harmlessly to the south of me: 'Co-op Grain Ship' I read on her side. *Morningtown* had managed to raise them on the radio and, after a few language problems, made them notice the windsurfer on their bow which belonged to the ketch to starboard. They had been blissfully unaware of us both.

Bumble arrived and we had a hectic time unrigging the 9m sail in the fresh breeze. Amidst our confusion, the alarm on Charlie's watch went off with a piercing electronic jingle and we all started to laugh. Haydn pointed out that it was time to get up and I looked at the watch which said 8.30am. Here we were being blown about in the

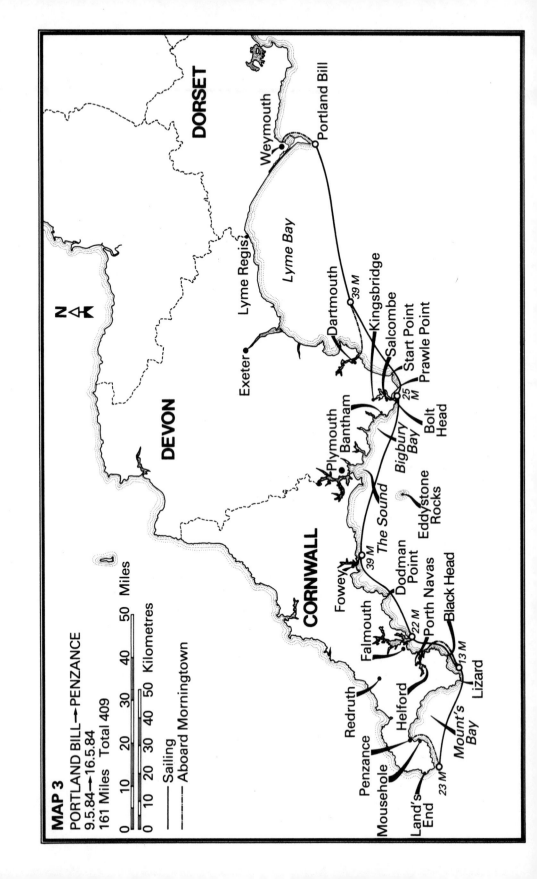

middle of the English Channel, having just clashed with a large ship, when we might have been waking up gently to Capital Radio and a cup of tea home in London.

With typical perverseness, the wind dropped some fifteen miles before Dartmouth and I changed back to the 9m sail, pottering on until the sea became dead calm. The lull seemed like a good moment to stop for lunch and *Morningtown* steamed back to me. I was about to jump on board when a shy puff of wind ruffled the surface of the mill-pond so I carried on a little further, not wanting to waste any precious wind. Half an hour later the wind vanished again but reappeared as soon as I made moves towards lunch. It was another hour and a half before I snatched time to drink some soup.

For a short stretch after lunch the breeze was enough for me to plane and I kept up with *Morningtown* at full speed – so close that I was almost able to talk to them. Then the wind died and I began to drop back. *Morningtown* steamed on ahead and in a short time was a couple of miles in front and barely visible. I thought it odd that they were maintaining such a speed and stopped to radio them. They had not noticed I was missing. After the first couple of days a 'Timwatch' system operated whenever I was on the water without *Bumble*: the crew would take turns watching me through the binoculars from the aft deck. The sight of my bright yellow sail must have made them dizzy after a while and, on this occasion, the Timwatch had obviously either dozed off or gone below. The incident brought home how easy it would be for us to get separated and from that moment on *Bumble* was almost always on the water with me.

This safety measure had a precious spin-off for me. With *Bumble* generally in hailing distance I felt much less cut off and lonely – and quality of life on the board was definitely improved.

There being no wind and, looking at the sky, little prospect of any, we stopped for the day at 1.20pm, just nine miles short of Dartmouth. After a thirty-nine-mile run I had broken the back of Lyme Bay. We would return the next morning to our Decca spot and carry on westwards to Salcombe.

Approaching Dartmouth from the sea is one of those unforgettable moments. Rugged Devon coast melts into tree-lined hillsides rising up on both sides of the River Dart, dotted with pretty houses. We all went ashore and Jill treated us to a magnificent Devonshire cream tea of scones, clotted cream and strawberry jam. She was leaving today and would be missed, not least for her insistence that we had free berths wherever we went. At Dartmouth we were berthed in a prime position on the town quay just behind a sleek French sloop.

That evening we were visited by Stephen Coombs, a local

windsurfer and marine biologist who, with his brother-in-law, sails a tandem board. We had exchanged letters before the trip began and he wanted to join us for a day somewhere in Devon. I was all in favour of some company and, to make matters better, he had brought a cheque for the RNLI and a half-gallon of J & B Whisky (his sponsors). He is an amusing talker and his board sounded incredible: with enough volume to support eleven people and special compartments for spare sails, food and, naturally, a lot of whisky. I was looking forward to our ocean meeting.

Next morning I lingered in bed, knowing there was at least an hour and a half before I needed to be ready. My next recollection is of bouncing up and down in my berth: *Morningtown* was obviously motoring into quite a sea. I lay for a bit longer, trying to imagine what was going on outside when Paul came into the cabin and spelt it out: 'Better get up, buster, it's blowing a good 6 out there . . . pretty rough . . . you'll need a 3 or 4m sail.' This news, delivered while I was still warm and cosy in bed, alerted butterflies in my stomach. I dressed with some difficulty owing to the pitching of the boat and by the end of the exercise felt rather queasy.

Struggling out onto deck I took in both the wind and the grim faces of Rodney and Paul. I sat in the cockpit and drank half a cup of tea before going below in search of sections for my boom to fit the small sails. On the way I was suddenly gripped by a simultaneous attack of diarrhoea and seasickness. I got the nearest person to unzip my drysuit and dashed to the aft head. Someone was in there so I stumbled forward and just reached the other head in time. With the terrible crashing of the bow I had great difficulty in steadying myself and water leaking through the hatch made the whole experience even more unpleasant. Back on my bunk I lay retching and sweating in my thermals until Alice helped me undress and Paul came down to see how ill I was. 'I hope you're going to do something soon, because Rodney is pressing to go back to Dartmouth,' he said.

I knew that to give in now would be to jeopardise future sailing whenever the sea was rough, which would be a great handicap to the trip. Seasickness had been a worry before the trip and had to be beaten now or never. 'I think I can make it, Paul, if you get everything ready . . . just chuck me onto my board,' I groaned, not convinced by what I was saying. When the moment came I was still just on the right side of total helplessness and managed to crawl back into the drysuit. Lurching through the saloon, I caught sight of several uneaten breakfasts and green faces – at least I was not the only one. Unsteady on my feet, I was at last on deck and looking at the sea – so changed from the mill-pond of the day before – seething and boiling like water in a great cauldron. But it was the most wonderful place in the world at that moment as I swung myself gratefully off *Morningtown*'s heaving deck.

For a while I just sat on the board, chilled as the cold wind stabbed through my suit drying my damp skin, but feeling better every minute as the sickness subsided. I slipped off the board into the sea and quickly popped out again with a waterstart, sailing off unsteady at first, but as my balance returned, beginning to enjoy the wild conditions. I was using the Klepper S205, my smallest and lightest board, and kept it planing at high speed with the 4m sail, gybing and surfing my way westwards with the wind.

It was a beautifully clear day with ragged white clouds racing high overhead. The large waves meant that visibility at sea level was poor and *Bumble* kept right behind me all the time: I could hear the engine above the noise of the wind and, if losing it for a second, stopped to check they were still there. At one point I sliced past *Morningtown*'s stern, gybed and hurtled off down a wave; I could see from the faces of those on deck that they were amused by the spectacle of *Bumble*, the faithful hound, on my shoulder as I sailed along. It was the comic caterpillar motion of the inflatable clawing its way to the top of a wave and slithering down the other side that inspired the name.

After the chunky white lighthouse at Start Point only the headland of Prawle Point lay between us and our destination, Salcombe. Once past, I caught a series of long waves which carried me all the way to the Kingsbridge estuary. Stopping adjacent to a white house on Bolt Head I clambered into *Bumble* and we motored in, towing the board. My parents were on the quay, a lovely surprise, and Mark was beside them, a bottle of champagne at the ready. Considering that morning's twenty-five miles, I was in the mood for celebration. A cameraman from TV South West also arrived and persuaded me to get back on the board so that he could film me 'sailing in'. Cajoling my cotton-wool forearms and rubber legs, I sailed across the river and back, falling in towards the end but trying hard to make it look deliberate.

Charlie had worked in Salcombe for several years and seemed to know everyone there. Beret-clad, he strode around authoritatively and provided us not only with lunch but also a big party in the evening, by kind courtesy of the Victoria Inn, which raised over £100 for the appeal. He even managed to get hold of fresh bread early the next morning and after this was nicknamed 'Salcombe Charlie'.

For me, the highlight of the day was a long hot bath at the hotel where my parents were staying – a chance to soothe away the aches and memories of seasickness. Fresh problems were already on the horizon with our land support. Yet again, David had returned home to Oxford leaving Mark on his own, and it was becoming clear that

David's heart was no longer in the job. Oliver Moore and I discussed the matter on the telephone and agreed that it would be better in the long run for David to quit now. He was told later that evening and Mark subsequently took charge of the PR and the truck.

The strong north-easterly winds continued the following day, Saturday 12 May, and we planned a forty-mile run, all the way to Fowey. Starting at about 8am with *Pytheas II* and the 5m sail, I picked up the wind just beyond Bolt Cliffs and met up with the tandem boys, who had sailed out from nearby Bantham, a Devonian Mecca for windsurfing. I greeted Steve and his brother-in-law who were both wearing crash helmets and looking ready for anything. They were just finishing a shot of Scotch and a sail change down to their small rig and told me to carry on and they would catch up.

Imagining something of a race I set off at a cracking speed across Bigbury Bay towards Plymouth. Quite carried away by the sailing, I did not look round for some time and failed to notice that the tandem, *Bumble* and *Morningtown*, were trailing behind. They were all several miles back when I tried in vain to raise them on the radio and I had to sit and wait on my board, rather irritated at wasting the good breeze. A short time later a fishing boat came along and wanted to rescue me. I had quite a job convincing the skipper that there was no need but he was obviously determined to rescue something and on leaving me made a bee-line for the tandem. Steve and his brother-in-law stoutly resisted arrest and those on *Morningtown* described the sight as it tried to elude the fishing boat, looking like a wounded butterfly, its yellow sails flapping. Later we heard on the radio that the tandem with all its valuable cargo had been towed reluctantly into Salcombe.

Bumble eventually caught up after sorting out some engine problems. They passed on a message to me from Rodney: 'If you ever get that far ahead again, the contract is terminated!' Knowing better than to argue, I ignored this threat and we continued. To our right now was the wide mouth of the Plym and on the horizon to our left we could see the tower of the Eddystone lighthouse.

The wind slackened and we tried a sail change in *Bumble* which took over half an hour and still resulted in a baggy mess. We all blamed each other and then laughed about it. The boat was really too small with four of us crawling around trying to thread ropes, tie knots and slot in battens. We never rigged sails in *Bumble* again as it was obviously more efficient to do so on *Morningtown*'s foredeck.

These delays cost me dearly. The wind was dying away by the hour and I was running out of time to reach Fowey before the tide turned. In uncomfortable conditions I became bad-tempered and *Bumble* wisely kept for the most part out of earshot! While I sloshed slowly along, the Fowey lifeboat came out to join us and evidently found 'the scene' boring compared to the eighteen-knot excitement they were accustomed to on board a new Brede Class lifeboat. They enlivened the afternoon by making repeated fast runs towards me and sheering off at the last second. When Chris started to make a photographic record of this windsurfer-baiting, *Bumble* became the next target for hostilities! It was good light relief for which the lifeboat boys were rewarded with swigs from our half-gallon bottle of whisky, swung across to them from *Morningtown* on a rope.

Just east of the entrance to Fowey, mind, body and tide all conspired to make me stop and we motored a mile up the river to anchor for our first night in Cornwall. Mark was in Fowey, cheerful after his first day in control of the PR, and requesting me ashore immediately for a live phone-in on the local radio. After reviving myself with a tall glass of sweet sherry, I complied.

We woke the next day, 14 May, to a still, clear morning. The river looked magical, sparkling in the sun where the odd ripple disturbed the surface. My enjoyment of the gorgeous weather was spoilt by the knowledge that light airs would doubtless make for a slow, uncomfortable day at sea. Charlie and I motored to the mouth of the river to make sure of the sail choice – there was no wind. Armed with the 9m I started off towards Gribbin Head on the first step to Falmouth.

I had not gone far when, to my astonishment, vigorous gusts of wind came sweeping off the hillside behind me and in an alarmingly short time the breeze reached such a strength that I could hang onto the sail no longer. I radioed *Morningtown* for a smaller sail but was being blown rapidly ashore and should have anticipated their reply: 'You're too close to the rocks, we can't risk coming in.' With no chance of another rig in a hurry, my only option was to jump into *Bumble* and motor out of trouble. In the scramble to dismantle the big sail we forget to take a fix of my last position and, with a sinking feeling, I realised that I would have to return to the mouth of the river and start all over again. The whole episode cost me about an hour and, to make matters worse, the wind began to die shortly after I restarted. It was going to be one of those days: the boom was absurdly low on the mast, and the leg-straps on my harness jacket, wrongly positioned, cut into me whenever I stood up straight!

It was a long, tedious session to Falmouth, wobbling precariously in the large swell. Such days of choppy sea and light wind were the worst for me, although the most peaceful for those in *Bumble* and *Morningtown*. A faint but consistent sea breeze picked up and carried me the last stretch to St Anthony's Head and it was with great relief that I finally halted by the lighthouse in the mouth of the Fal. I had covered just twenty-two miles in five and a half hours, making my average speed a pathetic three and a half knots. Collapsing in a heap on *Morningtown*'s aft deck for the run-in to Falmouth, I reflected that these last two days had been reminiscent of the ghastly first two – the voyage was becoming a slog again. I was barely more than a fifth of the way round; things had got to speed up.

I was reminded of my comparatively slow progress, meeting in Falmouth marina the crew of a large yacht on their one stop-over from Southampton to Dublin. Whereas I had passed Southampton a week ago, they had been there the morning before and hoped to be in Dublin the next day!

We were met in the estuary by the Falmouth lifeboat and entertained no less than eight lifeboatmen to a beer when we berthed in the marina. The coxswain intrigued us by saying that few call-outs these days were to vessels in real distress and that most were to incompetent yacht owners. 'The other day we were called out to a catamaran in trouble,' he said, 'and found that at the first sign of weather, the owner had frozen up and forgotten how to turn on his engines or put up the sails!'

We took a rest day in Falmouth to carry out maintenance work on *Morningtown* and to fill up with diesel and water. I bought myself a new pair of rubber windsurfing shoes – the soles on my first pair were worn through – and also reorganised my masts, sails and booms with a view to making sail changes more efficient. With this in mind I held a rigging 'surgery' on the quay for any crew not already *au fait* with luff, clew and leech.

Later, Liz and Mark had their first attempts at windsurfing, the former rather more successfully than the latter, who seemed much more interested in the swimming side of things! Charlie and Chris, already accomplished at the sport, raced across the river and back fully clothed. Despite falling in, Chris was the winner, earning, I think, six pints of beer and two free games of pool. Jack, uncle as he was affectionately known, went home from Falmouth leaving Rodney now as the lone oldie among us youngsters.

Next day, Tuesday 15 May, looked like being yet another slow one. When we reached the mouth of the river at 9.30am, the sea was glassy smooth with not a breath of wind anywhere. I took the specialised, light-wind Division II board with my biggest sail and waited. For once I was glad to listen to the cassette player. While I lay on the board resigned to a sleepy day, Paul in energetic mood persuaded everyone on *Morningtown* to swab down the decks – and, bad luck for them, there was no tot of rum as a reward.

I was disturbed from my mid-ocean rock 'n roll by the growl of approaching engines and looked up to see a tall red ship bearing down on me in determined fashion. I gestured to them my lack of power and pointed away, but either the skipper misunderstood my sign language, or the answer was 'No' because it steamed resolutely on, aiming straight at me. I looked around. A few hundred yards away was a man fishing from a rowing boat and beyond him *Morningtown*. Between us we must have been blocking the deep-water entrance to the Fal, but why had I been singled out for attention?

There was no time to debate the point so I got to my feet and began pumping the sail strenuously. Fortunately, a flicker of breeze began filtering in from the south and I was able to edge effectively out of the way, noticing the tug's name as it passed, *The Invincible*. I carried on sailing and aimed for a chocolate-brown smudge on the water further out that indicated more wind. It was spring tides and once out into the main stream I hoped to make one and a half knots in the tide alone.

I crossed the estuary, passing a great ship at anchor and, nearby, a bombing range where an antiquated plane was making repeated drops over a large orange buoy – and missing each time by miles. Then I was passing The Manacles, vicious shark's-fin rocks, that have claimed many a brave ship and crew. Today, there was little chance of a shipwreck, the conditions being so gentle. I was impressed by the performance of the Division II board, able to glide along in the lightest of breezes and steal ground upwind. Sailing today was like being on a reservoir, so refreshingly different from the bumpy sailing I had experienced till now.

I made several tacks and headed, close-hauled, for a headland which by its shape I took to be the Lizard; the staircase of jagged teeth looked just like a lizard's back. On reaching it I realised that, not for the first time, I had misjudged the distance. This was Black Head and there was a six-mile-wide bay to cross before the Lizard itself. I was determined to round the headland this afternoon, but the tide would turn at about 3pm, in an hour or so, and it became a race against time. I put on all speed, driving myself forward across the bay, not stopping to draw breath, even though I had been sailing for close on five hours without a break.

I reached the Lizard, sailed well past the lifeboat station east of the point and was nearing the lighthouse before I realised that something was wrong. A black buoy marking a lobster pot bubbled past me at some speed, and then another one – the tide had turned already and was carrying me backwards! Having put so much effort into the thirteen miles to get there, I did not feel inclined to give up so easily and tacked offshore further into the race looking for less tide; if anything, it was stronger. *Bumble* came over and Chris urged me to stop. I glanced at the headland which looked innocently back as if to say, 'Don't worry, I'll still be here tomorrow', and dropped the sail in resignation, just off Bass Point. I guessed, and guessed right, that it would be a lot nastier the next day.

Our plan to be in Penzance for the night thwarted, at about 3.15pm we headed back towards Falmouth to anchor in the Helford river. On the way, passing The Manacles, Rodney spotted a Wayfarer dinghy through his binoculars several miles out to sea and heading east. We surmised that the lone sailor was intrepid rather than in trouble but notified the coastguard just in case. Motoring into our quiet anchorage, I was glad we had been delayed at the Lizard. Helford river, inspiration for Daphne du Maurier's *Frenchman's Creek*, is enchanting, with green, thickly wooded banks broken by lazy tributaries winding down to the main stream. We anchored up-river opposite the little village of Porth Navas and radioed Mark to make arrangements for the evening.

Rodney stayed on board to watch ship and, minus Liz who fancied an early night, the rest of us went ashore to have dinner with Tris Cokes, my board-builder. We left *Bumble* tied to the quay, calculating our return for 11pm so as to avoid being stranded on the mud as the tide retreated. Packed into the truck, Mark drove us through the Cornish countryside. What a contrast it was to see a valley in full spring bloom after so much bare ocean: palm trees, rhododendrons and wonderful colours in flower-beds and on hillsides. We arrived at Tris's house in Redruth and spent a riotous evening with everyone in party mood. It was good to see the team so well knit. Tris and his wife had gathered dozens of mussels from the beach which were marinated in wine, and there was pizza and chicken as well as more wine. We left Redruth hurriedly at 11.10 and arrived at Porth Navas just after 11.30. Mark dropped us in the village and drove off to find a place to park for the night. Five minutes later we bitterly regretted his going.

Bumble, still attached to the quay, was now separated from the main channel by several hundred yards of deep mud. There seemed little hope of getting out to *Morningtown* till the tide came back up at about 3.30am. Chris, however, with characteristic optimism, announced loudly that it would be easy to push *Bumble* across the mud to the water. 'We do it all the time at home in Essex,' he added. At that he stripped off from the waist downwards and advanced into the thigh-deep sludge. Giving *Bumble* a mighty heave, he managed to shift it about a foot. 'Only three hundred more like that', I thought. Paul and Haydn had already stripped off and were wading in to help; they had spotted a little channel down which a trickle of water was flowing. Charlie, unconvinced, but not wishing to look unhelpful, reluctantly removed his shoes and trousers to join in. Alice and I had less conscience and just watched with Chris's camera. They heaved and heaved at the stubborn boat. The little stream dried to nothing and, giving up at last, everyone came panting back to the quay, covered in mud.

While waiting for the tide to rise, we made ourselves as comfortable as possible and tried to get some sleep. Chris crawled under a nearby boat which soon began to rumble with the sound of his snoring. The rest of us curled up on the concrete and had rather less success. Some time later, Paul found an unlocked garage containing a variety of aids to comfortable sleep. He ended up on top of a freezer, Alice and I between two carpets, Haydn under a bean-bag and Charlie in an armchair. At last 3.30 came and enough water to rejoin *Morningtown*. We were all assembled except Charlie. Only a fearful coughing and retching could be heard which startled Alice until Paul reassured her it was only some 'old marshman'. At this, a creature appeared, and materialised into Charlie, complaining of food poisoning and blaming the mussels.

After what seemed like a sleepless night, we weighed anchor and set off to tackle again the formidable hurdle of the Lizard. At 10am I started windsurfing about a mile east of Bass Point on *Pytheas II* with a 7m sail. The wind was about the top end of force 3 from the north-west and blowing against the tide. An enormous sea had been thrown up and the place was unrecognisable from the comparative calm of the day before. I charged off into the race sailing close to the wind on starboard tack to stay as far north as possible. I had never encountered standing waves like these – sheer walls of water up to twelve feet in height. Somehow I gained enough momentum to ride up them only to drop down the other side landing with a crash that jarred my legs and spine. Totally in the grip of the tide I was being pushed and shoved by the swirling water, trying to keep the board moving forward to give me as much balance as possible. I felt very separated from the others. *Morningtown* was some couple of hundred yards away, see-sawing wildly and, in the troughs between waves, I could barely make out the top of her mast. *Bumble*, only twenty yards or so behind, was completely obscured by the sea.

Before long, *Bumble* came alongside as best they could to warn me that I was heading for the Canaries on the tide! They kept shouting 'Tack! Tack!' I was all in favour of the Canaries at the time and, in the heat of the moment, trying to keep my heaving board in contact with the sea and myself on top, I yelled back, 'Would one of you like to come and take over? I'm doing the windsurfing and I'm not tacking now!' Tacking in this sea meant falling in and being unable to start again, so I hacked on until clear of the worst. Then I tacked and fell in, spending a frustrating few minutes getting going again. I tried waterstarting but the wind was far too disturbed on the sea's surface and I swallowed mouthfuls of water. I uphauled instead and, succeeding at last, sailed off – now on port tack.

I clawed back the two miles that the tide had stolen and tacked again, this time managing a slick enough movement to cheat the sea. I followed *Morningtown*'s line across Mount's Bay, relieved and proud to have put this obstinate headland behind me. Would the next one be as difficult, I wondered?

I had a glorious two-and-a-half-hour run across the fifteen-mile stretch to Land's End. When the hump of this landmark came into view I looked back and could still see the Lizard poking up from the horizon. Soon it was gone and Land's End drew closer and closer. The wind having switched to the north-west today, I was planing close to the wind for about the first time. It was a comfortable point of sailing, not too close to have to adjust constantly but close enough to be able to relax fully into the harness and let the body's weight balance the force of the wind in the sail. I tried to keep as still as possible and steered the board with the pressure of my feet on its edges – a little on the far rail to go closer to the wind, a little on the near rail to bear away more. Sometimes in the stronger gusts the board suddenly surged with life and I would have to restrain it, pulling the rig back towards me with my stomach muscles.

On the two or three occasions when I had visited Land's End before, there had always been a formidable sea running. Today was no exception: a long, lazy swell was rolling past, probably generated thousands of miles away by some mid-Atlantic storm – even now still going strong. I had sailed twenty-three miles in only three and a half hours, a good average of six knots, and Paul and Rodney both shared my pleasure, commenting, 'Just shows what you can do with the right wind and no stops or falls!'

Just before 2pm we headed back to Penzance for the night to prepare for one of the most difficult sections of our journey – round Land's End and across the Bristol Channel to the Welsh coast. I ate a good lunch of toasted cheese sandwiches and home-made tomato soup sitting on deck gazing at the rugged Cornish coast. We were passing the Minack open-air theatre at Porthcurno and everyone clamoured for the binoculars to study this unique stone structure. Considering the frequency of roaring gales along the coast here, I wondered how the actors ever made themselves heard above the wind. We passed the famous village of Mousehole and then, with the fairy-tale castle of St Michael's Mount as a distant backdrop, docked into the small inner harbour at Penzance.

I slept in the afternoon and woke in time for supper to the sound of

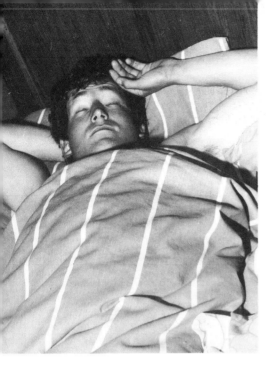

(*above left*) Waking up; (*above right*) Rigging the sail; (*below left*) Lunch; (*below right*) Off with the drysuit

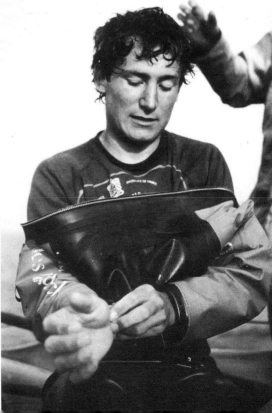

(*above*) Rigging surgery at Falmouth; (*below*) Haydn, Chris and Paul in the Helford River mud

an old fisherman talking loudly in the saloon. He was narrating his life story to anyone who would listen while Rodney quizzed him about ports along the west coast. 'Douglas, Isle of Man's a super harbour, but watch out for the sands to the north . . . Fishguard, now that's a terrible place. I wouldn't go near it if I were you . . . Lundy, there's a great anchorage there. Milford Haven? Fine harbour. Married my third wife in Milford Haven!'

From this and information gleaned from both cruising books and other locals, we realised there were no 'safe' harbours for us between Penzance and Milford Haven. This was a stretch of coast where *Morningtown*'s deep six-foot keel was at its most restricting. Padstow was too shallow and most other harbours up the north Cornish coast dry out completely at low tide. As the majority of anchorages would be exposed to weather from south-west through to north-east, we had to think in terms of two or three nights at sea. I hoped the weather would be kind as I did not relish the prospect of long, hard days on the board, punctuated by sleepless, seasick nights.

5 LAND'S END TO LUNDY

17 May started cold, grey and windy. We listened intently to the shipping forecast, hoping the wind might shift out of the north and allow a fast sail across this long stretch, but it seemed firmly anchored: north-nor'westerly 5, possibly 6, was forecast for sea area Lundy. Had there been a hint of 8 in the forecast we would certainly not have set off, but force 6, even on the nose, was within my limit. We planned to leave in the afternoon.

Morningtown was prepared for passage, anything stowed that might fly around in rough seas and all clothes and bedding sealed in black dustbin liners. Rodney lectured us on how tough it was going to be: 'Be ready for it to be appalling and it won't be much worse!' he said in his sternest voice. Organising the watches, he decided that we were short of people with himself counted out as navigator and me as windsurfer. He was pondering over some changes in our routine, but when Chris interrupted with an offer to help, Rodney flew off the handle and snapped at him to shut up. At that moment the nearby Scillonian ferry gave a deafening blast of its horn that mercifully diverted everyone's attention.

A short time later Tris appeared with the new board. It was indeed a monster and wide enough, as Tris had said, to accommodate a deck chair if I got fed up. Despite being so large, the board, like all Tris's creations, had an elegant line. He had painted the nose and tail fluorescent orange to aid identification (which proved useful on several occasions). I fell in love with this new weapon, which came to be called the *Log*, and could not wait to try it out. The new arrival, however, rekindled Rodney's temper. He refused to let an extra board be carried on *Morningtown*. Two were already stored on the stern quarters and a third, he declared, would handicap the yacht's performance, and perhaps put all our lives at risk. Though I could see the disadvantage of cluttering *Morningtown*'s foredeck, I did not wish to be limited to two boards, which would mean abandoning the Division II and thereby sacrificing good upwind performance in light airs. I thought it best not to pursue the argument with Rodney and left Paul to sort out a compromise. Thanks to his tact it was eventually agreed either to tow or to tie the third board onto *Bumble*, so only two boards would be on *Morningtown* at any time.

It was clear that Rodney was under pressure as master of the ship — with effective responsibility for the operation — and this was

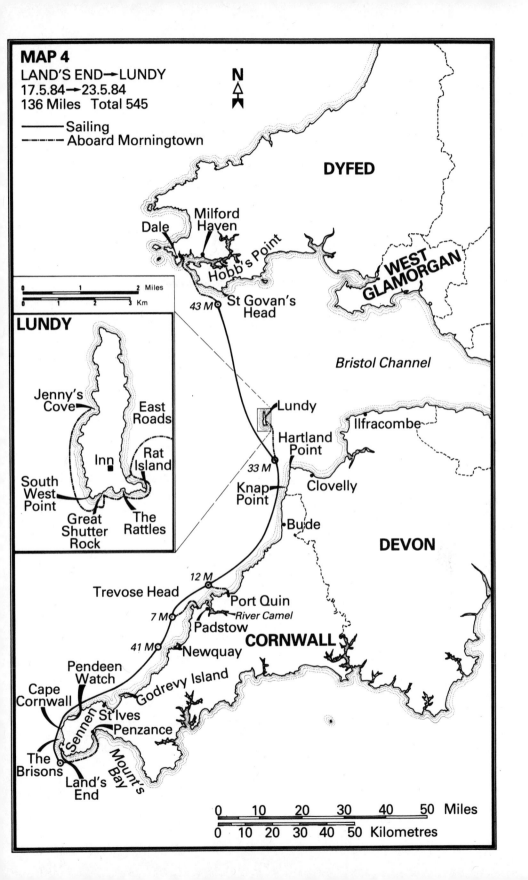

MAP 4
LAND'S END→LUNDY
17.5.84→23.5.84
136 Miles   Total 545

——— Sailing
—·—·— Aboard Morningtown

N

DYFED

Milford
Haven

Dale

Hobb's Point

43 M

St Govan's
Head

**WEST
GLAMORGAN**

Bristol Channel

LUNDY

Jenny's
Cove

East
Roads

Inn

Rat
Island

South
West
Point

Great
Shutter
Rock

The
Rattles

Lundy

Ilfracombe

Hartland
Point

33 M

Knap
Point

Clovelly

Bude

DEVON

12 M

Trevose Head

Port Quin

River Camel

7 M

Padstow

41 M

Newquay

CORNWALL

Pendeen
Watch

Cape
Cornwall

Godrevy Island

St Ives

Penzance

Sennen

The
Brisons

Land's
End

Mount's
Bay

0   1   2   Miles
0   1   2   3 Km

0   10   20   30   40   50   Miles
0   10 20 30 40 50 Kilometres

Board comparison:

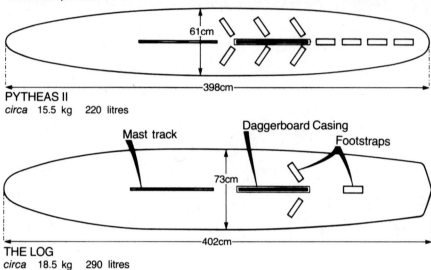

PYTHEAS II
circa 15.5 kg 220 litres

Mast track

Daggerboard Casing

Footstraps

73cm

402cm

THE LOG
circa 18.5 kg 290 litres

Side sections:

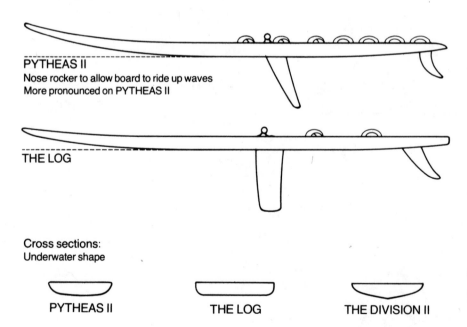

PYTHEAS II
Nose rocker to allow board to ride up waves
More pronounced on PYTHEAS II

THE LOG

Cross sections:
Underwater shape

PYTHEAS II   THE LOG   THE DIVISION II

exacerbated by our close involvement with both the RNLI and coastguard. Rodney's disquiet, however, brewed tension among the rest of us and we began to feel as if we were heading out into the 'roaring forties', not just across the Bristol Channel. The grey weather did not improve the atmosphere and, after the events of the morning, Liz decided that she had had enough. Complaining of a personality clash with Rodney, she quickly packed her bags, said goodbye and left. It was a sad moment. Liz was the second casualty in under three weeks; I began to wonder who would be next.

There were several mechanical problems to be put right before we could get away. *Morningtown* had a cracked auxiliary starting motor which had to be replaced and the ship was swarming with Rodney's men from his local yard. They also repaired *Bumble*'s large radio set which Haydn had accidentally 'blown' in Falmouth. Meanwhile, Mark collected some new radios, forwarded to St Ives by Thanet Electronics from Kent. The waterproof bag containing my radio had punctured on the way from Fowey and sea water had since destroyed the set. It would have been unthinkable to set out on this leg without all our radios in working order – communication was vital.

I needed a back pouch sewn to one of my harness jackets and went in search of a sail loft. I found one up a side street and was confronted by a silver-haired old man who eyed me suspiciously, saying he would not do the job until I told him what the jacket was for. When I had explained he still would not help me unless I gave him a good reason for the crazy idea. I mentioned the *Guinness Book of Records* and then the RNLI, but he was unimpressed. 'Well, OK,' I said finally. 'It keeps the flies from settling and the moss from growing under the feet.' 'Now there's a reason!' said the old man with considerable satisfaction, and told me to come back after lunch.

Everything was ready at 2pm and we could at last leave Penzance and its rather tainted atmosphere behind. There were now several 'extras' on board: Maurice, the coxswain of the Sennen lifeboat, kindly acting as our pilot round Land's End; Dennis, a freelance photographer; plus a BBC TV cameraman. Maurice, a salty seadog with a great beard and a mischievous gleam in his eyes, immediately took charge. He saved us several miles by taking us close in to the shore near Penlee Point. Paul and I were slightly taken aback, noticing submerged rocks marked on the chart. 'You know its low water springs, don't you?' I pointed out to Maurice. It was a case of trying to teach your grandmother to suck eggs and he grinned broadly. 'We 'aven't 'it anything yet, 'ave we?'

Approaching the Runnelstone buoy an attack of nerves hit me. The TV cameraman kept asking me about the voyage and although his questions were well meant, I was not in the mood to answer them. Today's sailing was going to be very testing – a hard beat round this awesome landmark into whatever lay beyond – and all my efforts were going to be recorded by cameras. 'It'll be rough up there with a breeze against the north-running tide,' Maurice said, as if to key me up even further.

There is a limit to how long you can sit waiting with the adrenalin flowing and, for once, I was really eager to get onto my board and engage with wind and sea. For the fast planing I had chosen *Pytheas II* and the 6m sail. I kicked the daggerboard down to give maximum lift upwind and pulled the sail up. Streaking off towards the cliffs south of Land's End, I felt a painful twinge in my stomach – the muscles must have been strained by the close-hauled sailing across Mount's Bay the day before. It was a niggling worry but would have to be a lot worse to force me to stop now and I found a position in the harness that kept the discomfort to a minimum.

The waves were large, eight feet or more, and wherever the tide ran strongest there were areas of heavy overfalls. Concentrating hard on the broken sea ahead, I zigzagged north making as few tacks as possible since I risked a ducking with each one. The waves made forward progress very staccato, but the healthy tide under me meant I was soon drawing level with Longships, the Land's End lighthouse, distinguished from this distance by the flat top of its helicopter pad. I tacked just south of the rocks, the sea bursting up around them like a great live carpet, and headed towards the heap of square granite blocks that is Land's End itself.

An aircraft flew over and circled above my head. It was the Scillies British Airways helicopter. I was reminded of my last sighting of the helicopter as a distant speck when lost off St Mary's eight months before. I wanted to give them a wave but only managed a rapid jerk of my hand off the boom, spotted by Charlie (and later imitated!) coming up behind in *Bumble*. *Morningtown* was now steaming towards me at full speed and veered off at the last moment to allow the photographers their pictures: through the waves I caught a glimpse of Maurice's grinning face at the wheel. He laughed out loud a little later when a big green wave broke over the boat, catching both cameramen unawares as they craned over the side.

I was past Land's End now and feeling well pleased. We had turned an important corner and were heading north for the first time. For the most part buried from sight by the waves I popped onto a crest to see a fishing boat bobbing close by – all heads on deck were turned towards me and wearing looks of total astonishment. I wished I could have stopped to explain. We were off Whitesand Bay where Sennen Cove lies. Facing directly west, this bay is pounded by the full might of the Atlantic weather and its sandy beach offers some of the best surfing in Britain. Maurice piloted *Bumble* through the breakers and, his job done, waded ashore with the two cameramen.

Maurice's departure triggered a subtle change in the mood of the afternoon. The wind was freshening and the waves seemed larger, the sea wilder and the rocky shore more forbidding. The tall chimney of an old tin mine marked the bluff of Cape Cornwall up ahead and I worked my way towards it uneasily, feeling some pain in my ribs from heavy use of the harness during the day. I squeezed through a narrow channel between the mainland and some outlying rocks called The Brisons. The sea was smashing against them and the noise and the spray reminded me to take care. One slip here and I would be on the granite. I waited for a wave to go by, then tacked gingerly before the next one. Just south of the cape itself I found myself opposite a little scoop in the cliffs called Priest's Cove. Several men were moving about on the shingle near a couple of wooden boats; though only a few hundred yards away, ashore they seemed in a different world.

Once past the cape and heading for Pendeen Watch, I encountered the most severe conditions of the day. The fresh wind was propelling me along too fast for the state of the sea. The waves were tall, steep and close together, and on each one I was flung into the air and barely had time to land and steady myself before the next collision. More from exhaustion than error, my feet eventually slipped from the footstraps, and I splashed upside down into a tunnel between two waves.

I needed a break, but Charlie found it difficult to get close and made three attempts before throwing me a line. I tied up the board and flopped into *Bumble*. While exchanging a few pleasantries about the conditions, I poured myself a cup of coffee. 'What's the matter? Isn't it hot?' asked Charlie, seeing the look of disappointment on my face. The Thermos was full of broken glass and I had been looking forward to that coffee for two hours. We threw the flask away and watched it vanish over a wave top. The fearful slamming against the waves in *Bumble* had not only broken the Thermos but also the main radio, as well as damaging Chris's cameras. It suddenly dawned on me what Chris and Charlie went through on such rough days: today had been particularly harsh on Chris who looked exhausted and had already been sick once. All things considered, they were both remarkably cheerful. In their shoes I might well have been wondering what on earth I was doing there in the first place.

It was about six in the evening and we radioed *Morningtown* for a quick conference. Rodney suggested the alternative of stopping here and hoving to for the night rather than carrying on. Lying overnight in this monstrously disturbed sea with our backs to inhospitable cliffs was not at all an attractive proposition. Carrying on had to be preferable.

I gritted my teeth and heaved the board back into action. The next two or three miles were tough, but once past Pendeen Watch the coast slopes away north-east and I was able to bear away onto a close reach, cruising with a steady rhythm twenty-five miles up the north Cornish coast. I passed St Ives, then the white pillar of Godrevy lighthouse, of Virginia Woolf's *To the Lighthouse* fame, and by 9pm was level with the glittering lights of Newquay. During this stretch I was exhilarated by the swift sailing and the miles slipping by under the board but, as the evening wore on, the impulse to stop occurred more and more frequently. Whenever this happened I either distracted my mind till the urge retreated or reassured myself with false promises that I would 'stop in a minute' – anything bar actually laying down the rig.

Playing this cat-and-mouse game I became almost hypnotised by the need to carry on regardless. Had Chris and Charlie not broken me from my trance I might in this way have sailed right up the coast of Cornwall. Rodney thought it prudent that we stop before night set in and, some forty crucial miles covered, I dropped the sail.

Bumble manoeuvred in close to pick me up and we all had a fright when *Morningtown* caught a wave and was swept almost on top of us before Rodney managed to put her into reverse. With some difficulty, Charlie took *Bumble* alongside to pass the mast and boom up to Haydn and, waiting my moment, I leapt for a shroud and pulled myself aboard. Chris began passing the rest of the gear up from the drenched inflatable and had hardly enough energy to do so. As he came to climb aboard I watched, concerned, rarely having seen anyone so utterly exhausted. He lunged for the shrouds, missed and fell heavily against *Morningtown*, nearly pitching into the sea between the two crashing boats. Fortunately, he did not seem to be hurt; perhaps was too tired to care. Haydn and Paul quickly helped him aboard and he went below for a wretched night of seasickness.

I did not feel much better myself. Getting off my board after so many hours gave me a feeling of amputation, rendered much worse by the contrast between the even surfing of my craft and *Morningtown*'s evil rolling. I looked at the lights of Newquay only a few miles away across the dark choppy sea. How much I would have preferred to be there – on solid ground. I half thought of surfing in

(*opposite above*) Engaging hovercraft, Dover; (*below*) Radios out in Porth Clais after an attempt on St David's Head, south-west Wales
(*overleaf*) *Morningtown* and sailboard flat out down the Sound of Jura

and beaching my board on Fistral beach, an old haunt, but I did not entertain the idea for long. I could not have left everyone else behind and the mere suggestion would not have gone down well with the ship's master!

I went below to remove my clothing. The knees of my drysuit had worn through and now the legs filled with water. I peeled off the suit and poured the water down the drain in the aft head. The ship lurched violently. I began to feel sick and wanted to lie down – all the aches and pains that had developed and been suppressed during the day were surfacing. I dried off as best I could and went into the aft cabin where I was sleeping for greater comfort while we were at sea. Alice came and offered me some supper but I felt too tired and too sick even to lift my head up and eat. She later told me of her cooking disaster that evening, when the oven door had opened and shepherd's pie had erupted all over the galley; it spread in all directions, even penetrating the hatch into the engine-room. She had scraped it back into the dish (no one saw that!) and spent the next hour scrubbing grease off the floor to make it non-slip again.

We hove to for the night where we were and the boat rocked backwards and forwards with the yankee acting against the mizzen, keeping us almost on the same spot. It is a relatively comfortable way to kill time out at sea – the same sensation as moving gently forwards – because you meet the waves full on and there is minimum roll. I still felt uncomfortable, not being much of a sailor stomach-wise. The wind and waves always sound more fearsome when you are stuck below and it was difficult to snatch more than brief bouts of sleep before I would be awake again, listening and wondering about the morrow. Once I sat up, frightened out of a doze by the conviction that the boat was sinking. I looked around the cabin and was sure that the floor was awash with water: I was too tired to do a great deal and would probably have gone down quietly with the ship. Then Rodney walked in at the change of a watch and did not seem to be bothered by knee-deep water so, realising my mistake, I flopped back in the bunk and closed my eyes again.

The next time I opened them a grey light was filtering into the cabin and I lay there for a few moments, quite still and comfortable for once; the wind seemed to have died down. I heard Rodney say in an urgent voice to the ship in general, 'It's five o'clock, let's get him in the water!' which put me straight into a bad mood. I was not an object to be chucked in and pulled out at his whim. I felt stiff and

(*above*) The reefing sail in action off the Isle of Man coast; (*below*) Paul and Liz make light of rough weather off north-west Scotland

tired and not in the least like getting up to go windsurfing, so I staged a small lie-in demonstration. Alice eventually cajoled me out of this by playing on my conscience: 'Everyone else is up, some have been up most of the night, so why should you stay in bed?' It was a valid point. What were all these people doing here, if not helping me round Britain? It seemed a remote goal at the moment but I rose, still feeling that I was getting a raw deal.

In the cabin while I drank some tea and ate Marmite on toast, Rodney muttered something about it being 'not on' for me to linger in my bunk. This I thought was unnecessary but said nothing and waited till I was away on the board before letting off steam to Haydn and Charlie in *Bumble* (Chris had been left in his bunk to rest). I started with a 7m sail and *Pytheas II*, but the breeze was dying steadily and feeling ghastly I soon stopped for a welcome cup of coffee from Thermos II and a Penguin biscuit. Afterwards, I tried the *Log* for the first time with a 9m sail. The stability of this new board was a joy, so much so that I should perhaps have made a sacrifice to the gods on the spot. I knew then what a difference the increased comfort would make to the rest of the trip.

After a while, not even this new delight could keep my tired body interested. I was having difficulty even uphauling the large sail. On the move I kept nodding off to sleep – as one does on motorways during long car journeys – and jerked awake with a start when I took in my surroundings. It was not as dangerous a habit as falling asleep at the wheel but just as unnerving. Before long I stopped and sat on the board. There was no breeze worth talking about and progress was minimal: just seven miles towards Trevose Head in nearly four hours – by far the worst average to date. At about 10am the tide turned and we had no choice but to call it a day, for at least six hours anyway.

Rodney reported a strange radio call from a nearby boat, *The Diligence*. 'Wem-u-too?' a voice enquired. This was said so fast as to be incomprehensible and Rodney took it to be an enquiry after our recent movements. 'We've come from Newquay this morning,' he replied. 'Yer, I know thaat but werem-u-too?' *Diligence* asked again. Rodney then twigged; he wanted to know where we were headed not where we had been! The skipper of *Diligence* turned out to be the coxswain of the Padstow lifeboat and when he heard we had no particular destination, he invited us to use the lifeboat mooring in a little cove just round Trevose Head towards Padstow.

This was excellent news. We motored as fast as we could towards the haven – Haydn made coffee which we drank on deck and, as the cook was asleep, we took the opportunity to demolish a chocolate cake. Everyone's spirits lifted. Chris had surfaced and looked totally recovered from his unhappy previous day and I, too, felt much better, the trials of the last twelve hours receding fast into memory.

The cove was so well concealed behind a semi-circle of broken-down cliffs that we almost missed it. A squadron of gulls flew up to announce our arrival and we noticed how the rock was whitened with guano. It was a beautiful little bay, well sheltered from all except nor'westerly winds and dominated on the south-west side by a spectacular lifeboat house and slipway, jutting out of the rock wall. What a perfect spot. You would never know it was there without local knowledge, without *Diligence* in this case.

Safely moored to a sturdy buoy, we were able to relax. I went below to sleep and woke to hear excited voices on deck. *Diligence*, a little blue fishing boat, had arrived bearing a gift of six enormous crabs. The skipper's name was Trevor England and we invited him on board for a beer. He is an entertaining man full of life and bounce, with sparkling blue eyes and a youthful appearance that belies his years of experience at sea. We got on so well that he and his mate stayed to share our lunch of boiled brisket. Trevor was interested to hear about Maurice being our pilot around Land's End. 'He's a good mate of mine is Maurice. And a very brave man indeed,' he said, pausing artfully before continuing. 'Sennen's a small place and it's a brave maan tha' could leave his wife and take up with another woman in the syme village!'

After lunch, Trevor gave Chris, Alice and me a lift into Padstow. He showed us some local sights of interest, such as the dreaded Doom Bar across the mouth of the River Camel that earned its name for wrecking so many ships of old and, more topically, Boobies Bay, reputed to be Prince Charles's favourite surfing spot. On the way Trevor hauled up from a sea-bed store several crates full of spider crabs destined for the export market. Despite being sweeter than the ordinary crab, they are not popular in Britain and almost all the Cornish catch is sold on the Continent, particularly to Spain.

That night we slept well after a magnificent meal of crab and woke in the morning, 18 May, to find no change in the wind – there was still very little – and on top of that we were surrounded by dense fog. Paul, Chris and Charlie went to Padstow in *Bumble* and had to pick their way from rock to rock along the shore. A little later we heard an engine through the mist and *Diligence* appeared. Trevor, as usual beaming, handed Alice a large, freshly caught grey mullet, which she turned into a delicious lunch. I spent the morning repairing the nose of the *Log* which had been damaged in the night, banging against *Bumble*'s engine. Rodney chatted to the lifeboat honorary secretary who had also come to meet us. We had eaten all but the head of our delectable mullet when Trevor turned up with more fish. This time it was pollack and we traded it for a bottle of Charles Heidsieck.

The rest of the day was on the whole quiet and peaceful. Most people read books and one or two jokes circulated about our lack of progress: Rodney kept asking Alice if she had remembered to bring the turkey! Being becalmed for a day and a half certainly rubbed in how completely in the hands of the weather we were, and potentially what a very long time the journey could take. For me it was partly this uncertainty – so infinitely preferable to the predictability of motorised travel – that made the trip worth doing.

We tried unsuccessfully to reach Mark on the radio and guessed the truck would be on its way round to meet us in South Wales. Unknown to us, however, it had broken down and was sitting at the time in a garage in Exeter.

In mid-afternoon the mist suddenly lifted to reveal a sunny sky and the ruffle of a decent little breeze further out to sea. Plans were quickly made. 'Let's get moving,' Rodney urged. 'We've still got time to reach Lundy tonight.' The boat was cleared and ready to leave when we noticed that Chris was missing. He was located near the shore, swimming with his seagull hat on, and we had some difficulty making ourselves heard above the din of courting gulls before he swam back.

On the way out to Trevose Head, elaborate lighting plans were made for the night sailing that would be entailed in reaching Lundy. But by the time we arrived at our spot at about 4.30 the breeze was petering out and a long haul did not seem so likely. I started sailing with *Pytheas II* and the 7m but was never comfortable. Before long a change to the Division II and the 9m sail was precipitated by the rig collapsing and plunging me backwards into the water. It was a strange sensation – I heard a sawing sound as Haydn's clever little rigging knot slipped off the sail and I was landed in the sea, the sail on top of me.

The wind became so light that at one stage Chris and Charlie were giving me a good race by rowing *Bumble*. The tide, however, was with us and, to my surprise, I covered twelve miles in just over two hours. We stopped for a quiet night at anchor off a little village called Port Quin.

Port Quin is noted for having become a ghost town in the eighteenth century. All the local fishing boats were lost one night in a violent storm and the surviving population subsequently emigrated to Canada. Alice, Paul and I stayed on board *Morningtown* while the others went ashore to see if the village had a pub. They met a young lad on the jetty who directed them to an inn two hundred yards down the road. It turned out to be nearer two miles and drinking time was substantially cut down!

Next morning I was awake at 4.30am and went on deck to see if the wind warranted a really early start towards Lundy. There was no wind at all – the sea was as smooth as old glass with a thin grey mist hanging over the surface. I woke again at 6.25am for the shipping forecast. The Meteorological Office was evidently expecting a lot of wind from the north but did not seem able to say quite when. There was just enough breeze to start and by 7.30 I had set off with the Division II and the 9m sail. It was a fickle breeze and progress tedious. Rodney, carrying on the theme of being at sea till Christmas, put some carols on the cassette player and blasted them out across the water. *Morningtown* was several hundred yards away so the music was quite faint and Chris, who heard the sound first, thought he was either hearing mermaids or going crazy (or both!). The tide turned foul at ten o'clock and we stopped and hove to opposite a ruined church near Tintagel Head. We had a six-hour wait and in the calm haze were visited by a tiny inquisitive swallow and a huge orange jellyfish that floated lazily past.

To everyone's delight a healthy breeze had filled in from the north-nor'west by 3.30. At last we might make Lundy and I began (with *Pytheas II* and the 7m sail) a long beat towards Hartland Point. I was using the leg-strap harness with the lower hook to give my chest a respite from the bruising it had received three days ago around Land's End. On good sailing form otherwise, I was full of energy for the strenuous job of keeping the board sailing close to the wind. Toes jammed in the footstraps, I tilted the board to leeward to give the daggerboard more bite, leant out over the water in the harness and zigzagged up the rough Cornish coast across Bude Bay, prising miles from the eye of the wind.

After a couple of hours the breeze began to gust above force 5. For a time I battled on, throwing all my weight against the fierce blasts, but I was feathering the sail more and more to spill wind and being driven off line. I stopped to change down to a 6m sail which took a long time in the choppy conditions, *Morningtown* finding it hard to come in close.

Approaching Knap Point, a short blue pencil line appeared on the horizon and gradually grew into the oblong lump of Lundy island. Sailing towards it I so badly wanted to get there that I was as excited as if Lundy were the finish of the whole journey, the end of the rainbow, not just a stepping stone across the Bristol Channel. But the long day of beating had taken its toll and I began to tire. The wind dropped and I changed first to a 7m then a 9m sail, swapping *Pytheas II* for the *Log*. When the wind freshened yet again I was reluctant to make the crew perform another sail change and kept going, straining to subdue my large sail in the rising breeze.

Just after the sun had disappeared – a red orb so like molten metal that one expected a whoosh of steam as it sank into the sea – I gave one wrench too many on my sail and felt something go in my stomach. I stopped immediately, certain I had incurred some deep muscle or hernia injury. It turned out to be a false alarm (the body's trip-switch perhaps), but until the discomfort receded I sweated and fretted like the most hypochondriacal of professional sportsmen, too appalled at the imagined wound and its consequences (goodbye Southend!) even to mention it to anyone.

We had stopped just short of Hartland Point, the promotory of Hercules, where in the gloom of dusk the white skeleton of a wrecked coaster could be seen hard up against the rocks. We were ten miles short of Lundy, but I had covered a good thirty-three miles which amounted to about double the distance of the previous two days. We motored for an hour and a half towards the island through roughish seas, using our radar in the darkness as we approached. Once anchored in the East Roads, the towering cliffs looked quite spooky, lit up every few seconds by the flash of a nearby lighthouse. After a late supper of fish pie and a rare treat of wine, everyone appeared to be in good spirits and the morrow, 21 May, was unanimously declared a day off to explore the island.

Lundy is spectacular in daylight. Three miles long by three-quarters of a mile wide, the island is bordered on all sides by four-hundred-foot cliffs rising almost sheer from the sea. Surfacing at about 11am, we went ashore in *Bumble* and beached on a small apron of shingle under the cliffs. We were met by John Puddy, a bearded, youngish man, who introduced himself as 'The Administrator' (very *Brave New World!*) and asked for £1.50 from each of us as a landing fee. The charge was waived when we explained our mission. 'I don't think anyone has visited Lundy by windsurfer before, though an Egyptian fellow did try and swim over once,' said Mr Puddy.

We climbed a steep, winding path up the cliffs and in a grassy hollow near the top came across a large elegant house, once inhabited by the 'King' of Lundy. It commands superb views across the sea to Devon and is nicely sheltered from the west, about the only place on the island that is. Here we bumped into the island's lighthouse-keeper-cum-coastguard and, following his directions, arrived at the focal point of Lundy life, the Marisco Tavern.

Over a pint of local brew we got talking to several more of Lundy's twelve inhabitants and were able to raise some considerable interest for the lifeboat appeal (our greatest return per capita in any area of the country!). They were forewarned of our arrival watching us rounding Land's End on television news. We chatted about life on Lundy, the frequent storms and the isolation. In the past the island has been the haunt of Vikings, Normans and pirates but is now most popular with writers and bird-watchers. Weekly supplies are delivered weather permitting by the island boat, the *Polar Bear*, and about a dozen times a year, Lundy is visited by *The Waverley*, the world's last ocean-going paddle-steamer, crammed with tourists from Ilfracombe. As luck would have it we had picked one of those days!

We took the precaution of stocking up with beer and sandwiches before the hordes scrambled their way up the cliffs to the inn. They were a varied group, a fair proportion of them on a break from school. Later we were in the tavern when an elderly couple came in complaining that their cottage had been raided and stripped of alcohol and cigarettes. When the paddle-steamer docked back at Ilfracombe the police were in position, hoping that not all the evidence had been consumed!

Rodney and Paul joined us for lunch at the Tavern, having walked right round the island. Rodney took the opportunity to announce that he would be leaving *Morningtown* for a while as soon as we reached the Welsh coast. His marine business needed attending to, but we all thought he simply wanted a break. I felt ambivalent about his going: on the one hand there would certainly be less tension on board but on the other, we might seriously miss his seamanship and experience. Paul, though, was evidently confident. He did not look at all perturbed by the news that he was soon to take over as master-in-charge.

After lunch, Alice and I took a walk across the island. It is a bleak place – just a few hundred acres of rough pasture and one or two scrubby trees. The grazing is for a small herd of cows, Lundy ponies, sheep including some rare Soay sheep and, even rarer, some Sika deer plus the odd goat. We stopped and sat down on a steep grassy slope overlooking a blue cove full of darting puffins, razorbills and guillemots. Shortly, the beer and warm sunshine took effect and we fell asleep, frightening ourselves when we woke and looked down at the rocks and sea just one roll away.

Back at the little settlement we came across Chris and Charlie with John Puddy filling jerrycans with petrol for *Bumble*. It being so hard to get supplies to Lundy, we felt guilty asking for fuel, but there was no real alternative and Mr Puddy seemed eager for us to have some. Having said our goodbyes we went down to the beach and found the tide out, fifty yards of rocks separating *Bumble* from the sea. Used to this sort of problem by now, we sat down to wait. Before long a barrel-chested man appeared and offered to help us lift *Bumble* to the sea, which he did almost single-handed!

After supper, Charlie and Rodney paid another visit to the inviting

Marisco Tavern. The wind, which had been moderate nor'north-
westerly throughout the day, was getting up, perhaps force 6 now.
At about 11.30 we saw the lights of a boat approaching the
anchorage and, as it came close, identified lifeboat 003, a Clyde,
which at seventy feet long is the largest class in the fleet. Based at
Clovelly on the Devon coast, 003 is permanently manned and
patrolling the Bristol Channel area. Rodney and Charlie paid the
crew a visit on their way back and discovered the secret weapon that
keeps them entertained during their ceaseless roaming of the ocean –
a TV and video!

The lifeboat anchored a couple of hundred yards west of us and we
flicked on the radio in case they wanted to talk. By coincidence, a
weather bulletin was on the air: 'There are warnings of gales in sea
areas Sole, Lundy, Fastnet.' I looked at Paul and could not help
grinning. This might scotch plans for moving on tomorrow, but I
was somehow excited by the thought of 'real' wind at last. We
waited up for a more detailed report from the shipping forecast at
12.25am which reiterated the warning of strong winds: 'Northerly
gales, force 8 expected soon.' It was going to be a bumpy night.

By six o'clock the next morning the wind was whipping up
towards force 8 and a considerable sea had developed. *Morningtown*
was rolling tirelessly and every few minutes an extra large wave
clubbed her side, sending a shudder through the boat. After listening
to the 6.25am forecast that continued to give gale warnings, we
weighed anchor, looking for somewhere to escape the direct path of
the weather. We rounded Rat Island on the eastern outcrop of Lundy
and tucked in under the cliffs on the south side in an anchorage called
The Rattles.

The anchorage was noisy. Anchor and chain continually scraping
against the rocky ocean bed and, a fair swell still penetrating this
more sheltered spot, it was by no means comfortable. We spent the
day reading thrillers, eating, and listening to the wind and rain
blasting over our heads. Alice commented that 'days like this just
eat up supplies and morale' and it was certainly on the gloomy side
with seven of us so cooped up. I did not even think of windsurfing;
King Kong would have been overpowered by a handkerchief-sized
sail. Only Chris, Charlie and Alice braved the elements, going out
into the cockpit for a smoke – there being a no-smoking rule below
decks – and coming back drenched. Because of the enormous surf at
the landing beach there was no chance of going ashore. Rodney
pointed out that more yachtsmen die paddling to and from their
yachts in little dinghies than out on the sea itself.

No respite came with the 2pm forecast: 'Northerly gale force 8
veering north-easterly and increasing severe gale force 9 imminent.'

(*above*) Passing Longships lighthouse, Land's End; (*below*) Whoops!

(*above*) Liz with ropes and onlooker, Portpatrick; (*below*) Paul, myself and Mark in serious mood with sail designer Willem Blaauw

In the afternoon our anchor dragged and we moved closer to the cliffs for more shelter from the wind and swell. Moving anchor was not my favourite activity as I invariably landed the job of hand-feeding the anchor chain into its locker. The manoeuvre involved crawling head-first into the forward locker and jamming my legs against the walls to avoid disappearing into the bowels of the ship.

Later that afternoon we radioed LB 003, surprised that they had not moved to our more sheltered spot. We found them motoring slowly back to Swansea into the heart of the storm, their main generator having broken down. It was widely tipped that the loss of TV had prompted this drastic action. In the early evening another boat turned up at The Rattles, a diving boat, the *Bessie Vie*. Over the radio we learnt that the two men on board had swum out to their boat through the heavy seas in the East Roads. They were wet and cold, without heating or nourishment on board, so we invited them to share our supper.

When Charlie ferried them over we recognised the barrel-chested man, John, who had helped us down to the sea with *Bumble*. Last year he had lost his diving boat in similar bad weather and with a force 9 forecast did not dare leave *Bessie Vie* at anchor unattended. After a jolly evening, John and his mate returned to their boat. We arranged to keep Channel 73 on the radio open throughout the night, should there be any need to communicate. We heard that the Padstow lifeboat had been called out to a fishing boat in distress off Doom Bar and we thought of Trevor. Watches were set and we turned in. The wind appeared to have slackened; perhaps the worse had gone through.

I woke up to the evil noise of the anchor grinding on the rocks. The wind had got up again. Alice was also awake and we listened for a while to the rasping of the chain across the sea bed and the wrench as more chain jerked loose. But there could surely be no real problem or the watch would have done something, and we dozed off again. Later I woke up sweating after a nightmare that the boat had foundered on the rocks. The dream was so vivid that I got out of bed and went into the cabin to ask Haydn, who was on watch, if everything was OK. 'No problem,' he assured me, and I went back to sleep.

The third time I woke, Paul had just taken over watch and was rousing the ship. The force 9 was now here and honking from the east not the north – we were right in its way. The anchor was dragging and, according to the radar, *Morningtown* was within yards of Great Shutter Rock directly to our backs. *Bessie Vie* was safe several hundred yards to windward and, as we later found out, they had seen us dragging in the gale, but were unable to reach us on the radio. Somehow the squelch button on our set had been turned right down (possibly to blot out some Spanish fishermen who were gabbling continuously on Channel 73).

I waited in the anchor locker for the engine to start and heard Rodney turn it over. Nothing. The batteries were flat. There was a petrol generator for such emergencies which did start and eventually the engine started too. The anchor took three attempts to lift, getting snagged on the rocks each time. To everyone's relief we were finally away and heading for shelter on Lundy's west coast at Jenny's Cove. We gave the island as wide a berth as possible to avoid any outlying rocks but hit bad overfalls off South West Point. A set of three massive waves made *Morningtown* pitch as if she were falling into a ravine and on the third wave there was a loud twang and the heavy, six-pronged radio aerial crashed onto the deck from the top of the mizzen mast. It missed Paul's head by a foot. 'Lucky it didn't fall overboard', said Rodney, calmly throwing the wreckage down below.

Once we reached the west side of the island we were sheltered from the worst of the sea, but out in the cockpit one could still see the fury of the gale. The moon would come out briefly from behind the fleeing clouds and illuminate the seascape – an eerie sight – long white streaks of foam glinting across the water. The darkness was somehow more frightening and I half expected a sickening crunch as *Morningtown* ran across a rock perhaps not marked on the chart. Haydn made coffee and produced more pineapple chunks from somewhere. Then at last we were safely in Jenny's Cove and, in comparative shelter, could drop our anchor and get some rest.

I woke for the 6.25 shipping forecast which gave easterly 6, backing northerly 3 – it looked as if we would be able to move on at some stage today. In the daylight I recognised Jenny's Cove as the place where Alice and I had dozed off the day before. I stayed up on watch for a couple of hours writing my log and watching the tiny puffins whizzing across the cliff face, with their staccato wing beat more like bats or mechanical toys than birds.

When Paul woke me at 10.30am the wind had eased and Rodney was becoming edgy, muttering about going back to Ilfracombe if we did not move on from Lundy soon. He was not the only one keen to depart so, saying goodbye to *Bessie Vie* who had joined us in the cove during the night, we made ready. We felt close to the two divers, having come with them through the storm. As we left, their breakfast was being lowered down the cliffs to them by friends.

We sailed back towards Hartland Point and our last stopping-place. On the way we received some radio calls from the mainland and I did a couple of interviews with BBC Radio Oxford and Radio

London, both live. It was encouraging to know that people were still following our fortunes.

After the storm the sea was still jumbled and violent, although no longer on the attack – the wind had lost some of its venom. For a fast reach I chose *Pytheas II* with a 6m sail. A waterstart and a shuffle of feet into footstraps and I was away and going like smoke towards Lundy. There was still a punch left in the breeze and I was sailing right on the limit, careening down the waves, up the backs and exploding off the crests. I quickly overtook *Morningtown* and left her well astern. The familiar lump of Lundy came closer and closer. How exhilarating to be making miles after the inactivity of the last two days. My only concern was blinking away the showers of spray so that I could see as I dashed through the forest of waves.

I fell once in the confusion of waves off South West Point where we had snapped our aerial the night before, and then I was purring along the island itself. One last look at Jenny's Cove with its purple rocks, a visit from some inquisitive puffins and I was past and steaming on, aiming north-west towards Milford Haven and the Welsh coast. 'At this rate I'll be in Pembrokeshire in no time,' I said to myself, but spoke too soon. After an hour and a half in which I covered an incredible eighteen miles, the wind died away. With twenty-five miles left to Milford, it looked like being a long day.

I let *Bumble* catch up. The slamming that day had been so bad that for the second time their main radio set had smashed; the hand-set would have to do from now on. Chris casually reported to Rodney that the radio had 'jumped up and down on their sandwiches', which incensed him as well as annoying the cook! When *Morningtown* caught up and I requested a larger sail, the reply was 'Negative'. Rodney was feeling rather unwell and being left behind had darkened his mood. He decided that *Morningtown* would keep up better if my sail was too small.

After a period of stalemate while I sat idly on my board, it became clear that there was no need to clip my wings, and I was given the 9m sail and the *Log* to get going as best I could. The wind had backed to the north and died away to almost nothing. What was left of it now changed direction no less than three times. I quickly became disorientated and ended up heading in the direction of, Rodney informed me, Mexico. I about turned and went the other way.

A couple of hours later, when I felt that I might be condemned to spend the rest of my life in the Bristol Channel, the breeze finally stuck in the north-west and I sailed off at a respectable amble on port tack. Thanks to Paul I made the rather late discovery that, by using a large fixed wooden daggerboard rather than the small plastic retractable one, I could increase the *Log*'s performance upwind by several tens of degrees. I was going to grow very attached to the *Log*.

It was a relief when the coast of Wales eventually appeared on the horizon; the bogey of the Bristol Channel was conquered at last and I spotted the oil towers of Milford Haven. The wind vanished at 8.30pm and we called it a day, stopping off St Govan's Head, ten miles short of Milford, but with forty-three vital miles behind us.

I showered, ate and then slept till we reached Dale, a sheltered anchorage to the west of Milford Haven, Britain's largest natural harbour. Everyone was eager to get ashore and we reached a pub just in time for last orders. Waiting inside – drinks lined up on the bar – were Mark and Alan Griffin. It was great to see Mark and exchange news after almost a week out of contact. Alan, without doubt our most faithful supporter, had driven across from the Midlands to check our progress. He had by now personally raised over £700 for the appeal and we drank to his achievement as well as to our arrival in Wales.

6 MILFORD HAVEN TO HOLYHEAD

Rodney left the next morning, 24 May, wishing us luck on our journey up the Welsh coast and saying he would meet us again on the Isle of Man. Our numbers stayed the same on *Morningtown*, however, as Liz had decided to rejoin us.

Morningtown needed to take diesel and water on board before we left Milford. To make the most of sailing time, we had planned for *Bumble* and I to set off ahead and meet up later, but this idea was upset by the weather. The wind was back in the north and blowing at about force 7. For safety's sake we had to stay together and leave when the yacht was ready, probably the next morning.

It was ten miles from Dale to Hobbs Point at the other end of the haven where we went to pick up the diesel. On the way we passed Milford Haven's vast supertanker oil jetties, some of which are more than a mile long. Milford has long been an oil town; originally it was sperm whale oil but this industry collapsed with the introduction of gas lights. Now, of course, the town flourishes on oil of a different kind.

After refuelling at the quayside we moved *Morningtown* out into the bay at Hobbs Point, picking up a large mooring buoy among thirty or more other yachts. Half of the team were in town: Alice, Charlie and Chris had hitched a lift to the nearest launderette with the ship's washing which, to the attendant's amazement, filled all seven machines. Haydn remained on shipwatch while Paul and I went ashore to the chandler's. We had just assembled our goods on the counter when a man came into the shop saying, 'Does anyone know anything about a yacht that appears to be dragging her mooring in the bay?' We shook our heads, thinking that it could not be us. Out of curiosity we wandered out of the door just to see which idiot's yacht was moving. With horror we saw it was *Morningtown*. In the fresh breeze she was drifting at several knots, trailing her buoy through the fleet of yachts towards the rocky shore. What the hell was Haydn doing? We sprinted down to the quay and leapt into *Bumble*. The engine started first time and we roared out at top speed towards *Morningtown*, still blowing fast across the bay. In the short time it took us to cover three hundred yards she had covered thirty, passing within inches of a green fishing boat and heading for an

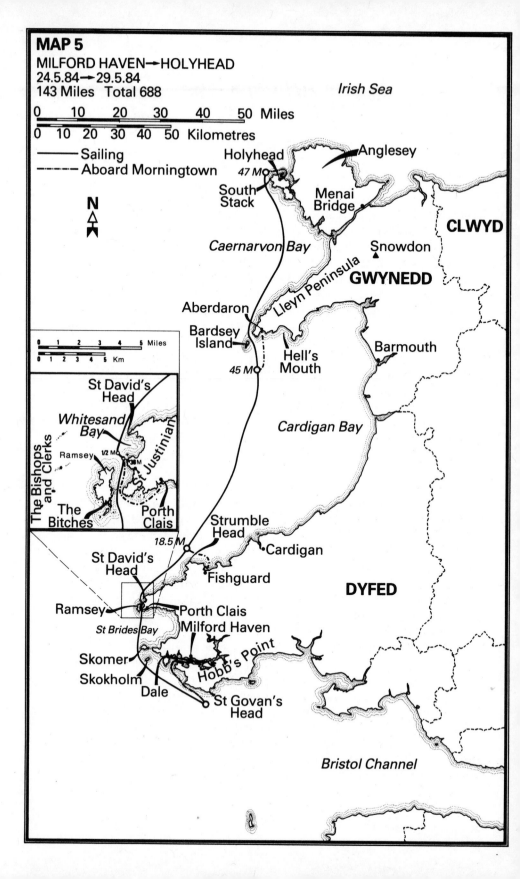

MAP 5

MILFORD HAVEN ➜ HOLYHEAD
24.5.84 ➜ 29.5.84
143 Miles   Total 688

0   10   20   30   40   50 Miles
0 10 20 30 40 50 Kilometres

—— Sailing
–·–·– Aboard Morningtown

N

Irish Sea

Anglesey

Holyhead
47 M
South
Stack
Menai
Bridge

CLWYD

Caernarvon Bay

▲ Snowdon

GWYNEDD

Aberdaron
Lleyn Peninsula
Bardsey
Island
45 M
Hell's
Mouth

Barmouth

Cardigan Bay

St David's
Head
*Whitesand
Bay*
Ramsey *½ M*
St Justinian
The Bishops
and Clerks
The
Bitches
Porth
Clais

Strumble
Head
18.5 M
• Cardigan

St David's
Head
Fishguard

DYFED

Ramsey
Porth Clais
Milford Haven
St Brides Bay
Skomer
Hobb's Point
Skokholm
Dale
St Govan's
Head

Bristol Channel

expensive yacht, which was the last stop before the rocks.

Approaching *Morningtown* we yelled across to Haydn who emerged from below carrying a mug of tea as Paul jumped aboard and ran for the ignition. 'I didn't notice a thing,' he said. Paul had the engines going and we disconnected ourselves from the so-called mooring buoy and motored out of trouble. Miraculously, *Morningtown* had missed everything in her flight and, once anchored a safe distance away, we all burst out laughing. 'Rodney would have been proud of us,' said Haydn, which made us laugh even more. How we could have broken the news to him that his yacht was wrecked on the very day he left just did not bear thinking about. Later, Paul went out in *Bumble* and towed the mooring buoy back into position: it turned out that despite the buoy's impressive size and great hank of rope, there was nothing but a length of chain attached to it, the sea bed concrete block having broken away.

Back in the chandlery later on, I was enquiring about detailed charts for the St David's Head area and landed instead a lengthy caution from an old boy who had written a book on passage making in the area. He told us of the perils of a narrow channel called Jack's Sound. 'When the tide turns through there it's like a mountain river in full spate . . . aim for Wooltack Point between Blackstone and Anvil Rock. When you can see the surf breaking on Crabstones, tack west to avoid being set onto Tusker Rock . . .' I began to write all this information down and gave up in dismay. 'Is there an alternative to Jack's Sound?' I asked hopefully. 'Right enough, you can go west of Skokholm and Skomer Islands but that means passing through the Wild Goose Race,' he said lowering his voice ominously. 'What's special about the Wild Goose Race?' I asked, impatiently. 'I've only been through it once,' he continued. 'It was a calm night but you could feel the evil of it – I've never been so frightened. The ocean bed is corrugated like a vast cathedral which causes the most unearthly turbulence in the waters above. Further north you've got Ramsey Sound; tide goes through there like an express train . . .' I began to wonder if there was any way out of Milford Haven.

There being little left of the day, departure was now officially postponed till tomorrow. Late in the afternoon Liz arrived by train from London, and Charlie entertained some of the locals with an exciting display of mono waterskiing. That evening we got rather embroiled with the occupants of a neighbouring yacht, a beautiful 55ft Swan. We chatted and drank with them till past one on board the plush racing yacht that made good old *Morningtown* seem more homely than ever. John, the skipper, was an old friend of Paul's father and delivered yachts all over the world for a living. He and his crew on *Pacer* had been heading up to Scotland for the Tomatin

Trophy but had called the trip off owing to the northerly gales. On our way back to *Morningtown* I noticed how cold it had become and shivered as I thought about what lay ahead in the next couple of days.

We could not recommence until the afternoon of the following day, 25 May, as our spot lay offshore in the middle of another firing range. We had to wait until a ceasefire had been called. All the talk on board about shelling must have affected our instruments as on the way both the Decca (Desmond to his friends!) and the Satellite Navigator were refusing to work. We returned to simple compass bearings to ascertain our position.

It was an overcast, bitterly cold day and even at 2pm when I eventually got started, the temperature was low enough to numb my hands inside my gloves. I was using *Pytheas II* and, for the first time, the reefing sail. Beating into a fresh breeze from the north-west, after a while I found the sail area a little too much and removed one of the zipped sections of the sail, reducing it from 6.5 to 5.2m at a touch. When the wind eased I simply zipped the section back in. This was very quick and convenient and was the beginning of quite a craze for the reefing sail.

I was now approaching Skokholm Island. We had plumped for the Wild Goose race as being the most direct route. Remembering my conversation in the chandler's I was somewhat nervous but, when we reached the island, the sea was almost mill-pond flat. I appeared to have escaped lightly, but about half a mile later I encountered a very localised area of overfalls that mysteriously appeared in front, advanced towards me, tried to knock me in and then receded in the direction of Skokholm lighthouse. After that I was in no doubt that here was an uneasy place of restless currents that would throw up a violent sea at the slightest provocation.

Skokholm Island itself has an unusual history, being the site of the first experiments on myxomatosis. Scientists could not understand why the island population of rabbits flourished despite regular introduction of infected individuals – until they discovered that Skokholm is the one place lacking the necessary type of disease-carrying flea!

I was soon passing the adjacent island of Skomer and, rather than rabbits, found it heavily populated with birds. I sailed close to the rocky cliffs to take a good look at the colonies of puffin and guillemot and their vicious co-residents, the skuas. Relishing the colour and interest, I reflected that, compared to miles of empty sea, there was nothing like passing a good chunk of land for making the time pass quickly.

I forged steadily across St Brides Bay and by early evening was approaching the narrow Ramsey Sound that runs between Ramsey Island and the mainland. I tacked once off the mainland, once off Ramsey Island and then managed to hold a line through the sound itself. The tide was beginning to turn against me and I inched past a reef known as The Bitches and on through the channel, past St Justinian to Point St John. Though travelling quite fast through the water I was barely making forward progress over the ground and, after a tack near some needle rocks off Whitesands Bay, I stopped. It was 8.45pm and I had sailed thirty-two miles – the last two had seemed to take forever but I was glad to have negotiated Ramsey Sound while conditions were relatively calm. There was never any telling what tomorrow would bring.

We motored back on our tracks and tucked round the corner, anchoring off a charming old Roman harbour called Porth Clais. Mark, having watched our passage through the sound, joined us for dinner. We turned in early in readiness for a dawn start the next day to get round St David's Head with the tide. My alarm went off at 4.20am and I lay awake with the thin light filtering into the cabin and listened. There was little evidence of wind here at our anchorage but I was sure I could hear a moaning noise in the distance. My ears had become very sensitive to the sound of wind (especially in a prone position in my bunk!). This noise indicated a great deal of wind and I suspected that it was coming from Ramsey Sound.

Over a hurried tea and cereal, I mentioned my wind theory to Paul. 'What the hell,' we thought. 'Might as well go and see!' The anchor was up by 4.45am and we turned into the sound fifteen minutes later. There was indeed a lot of wind – northerly force 6 and with wind against five knots of tide I had to rub my bleary eyes to believe the waves we were meeting off The Bitches. *Morningtown* stuck her nose in and popped up again at each one. Paul, at the helm, grinned with the thrill of it. The sound was a different place today, a mass of white water, and one could appreciate how it had gained its fearful reputation. Thousands of years of erosion by the sea have tunnelled out the rock underwater and the depth of the channel plunges from only sixty feet at each end to over two hundred feet in the middle, opposite the treacherous Bitches. This depth and the racing tide creates a turbulent sea that obscures the reef in bad weather and many ships have foundered on the ledge without even knowing it was there. The chasm at the bottom is a graveyard for both ships and men.

We punched our way to the northern end of the sound and I began sailing with the reefing sail, minus one reef, and *Pytheas II*. Within seconds it dawned on me that sailing against this fierce wind into such a confused sea was almost impossible. My board kept rocketing out of control, I suffered a continuous battering from the waves and the conditions exposed some flaws in my equipment preparation: the footstraps were too loose for my feet to stay in tight; the sail was set too baggy and the harness lines were so slack that my back was crashing along in the water. I stopped to make the necessary adjustments and took a reef out of the sail for good measure. In that short time I was blown some 150 yards back towards the rocks fronting Ramsey Island.

I resumed, but now the conditions had become even more outrageous, the wind having increased to force 7 or more. I seemed to be surrounded by rocks: they were ahead and to my lee, and to my west was a scattering known as The Bishops and Clerks. Everywhere there was livid spray and breaking waves. I tacked and headed at high speed towards St David's Head, my knees feeling like overworked shock absorbers after a few hundred yards. I cranked the sail low over my head to keep the board pointing to windward and then, in an explosion of water, the top of my mast embedded itself in the crest of a wave, like a pitchfork into a haystack, and the next thing I knew I was lying on my back watching the wave roll by. I swam to the board, clambered on and, straddling it, looked ahead, the wind a steady roar in my ears.

All I could see was a mass of white water. The closer I approached the headland the worse it would become. If I made it round, there was still a twenty-mile beat to Fishguard with a lee shore the whole way. As I sat thinking 'this isn't really on', I watched a wall of water the size of a house come rolling towards me. 'Help!' I thought with alarm. Fortunately, it was not yet breaking and simply picked me up and put me down again a little further south. I looked round to where the wave was now splatting against the rocks behind and turned back to see another on the way.

This was enough for me and in a short time I was in *Bumble* and on the radio to Paul; 'Let's get out of here before it gets any worse!' I gabbled. 'Say again, slowly, I didn't hear a word you said,' said Paul calmly. This was impossible as the radio batteries had now run out. After a tense couple of minutes while we changed them and watched ourselves blow even closer to the rocks, we got through to Paul again and, as expected, found he heartily approved the plan. We motored separately back through the sound past Scylla and Charybdis and met up again in the shelter near Porth Clais. It was a record day – half an hour's sailing and half a mile of forward progress! Our decision to stop was backed up by the 6.25am shipping forecast that gave northerly force 8. Back we went to our cosy anchorage for some very welcome sleep until lunch.

In the afternoon we went ashore to stretch our legs with a stroll to

St Justinian, the village with a lifeboat house that overlooks the sound. There we had a look at the state of the sea with northerly force 8 against the north-going spring tide. It was an awe-inspiring sight from above, great white-capped walls of water ploughing majestically down the sound, but it bore little resemblance to the raw fury I had felt and seen from my sea-level position on the board that morning.

By coincidence, in St David's we met up with a former housemaster of mine from Marlborough, Michael Birley, and were invited to dinner at his cottage, which enjoys a remarkable view over Whitesands Bay where we had been wrestling that morning. The next morning the Birley family got up early to watch my third attempt to round St David's Head. They later sent a postcard: 'Well done – we only saw you fall in twice!'

My third round with St David's Head began at 6am on 27 May. This time I won, if slowly and painfully. I was using the reefing sail, minus a reef, and *Pytheas II*, beating into a northerly force 5. The conditions were less rough than the day before but I fell in on almost every tack. Moreover, I was pointing at the poor angle of 50° to the wind, which I put down partly to lack of concentration and partly to the shape of the sail. With a reef out it lost the roach, or fullness, and became bottom heavy which impaired upwind performance. After five hours' hard planing at nine knots I had made a paltry eighteen miles in the right direction. Stopping to rest three times in the session I radioed Paul for a mileage count and each time was disappointed by the reply. Throughout the trip I had a habit of over-estimating progress, but on this day my miscalculations were particularly marked and particularly demoralising. The tide turned against me off Strumble Head and put me out of my misery. We motored the six miles to Fishguard and picked up a mooring buoy, by courtesy of the lifeboat, to wait out the foul tide.

The next harbour north that was deep enough for *Morningtown* was Holyhead, one hundred miles up the coast. After lunch we had a meeting in the cabin to decide whether to press on across Cardigan Bay this evening or to call it a day till tomorrow. There was a strong wind warning (6 plus) on the radio and if we left this afternoon it meant at least one night hove to in the middle of the bay. If we stayed in Fishguard and left very early the next morning we might conceivably be across Cardigan Bay in one day and in Holyhead in two. We agreed on the latter option, I for one being particularly glad to stay in Fishguard, feeling deeply tired after the morning's exertions.

Later, the local lifeboat crew came on board for a chat and a beer, the coxswain surprising us with leather jacket and flowered shirt as opposed to the more familiar RNLI guernsey. We recounted our experience in the storm at Lundy and they described how on that same night in Fishguard a spanking new yacht had broken free from its moorings, sailed right across the harbour under bare masts and smashed itself to matchwood on the rocks at the far side.

We turned in early for bed. I lay awake for a while and could not help thinking about the bad turn that our progress had taken. Including today's eighteen miles, we had made a total of just ninety-four miles in the last week. At this rate it would take about fourteen more weeks to complete the remaining 1,300 miles round Britain. Where were all the westerly reaching winds I had been promised for this leg north? Things had to improve.

It was not yet light when Paul got up and switched on the engine to rouse the ship. I looked at my watch. It was 3.45am – this was really beyond a joke. I dressed and almost sleep-walked next door for some breakfast. Paul and I discussed the day's plan. The wind had refused to budge out of the north during the night as we had hoped it might. It was going to be a dead beat across Cardigan Bay and I was tempted to call it off until the wind backed or veered to give me a reach; but there was no point. The lifeboatmen assured me it had been blowing from the north for nearly five weeks now. How long would we have to wait?

We motored past the massive breakwater of Fishguard Bay and out into a lumpy ocean and a cold, blustery wind. Chris did not keep his breakfast down long and there was a fair amount of moaning and groaning from the crew about the hour and the general unpleasantness. When it was time for me to get onto the water I stopped briefly and looked north into Cardigan Bay. In the grey light of dawn the sea looked bleak and hostile, more so than any winter landscape, desert or leafless forest. 'Damn it!' I thought. 'Why are they complaining? I'm the one that has to get out there and wrestle with it.' I knew that Paul for one drew comfort from the fact that someone else was worse off as he looked at my grim face when I stepped off *Morningtown* at the start of a difficult day. I had read an entry in his log; 'The ritual of feeding Tim to the elements is a daily tonic!'

My system found the 4.30 start just a bit too early and I had to stop after an hour and a half and clamber onto *Morningtown* to use the heads. The wind was northerly 4–5 and I was using the full reefing sail and *Pytheas II*. I sailed well and, with a good lift from the tide, had made a magical twenty-five miles to windward by the time the tide turned foul at eleven o'clock. In contrast to the day before I was tacking through an excellent angle of 80° (40° to the wind). This made all the difference. There was jubilation on board that we had so easily broken the back of Cardigan Bay and I slept contentedly while we hove to for four hours or so.

We resumed at 3.15pm and again I made excellent progress, considering I was still sailing into the wind, or uphill. The day had turned out sunny and in the clear light I could distinguish fragments of the Welsh coast ahead – the volcano-shaped cone of the top of Bardsey Island where we were headed and, further east, the peaks of the high mountains of Snowdonia.

Towards evening the wind died gradually and I changed to the *Log* and the 8m sail. We stopped at 9.15pm, just past some turbulent water known ominously as The Devil's Tails and some dozen miles west of the prong of St Patrick's Causeway, a submerged reef that stretches for ten miles into Cardigan Bay from north of Barmouth. I had covered forty-five good miles in eleven and a half hours, my longest day so far. Before the trip began I would not have dreamt of putting in such long days; now, to my surprise, I did not feel particularly exhausted. As we motored the last six miles past Bardsey to anchor in Aberdaron Bay there was a lovely deep orange sunset to crown this productive day. Our luck seemed to be improving – I felt we had turned a corner. As if to prove this we had an exquisitely peaceful night at anchor in the sheltered bay. *Morningtown* was so still that it was difficult to tell that we were on the sea at all.

Paul and I rose just after 6am on 29 May to hear the shipping forecast, and Haydn sprang out of the pit shortly afterwards. The Meteorological Office were giving north-westerly/westerly 3 for the Irish Sea, but there was still no sign of movement outside. A morning mist blanketed the flat sea and, looking shorewards, there was a large graveyard dominating one side of the bay, its white gravestones grinning like teeth out of the tranquil haze.

Despite the lack of wind here we thought it worth motoring the six miles to last night's Decca spot. Sure enough, a gentle breeze began to stir and the mist to clear; it was going to be a magnificent day. Revising my sail choice from 8m to 7m I started off with the *Log* and the large daggerboard, close-hauled on port tack. At first I was pointing far east towards the bay near Abersoch known as Hell's Mouth (so called because of the danger to sailing ships of old of becoming embayed in south-westerly gales in this U-shaped bite in the coastline). Then the west-going tide lifted me, and my line improved till I was pointing back at Aberdaron village and finally towards Bardsey Sound. Soon I was gripped by the full strength of the tide rushing through the sound and got a tremendous yank upwind to almost half-way along the sound before I had to tack. On one side of me was Bardsey Island, purple, rocky and deserted, and on the other side mainland Wales. Now the domain of a solitary lighthouse-keeper it is hard to believe that Bardsey was once inhabited by a king with one hundred subjects. Approaching the mainland I heard a noisy eddy and tacked just in time to avoid the bubbling water.

There were just the glimmerings of white-caps on the clear blue water as I began to climb up the Lleyn peninsula. A Trinity House helicopter flew overhead, we guessed taking supplies to the lighthouse-keeper on Bardsey Island. Otherwise all was quiet. It was a glorious day for a sail, and *Morningtown* put up all her canvas including the huge white number two genoa, or ghoster, with which she rapidly drew away from me. These were the ideal peaceful conditions I had dreamt of: flat water and a gentle breeze. And what perfect surroundings, flanked on one side by the deep blue sea and on the other by the majesty of the Snowdonia mountain range.

We stopped at midday and hove to in the middle of Caernarvon Bay while a swift tide went dashing past. By 5pm the sea breeze had died considerably and prospects did not look good for covering the remaining twenty-five miles to Holyhead. I put up the 8m sail on the *Log* and incredibly was able to glide along at a steady four to five knots over the water – nearer six over the ground with the help of the tide. I fell in love with the superb shape of my large sail, the way it literally crept forward, forever increasing the apparent wind, and producing excellent speeds out of a mere breeze. Probably in common with others I find it difficult to judge my actual speed by facing forward, as the bow cruising into the waves and ripples gives an untrustworthy impression. Wind on the face is also an unreliable indicator as you monitor wind coming at you as well as wind caused by your own movement. I prefer to look at the wake behind the board; it is an infallible indicator of speed. I would be forever darting looks behind me at the stern wave and on calm days found that I could improve efficiency and speed by just looking behind for long periods.

Holy Island came into view long before Anglesey itself, which is very flat and looks as if one large wave could wash over the whole area. Off the western tip of the island is South Stack, a bird sanctuary surrounded by five-hundred-foot cliffs, and connected to Holy Island only by a precariously long and thin suspension footbridge. As I approached the lighthouse I met a roving patch of disturbed sea, similar to the curious overfalls off Skokholm Island. The swirling waters came at me from nowhere, tugged at the board and did their utmost to rotate and unseat me. Surviving this minor onslaught I now entered the overfalls off South Stack itself. I was in for a trying time. The wind, so kind all day, now decided it had better things to do and disappeared, leaving me to flounder rudderless in the slop between Holyhead Deep and Abraham's Bosom.

A little dory appeared with some well-wishers from the local windsurfing club. Mark was among them but I was too intent on keeping my balance to recognise him. Then *Morningtown* charged past me and someone shouted from the stern, 'You're too close to the lighthouse, follow us!' At this my peevishness developed into anger and I yelled my stock retort after them: 'Why doesn't one of you come and try it?' The situation deteriorated because of a problem that had arisen with the mast track on the *Log*. The track was coming adrift at one end and, to keep it from pulling off completely, I had to slide the mast far forward. In light airs this entailed straddling the raised track with one foot, but off South Stack this foot complained of a painful cramp, which I could do nothing to alleviate.

In a very grumpy mood I stopped just off North Stack with Holyhead harbour a few miles round the corner. Pulling the *Log* on board *Morningtown*, I caught it on the pushpit and, to my great annoyance, heard an ominous crack. Turning the board over I saw there was a three-inch gash across its belly which would undoubtedly let water in, if not repaired. What with this and the damaged mast track, my precious *Log* seemed to be falling apart! No one on *Morningtown* seemed to want to join in my sulk; on the contrary, they were all smiling. Paul then told me that it had been a record day with forty-seven miles covered – more than the day before and more than the day from Brighton to Gosport. And all had been done in winds of less than force 3 – it hardly seemed credible. I was delighted. Wales was behind us. Looking north across the Irish Sea as we motored to Holyhead, I could see clouds hanging over the horizon, with a hint of land beneath. That must be the Isle of Man; it could not be too far away.

Holyhead is a large, friendly, safe haven, sheltering behind a two-mile breakwater. We moored up and went ashore to the yacht club. Roger, a club official, was expecting us and we were plied with drinks and grilled about the trip. He is a heavily built man in his mid-forties and, after years of ocean racing on big yachts, is now addicted to windsurfing. He prefers it as a sport to yachting because there is no season and he can sail every weekend of the year. He lives in the perfect place for windsurfing; Anglesey, being an island, offers one safe shore for sailing, whatever the wind.

The next day, Wednesday 30 May, was declared a rest day, or in this instance a day when we all worked considerably harder! Everyone was busy: maintenance on *Morningtown* was an ongoing headache for Paul and Haydn – the bilges now needed pumping three times a day to stop the boat filling with water. Paul found a grease-gun and gallons of thick grease to pack the stern gland where most of the water was coming in. This kept it at bay for a while. *Bumble* was also in need of attention. Charlie and Chris turned her over on the yacht club slip and glued a total of fourteen patches to worn areas on the underside. Needless to say, they all fell off within a fortnight!

I rang Tris to discuss the crisis with the *Log*. Thanks to Paul's ingenuity, we had been able to mend the mast track, fixing a couple of steel plates that we had made up by a local engineer, but we only managed a temporary filler repair to the bottom. The board had been made so quickly that in parts it was almost egg-shell thin. What we needed was fibreglass and epoxy resin to reinforce it all along the middle of the underside. The resin did not seem to be readily available in chandleries so Tris forwarded some to Oban on the west coast of Scotland. The *Log* would have to last until we reached there. I also rang Tony Tilbrooke of Spartan who made my drysuits. I had now worn through the knees of all three of my suits so when I fell in the sea water seeped in and collected in the socks. Tony agreed to send a couple of new suits up to Lochinver (north of Skye), commenting that I sounded a bit low. I felt like saying, 'You would be if you had to face six weeks more of wet feet,' but instead muttered something about it being 'such a long way'.

It was not Haydn's day. He broke some expensive tools while trying to repair the self-steering gear and then capsized *Morning-*

(*above*) Charlie watching the dolphins off Eigg in the Sea of Hebrides;
(*below*) Storm brewing off Skye

(*above*) Head in the clouds, North Minch; (*below*) Hints from John Ridgway in Loch Ardmore

town's tiny rubber dinghy (which was in use while *Bumble* had her bottom patched). He came up spluttering in the cold water of the harbour, more upset at losing his peanut butter and jam sandwich which was floating away and soon to be greedily gobbled by a passing seagull, than at the plight of the 2hp Evinrude engine, now ruined after its ducking!

The incident must have affected his normal cool as the following day he suddenly announced that he wanted to leave at the earliest opportunity: responsibilities to wife and home were pressing. I remonstrated with him, reluctant to lose such a cheerful and hardworking member of the crew, but in the end agreed that he could go as soon as we found a replacement. The problem was removed the very next day when he said he had changed his mind and would stay after all. 'I won't muck you about again,' he promised, and didn't.

After our busy day in harbour, we all went off for the evening to a pub in Rhosneigr where Mark had arranged a party with the local windsurfing club. They were a lively bunch and gave us hamburgers and bitter and, as a special treat, windsurfing videos! Talking about the trip I found people unusually sympathetic to the problems. This was probably because several of them had experienced something similar, having windsurfed right round Anglesey the year before. It had taken three full days and, with the overfalls off South Stack and the notorious Swillies tide-race in the Menai Strait, it must have been rather like round Britain in miniature.

At the end of the evening we held a raffle in aid of the RNLI. Over £50 was raised but, to our amusement, Mark won the magnum of Charles Heidsieck which had been put up as a prize. Our hosts looked a bit sceptical (thinking this happened every time) until Mark gave them the bottle to be raffled again. He had a similarly funny experience a few days later when he visited Morecambe for the UK Boardsailing Association Captain Morgan Rum championship meeting. Mark was getting on famously with the organisers until he proposed raffling a bottle of Charles Heidsieck – it turned out that Captain Morgan belong to Seagrams, who also own Mumm champagne! Mark was doing a fantastic job visiting all the windsurfing clubs and keeping a smiling face even on the occasions when people evidently were not interested. Despite all his hard work, though, the appeal funds were not exactly mushrooming, with only £2,000 in the RNLI coffers at Poole. I must admit that at this stage the round trip was more important to me than the fund-raising. The money, I hoped, would come in if and when I crossed the finishing line.

I listened to the shipping forecast before turning in to bed, which

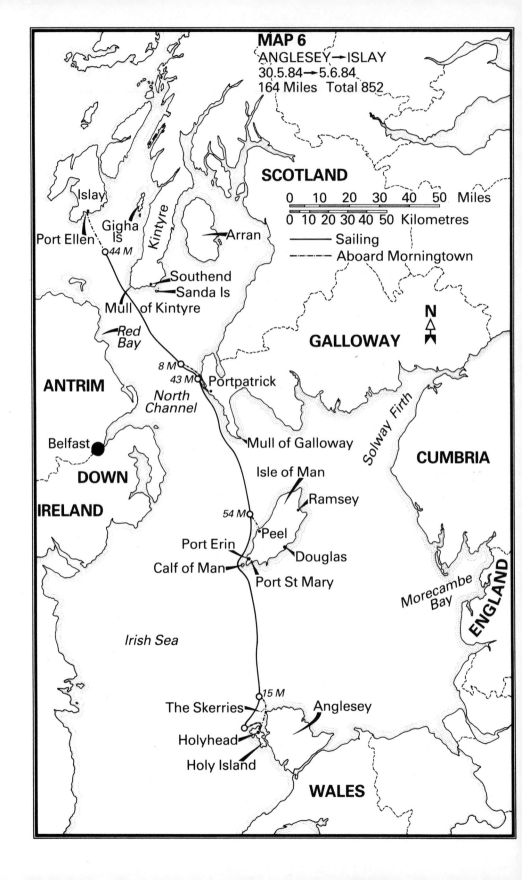

MAP 6
ANGLESEY → ISLAY
30.5.84 → 5.6.84
164 Miles Total 852

SCOTLAND

0 10 20 30 40 50 Miles
0 10 20 30 40 50 Kilometres
——— Sailing
—·—·— Aboard Morningtown

Islay
Gigha
Is
Port Ellen
44 M

Kintyre

Arran

Southend
Sanda Is
Mull of Kintyre

Red
Bay

8 M
43 M Portpatrick

ANTRIM

North
Channel

GALLOWAY

N

Solway Firth

CUMBRIA

Belfast

DOWN

Mull of Galloway

Isle of Man

Ramsey

IRELAND

54 M
Peel

Port Erin
Calf of Man

Douglas

Port St Mary

Morecambe
Bay

ENGLAND

Irish Sea

The Skerries

15 M

Anglesey

Holyhead

Holy Island

WALES

warned of possible southerly gales in the Irish Sea. When Paul woke me at 5am I went on deck and was greeted by a sharp blast of freezing wind whistling over Holy Island and across the harbour. My teeth chattered in anticipation of what was to come. To put us all in a better frame of mind, Alice cooked the number one favourite breakfast of beans on toast with sausages and we then began to nose our way out of the shelter of Holyhead harbour. I was up in the cockpit with Paul and Haydn, the wind beating me determinedly about the head so that I put my hands up to cover my ears. Before we had cleared the breakwater I turned to Paul and said, 'I'm not sure I fancy fifty miles running from this, right across the Irish Sea. What do you think?' 'Might be sensible to wait for the 6.25 forecast,' he replied. 'Agreed,' I said, and Paul was already spinning the wheel round to take *Morningtown* back into port.

We waited half an hour for the forecast and it gave south-easterly 6–7. I would have preferred a mention of eight, but we did not set out. Force 7 is still lots of wind and the Irish Sea a rough place to be caught out in. The Holyhead coastguards were very friendly over the radio, obviously amused by *Morningtown*'s about-turn in mid-exit. On their invitation several of us went along to visit the control tower just beyond the harbour. Their operations room was impressively ship-shape, well stocked with radio equipment and wallpapered with maps, bristling with coloured pins. Only one thing did not fit: there was a large picture window with a beautiful view, but it faced away from the sea. In my mind's eye coastguards always looked out over the angry sea, completely in touch with the conditions suffered by their distressed yachtsmen. Not any more!

When we returned from coastguard HQ it was still not yet 8am and everyone went back to bed for a couple of hours – what bliss to be able to sleep care-free during the day. The rest of the day was uneventful but by the evening a restless atmosphere had permeated the ship. Haydn had made his bid to depart and Charlie was in a rare bolshy mood, having spent most of the day sitting ashore in the truck with Mark. With Paul and Liz, Alice and I walked into Holyhead to see *Greystoke, The Legend of Tarzan*, and lost ourselves in the jungle for a while. Back on board *Morningtown* later, we lay awake for a while talking about how things had a habit of stagnating if we stopped for too long.

The following day Alice had planned to go home to a family wedding, but on my request she gave up the idea to avoid the rest of the crew asking for a couple of days' leave. Feeling insecure, I asked her how much the crew really cared about the trip. 'What would everyone do if I said I was packing it in?' I asked. 'They'd try and persuade you to carry on – but you wouldn't give up, would you?'

she replied. 'I might,' I said, knowing she was right.

On 1 June, we left Holyhead harbour at 5.30am and I was sailing at just after 6.30. The forecast was indifferent, variable 3 or less, which can be interpreted as little wind and from any direction it likes! It was one of those painful beginnings – after five minutes every muscle ached and said 'Stop!'. I slaved on, not wanting another lousy day, knowing that morale would pick up with forward movement. Why was I dogged by this feeble wind just when I needed a soldier's breeze? I passed the innocent-looking Skerries (that in worse weather have been the death of many a ship) and headed off in the general direction of the Isle of Man, out of sight on this hazy day. At about nine o'clock I hit a totally calm patch and the sky showed no prospect of any wind. Suddenly, it struck me that I was being unfair to Alice. Why should she not go to the wedding when I would probably be rooted to this same spot when she got back? Liz had volunteered to take over the cooking and I would cope with others wanting leave if and when the occasion arose. I went aboard *Morningtown* and woke up Alice – she generally slept for a while after cooking breakfast – and told her that *Bumble* was waiting to take her back to Holyhead. She was delighted. I watched them disappear towards The Skerries until they were a blip on the horizon and then blinked out of sight. There was still no wind.

Then we received a radio call from an RAF helicopter in the area who wanted to take some photos – could they have a detailed co-ordinate of our position? This we gave and there followed a mad panic to climb back into my harness, pull my gloves on and return to the board. Despite our faithful use of the Decca I did not think it would look good to be sunning myself on *Morningtown* the one moment that the RAF flew over, especially with a camera!

I was nearly ready when we heard the unmistakable drone of an engine and spotted a black dot fast approaching. We all began to giggle as I jumped over the side onto my board, and I was laughing uncontrollably by the time I finished pulling my sail out of the water just as the wasp made its first pass overhead. They must have wondered why they had such smiling, photogenic faces everywhere. The pilot soon discovered that he could get much better photographs by flying close to me so that I could plane on his down-draught. The first time this happened I was taken by surprise and clung on for dear life, convinced that a hurricane had suddenly hit me, before realising it was the 100mph wind from their rotor blades brushing towards me across the water.

It was a novel way to travel and I must have made a good quarter of a mile from the artificial wind. When the helicopter eventually flew off, I missed it as there was zero wind again and I ground to a halt. It was pointless not to return to *Morningtown*. We were in the path of the shipping route from Liverpool to Dublin and a couple of giants steamed past, but there was no *Bumble*. They had been gone one and a half hours now and we assumed they had broken down or lost their way back. The latter proved to be the case and after several plaintive radio calls and the dishing out of numerous compass bearings, they eventually reached us.

After one further attempt to make progress towards the Isle of Man, which lasted only five minutes, we decided to have a day of water sports in the Irish Sea. Paul tried swimming, but found the water so cold that he was back on board almost before getting wet. Charlie produced a waterski from the forepeak and *Bumble*, once stripped of all excess weight, made quite a serviceable ski boat. Throwing caution to the lack of wind I tried my hand at waterskiing, did a good impersonation of a submarine and had sea water dripping from my nose for the rest of the day. The last event in our Irish Sea Olympics was the Great Raft Race between Haydn and Chris. They were each given two fenders from which to build a raft and a paddle to propel themselves around *Morningtown*. Chris won because he cheated more than Haydn and the sight of Haydn being given artificial respiration on the foredeck was a fittingly hilarious end to an unproductive but morale-boosting day. At 5pm, with thirty-five miles still remaining to the Isle of Man, we motored the fifteen miles back to Holyhead. After supper we went ashore and met up with our friend Roger in the yacht club. He did not seem at all surprised to see us back there for the third time. As we left he gave us a teasing grin and said, 'See you tomorrow!'

He did not, thank heavens. On the next day, 2 June, and our thirty-second since leaving Southend, I sailed a record fifty-four miles which brought us within sight of Scotland. The day began, however, with a minor catastrophe. Paul pumped the bilges when he woke up and the pump promptly broke down; it needed a new impeller, the wheel that pushes out the water, and being a Saturday we had visions of a nightmare couple of days' delay waiting to obtain a spare part. After a tense hour-and-a-half wait, Paul contacted Rodney and heard the good news that a spare could be found in a cubby-hole in the engine-room, and it was duly fitted. Paul also learnt that Rodney would not now join us in the Isle of Man but 150 miles beyond in Oban.

Away at last, we motored north once more to the Decca spot, some fifteen miles away, and I was sailing by midday. The breeze was light, 2–3 behind me, and I used the *Log* and a 9m sail. For the first couple of hours the tide was taking me east towards Morecambe Bay and I was on port gybe. At about 2pm the tide turned and began sweeping me west so I gybed onto starboard. I stopped for a brief pasta lunch and was off again, the Isle of Man looming ever larger ahead. The afternoon was hot and, to avoid wasting time by plunging into the sea to cool down, Chris and Charlie threw buckets of water over me which they seemed to enjoy thoroughly!

Much later, the weather began to change and *Bumble* relayed me a radio message about gale warnings for the south Irish Sea. I kept a careful watch behind me and soon spotted a great purple mass moving up from the south-east. 'Here comes trouble,' I thought and tried to signal to *Bumble* to prepare for a hasty sail change. I did not want to get caught out here with my spinnaker! I could not attract their attention; they were far away, I later found out, hunting for submarines, or the tell-tale sign of a trawler being dragged backwards, Chris having seen from the chart that we were slap between two submarine exercise areas. *Morningtown* was also a long way off and looking for all the world like the *Marie Celeste* with everyone asleep except Haydn. Fortunately, the squall passed over well east of us and the wind rose by only a few knots. It was 5pm. I was now fifteen miles from the Isle of Man and in a unique position, almost equidistant between England, Scotland, Ireland and Wales.

Two hours later I was approaching the Calf of Man and, since progress was good, we decided to head for Port Erin on the west coast rather than our original target of Port St Mary, to the south. This meant we were to leave the Calf to starboard. As we got closer I became aware that we were heading too far east to pass west of the Calf, even allowing for help from a strong tide round the headland. I queried our course with Paul but he was unmoved. We drew nearer and I grew angry, checking our heading again with Paul, but still to no effect. The closer we got to the Calf the more angry I became. When Paul eventually began altering course – thereby, I thought, admitting his mistake – I swung my board the few degrees, tripped and fell onto the rig. All my pent-up frustration exploded and I gave the sail a mighty blow with my fist that punched a hole clean through it.

I looked at the ten-inch gash in my priceless 9m sail (that I would now have to do without for three weeks) and felt very sheepish. 'It was an accident, honest!' I said to Chris and Charlie, when requesting a replacement sail (it was not until the evening that I could admit the truth!). I changed the wrecked 9m for the reefing sail which was uncomfortably small for the wind conditions but, in guilty mood, I felt that sackcloth and ashes for a while would not be altogether a bad thing. The same masochistic spirit would carry me on for hours that night. We made it comfortably round the Calf without turning too much of a corner which excused Paul's navigation from blame for my sail damage.

Chicken Rock on the south-east tip of Man provided a welcome mood change. Lolling lazily on the water's edge were about twenty fat grey seals. 'What do you mean by idly wallowing while some of us are hard at it?' I shouted across at them. There was various snorting and barking but I was largely ignored. *Bumble* drove close in to try and assess how many of these blubbery creatures could be crammed aboard without the boat sinking. There were no takers!

Under the cliffs, a few hundred yards past the seals, I became trapped by a back eddy where the wind was blowing in circles. I was sailing backwards and leaning forwards against the mast to try and keep control when the wind reversed direction and I fell forward with the suddenness of a mousetrap springing shut. I landed heavily on the edge of the board before rolling into the sea. Dragging myself back on I knelt with my head down, growling through clenched teeth as I fought the waves of pain. I assessed the damage: one bruised left elbow, one twisted right thumb. *Bumble* drove up to see if I was OK. 'Could have been worse,' I said. I carried on; the injuries were minor and though painful would not stop me. I was shocked, though, by how quickly the accident had happened and knew I was lucky not to have landed on my face.

The wind was more true further offshore and built steadily as the evening wore on. I kept a good distance between me and the craggy Isle of Man coast, and started to make excellent progress. We passed Port Erin – our destination was now Peel – and still I kept going. There was a glorious sunset and under the orange clouds I could make out land, which had to be Ireland. Ahead now was also other land, a lump that was the tip of the long proboscis of the Mull of Galloway. We were nearing Scotland at last. As it grew dark we aimed for the white flash of the Mull of Galloway lighthouse. I sailed on, making a steady nine knots in the healthy, freshening breeze. There was incredulity from the crew on *Morningtown* and at one point they tried to persuade me to stop by sailing upwind of me so that I could smell the roast turkey that Liz had cooked for supper! I was enjoying the evening too much – the bright stars, the glow of the sunset to the west and the satisfying feeling of progress after the last few disappointing days.

When the lights of Peel were beginning to dim behind me I finally stopped and climbed aboard *Morningtown*. It was 11pm. I ate the delicious dinner and then lay back in the saloon, feeling exhilarated – totally, wonderfully exhausted and drained of all strength, as at the end of a long race, but very, very happy. I looked across the table where Charlie was already asleep: it had been a hell of a long day for everyone.

We tied up alongside a fishing boat in the little harbour of Peel at past midnight. There was nothing to be done but collapse into bed. The wind started to shriek and the rain to beat against the hatches; the promised gale had arrived, but I dozed off contented. I really had done my day's work.

During the night the gale snapped one of the spring lines holding *Morningtown* to the mooring, as well as crushing and bursting a fender against the quayside. Paul went on deck to make us fast again and had a strange encounter with the skipper of the neighbouring fishing boat. Paul was bending over to adjust the line, his head well muffled in oilskins against the driving rain. Hearing a noise, he turned round and found himself staring into a pig's head, held up by a grinning fisherman. Why fishermen are abroad in Peel harbour in the middle of stormy nights carrying disembodied pigs' heads we never found out!

The wind and the rain were still attacking us the next morning and we watched the onslaught through the window while eating breakfast, wondering if the skies would clear by 2pm when the tide turned north. Ramsey coastguard were reporting thirty-five knots of wind from the north-east but forecast a slackening and a shift to the south-east. At about 11.30am this happened like magic: in a matter of minutes the wind had veered to the south and the dark storm clouds gave way to a sunny sky, filled with bouncing white cumulo-nimbus clouds.

We took the opportunity for a hasty exploration of Peel and went in *Bumble* a few hundred yards up the River Neb to the town quay. With Mark taking the long way round through England the onus was on me to make the running for any appeal publicity. I made a bee-line for a telephone box, managing to connect straight into a live phone-in programme on Manx radio and left some sponsorship forms with a local windsurfing contact for him to distribute. I knew Mark would be pleased.

Later, walking down the promenade, I was astonished by the number of leather-clad men and the dozens of motorbikes either parked or gunning down the road. I asked about it at a tobacconist's and found that it was TT Week (Tourist Trophy) when the population trebles to 120,000 with the influx of motorcycle enthusiasts. Today was a special day, Mad Sunday, when unofficially no speed limit operates on the island's roads. Two people had

(*opposite above*) Picnic overlooking Loch Laxford; from l to r: myself, Alice, Colin, Charlie, Ivor; (*below*) Big seas round the corner from Cape Wrath (*overleaf*) Flat on my back and still sailing, Bamburgh Castle, Northumberland

already been killed in the orgy of noise, fumes and burnt rubber and we passed an open truck loaded with freshly written-off bikes. Mad Sunday is an understatement.

At 1.30pm we left Peel and motored north. For a short time I took the helm of *Morningtown* myself, in good spirits and blissfully unaware that I was heading for one of the worst stretches of the trip.

As it was downwind sailing yet again, I chose the *Log* and the full reefing sail; on the dot of two o'clock I was up and away. The sailing was comfortable for about half an hour until the wind dropped suddenly. Paul assured me it was the 'lull before the storm' so I waited before changing sails and, sure enough, the wind came. I watched cat's-paws approach over my shoulder and, when the main blast hit me, was swept away, hurtling along on the back inches of the board. My muscles ached as I clung on and in a few minutes I knew that if the wind did not ease something was going to break. With that thought I went flying over the sail and landed with a splash.

I swam back to the board and removed a reef from the sail. The wind spat spray into my face as if to say it was 'not just whistling Dixie' and, once on my feet again, I had great difficulty in bearing away on to a run. I sailed sideways like a crab for a few yards before ploughing into an elephant of a wave and plunging into the water again. I tried once more, sailed for a hundred yards and took another tumble. For half an hour the actions repeated themselves: start, lurch a few yards, fall in, up again. I tried broad reaching on both sides as well as running, but with the waves coming from all directions, no point of sailing seemed stable enough for me to stay upright for more than a few seconds. Eventually, I took one fall too many, came back to the board and just sat there sobbing with frustration. I felt thoroughly whipped.

It was the worst patch of sea that I had ever encountered and caused, I later reckoned, by a chance combination of factors: the gale the night before; the present strong wind coming from a different point of the compass; and two tides, one flowing west from the Solway Firth and the other south from the Irish Sea, both racing to fight their way up the North Channel. One thing was for certain; it was no place for a windsurfer, not a sane one anyway!

I nearly gave up and asked *Morningtown* to take me back to Peel. But, as always, the thought of admitting defeat, being still less appealing than the hell I was going through, spurred me to carry on. After twenty minutes of bobbing up and down, staring discon-

Waiting for the wind

solately at the grey water, I made myself continue, if only until I dropped from exhaustion. With fresh resolve, I pulled up the sail and steered the board carefully onto a run. Then I was away and bumping across the waves. A frond of seaweed dangled off the end of my boom – I hoped that meant good luck. My goal now was not to fall in at any cost. Several times I lost my balance and all but hit the water, somehow managing to pull myself back up straight. The advice of my former ski-racing coach came back to me: 'Never fall over. Never hit the snow, not even if it seems you have to . . . fight it!' I clung on for a quarter of an hour, half an hour and then miraculously an hour. I had regained my confidence. Now came the supreme test.

Some distance off to the north-east was the impressive horn of the Mull of Galloway. Half a mile in front of me and stretching as far as the eye could see were the white-caps of standing waves. All my previous experience of overfalls had been of small, localised patches, but facing me now were miles and miles of solid standing waves – close-packed, steep, wobbling walls of water. What a day! Just when I had thought the worst was over. Why didn't someone warn me about this place? Then I was amongst it. 'I'm not going to fall. I won't let this beat me,' I told myself, as the *Log* rode up on the first wave and began to be tossed around like a piece of driftwood. First one side of the board would be flicked up and I would tread heavily on it to restore my equilibrium, then the other side would twist up and I would throw my weight the other way. It was like riding a bicycle down a street with cobblestones the size of beachballs, only wetter! Somehow I kept my balance. Once into the last few hundred yards I knew I had won and smiled magnanimously at the snarling waves. I would never forget the Mull of Galloway.

Coasting in clearer waters my second wind came and the day changed utterly in character. I feasted on magnificent scenery, the lush fields of Galloway sloping back from the granite shore. This was Scotland at last. The air was crystal sharp as when the sun comes sparkling out after a rainstorm. Off to the left, Ireland was visible on the horizon, and across the blue sky were arranged hundreds of crisp white clouds of marvellous shape. Three elliptical clouds hovering up ahead looked like UFOs coming in to land on the Mull of Kintyre. The seabirds were also enjoying this perfect afternoon, a flock of gulls flying around me in close formation as if daring me to lift off into the sky myself.

The waves were long and regular and I concentrated on surfing them to increase my speed. As a wave reached me I walked forward to let the board lift and start planing, before dancing back to stop its nose ploughing into the wave in front, all the time playing the sail to avoid being catapulted forward by the gusts of wind. We approached a town clinging to the hillside ahead and before it a ruined castle. The town was Portpatrick and the ruin, Dunskey's Castle, formerly owned by a 'bloody' pirate who was unseated some three hundred years ago. Dunskey cut off the pirate's head and presented it to the king in exchange for the title deeds to the property!

The wind had freshened to force 6 or more and we decided to continue making miles while we could. We passed Portpatrick, where we were to spend the night; from two hundred yards off there was no sign of any harbour, just a line of rubble which looked to be simply a breakwater protecting the town from the ravages of the sea. I was at full stretch, galloping along on a run, easily matching *Morningtown*'s top speed, the coast flashing by at almost a mile every five minutes. We reached Black Head lighthouse and right under the light itself saw the wreck of a coaster, its back broken on the rocks. Dozens of wooden crates, presumably cargo, had been jammed by the sea into every available crevice and cave in the cliffs. A few miles further on we stopped, roughly opposite a farmhouse, a lonely grey dot amid miles of rolling green fields. It was 8.45pm and the day had been worth forty-three miles. I was very glad to have that stretch behind me.

The sea conditions were extreme now and I had to make a heart-stopping leap from the inflatable onto *Morningtown*'s shrouds. It was too rough to tow *Bumble* in and we motored separately the six miles back to Portpatrick. The sea was crashing onto *Morningtown*'s deck and behind us *Bumble* leapt into the air off the top of each swell, landing with a great splash and a cloud of spray. From the look on their faces, Charlie and Chris appeared to be loving it.

Arriving at Portpatrick we found that the little harbour was tucked in behind the breakwater and had to be entered through an exceedingly narrow channel in the middle. In these conditions Paul was going to need all his nerve to pilot *Morningtown* through the gap safely. Luckily, by this time Alice was in Portpatrick and had managed to find a friendly local to talk Paul in by radio. 'Keep close to Bread Rock, och,' he said. 'Pick up the leading lights, aye, now hard to port, och.' We could not believe there was enough water in the channel, seeing some seagulls walking around on a sandbank a few yards away. Paul was white-faced as he swung the wheel and I think I closed my eyes at one point. Then we were in and safe, and Alice was there. What excitement! We had reached Scotland.

The friendly local was Mac, who lived on a converted fishing boat and, despite sprinkling his speech liberally with 'ochs' and 'ayes', came, in fact, from Derby. This did not matter. Mac spotted me on *Morningtown* and must have thought I looked a bit cold and bedraggled. 'How would you like a bath to warm you up, och, laddie?' he asked. 'I'd love one, but where?' I replied. 'Right here aboard my boat,' said Mac, leading me onto his unique ex-trawler. Down below was a large bath, soon full of piping-hot water from his coal-heated tank. I luxuriated in the warm water; what a way to wash away the salt of five hundred miles of ocean! There was a knock on the door and an arm appeared holding a large glass of whisky. 'Get that inside you, laddie, ye'll feel a lot better, aye.' I did. Mac was a godsend.

I emerged from the steaming bathroom wearing warm, dry clothes and feeling reborn. Then Mac introduced me to Keith, a photographer from *The Mail on Sunday*. 'What a pity,' said Keith. 'I wanted to get some exclusive pictures of you relaxing in the bath after a hard day at sea.' I thought his taste in shots a little bizarre, but this was put very much in perspective by the extraordinary caption that eventually appeared in the *Mail* next to a picture of me: '. . . at night Tim sleeps with six men on a tiny ketch'!

Supper conversation was dominated by the day's big event on *Morningtown*. During the afternoon a racing pigeon had paid a visit, somehow finding its way into the hen-house (which bore a trail of evidence) and ending up inside Charlie's sleeping-bag. After supper, Mark arrived with a surprise, Willem Blaauw, my sailmaker from Neil Pryde in Ireland, and we all retreated to the quayside drinking house. Willem was on excellent form, particularly pleased because his protégé, a Dane called Tim Aagsen, had just won the first race in the windsurfing World Cup series using Willem's latest sails. Robbie Naish, the twenty-one-year-old Hawaiian superstar who has won every windsurfing World Cup since he was thirteen, was beaten into second place. Afterwards, he asked Willem if he, too, could have a set of new sails like Tim's. 'Sorry, Robbie,' Willem joked, 'these sails are only for the good guys!'

The next morning, 4 June, Paul and I went aboard Mac's boat to cadge some advice on possible anchorages for the night. We were heading into more uncharted territory and were eager for any first-hand information we could gain from old hands like Mac. One favoured option, Sanda Island, was ruled out because of the strong currents sweeping round the Mull of Kintyre and both Gigha Island and Islay were out of reach of a day's sail. In the end we plumped for Ireland and an anchorage in Red Bay.

We were kept busy until departure. There were visits from well-wishers, and Keith, the photographer, made us all pose for a group photograph on deck, insisting that we open a bottle of champagne. Willem gave Haydn, who had become an excellent sail rigger, some fine-tuning tips on setting sails, and we talked about my sail range.

Willem agreed to take away the 9m sail I had torn for repair and, anticipating light winds down the east coast, I persuaded him to make an even bigger sail. 'The sky's the limit, Willem! How about 10.5m?' He was excited by the idea and agreed to forward the sails to Lochinver, a couple of hundred miles further north.

We left Portpatrick at about 12.30 in order to catch the tide flowing north at 2.30. Keith would not join us on *Morningtown* as he was worried about seasickness but hired a bass boat in Portpatrick so that he could make a quick getaway if things turned rough. Sitting demurely in the front of the craft with the fisherman standing aft by the tiller, he looked for all the world as if he were on a gondola trip down the Grand Canal!

Willem borrowed the Division II board and joined me for a sail. In the light conditions we sailed in close formation, and it was a welcome change to have company for once. I was sorry when he stopped, saying half an hour in a straight line was enough for him, and I reflected that I was hoping for at least another eight hours in this straight line. But Murphy's law of the ocean struck (we were trying to get to Ireland!) and shortly after Willem and Keith had gone, flat calm descended on the waters of the North Channel. In the hazy sunshine we could no longer see land. After pumping for a while I stopped to sit and wait, killing time by reading the *Daily Mail* which ironically featured the tragic sinking of a tall ship in a squall in the Atlantic as the cover story. That amount of wind seemed a distant concept.

Chris went for a swim to cool off and got back onto *Bumble* rather suddenly saying he had spotted a giant jellyfish. He grappled with the two-foot-wide monster for some minutes before capturing it in a large bucket. Paul and Haydn then decided that Chris would look good wearing the creature as a bath hat, but somehow could not convince Chris to try it on. The episode ended with Chris going for another dip and the jellyfish slithering off into the deep.

There was still no sign of any wind and, only eight miles better off than when we set out, we motored back to Portpatrick. In the early evening the local lifeboat coxswain paid us a visit. He described the hazards of bursting out of Portpatrick harbour in the lifeboat in a westerly gale. 'You have to be going full tilt as soon as you leave the shelter of the breakwater and hope you get far enough out not to be dumped back on the beach by the first big wave!' The coxswain also explained the mystery of the wrecked coaster under the lighthouse. 'She was on her way from Ireland and, instead of turning south into the Irish Sea, she steamed at full tilt straight into the cliffs. The crew said they were lost in thick fog but I recall it being a clear night. I guess they must have all fallen asleep!'

We were woken next morning by a loud crack on deck. Mac's fishing boat had just slipped out of port, taking part of our guard-rail with it. 'Och, sorry,' called Mac as he steamed off. It was windy and would be rough out at sea. After all these miles the prospect of a rough day still made me nervous. We were not sailing till 12.30 and I walked a mile or so inland and found a sheltered, sunny glade where the air was warm. Sitting down for a moment and drinking in the sweet summer smells, it occurred to me how nice it would be to walk my forty miles today – just this once!

The ride out from Portpatrick was indeed bumpy and several of us were seasick. All sufferers congregated on deck, Chris, as was his habit, spreading out behind the mizzen mast before wrestling angrily into a drysuit! As usual I felt much better once on the board. The wind was north-easterly 5 and would have made Red Bay, Ireland, a dangerous anchorage. We aimed instead to shave the Mull of Kintyre, heading into the Sound of Jura to find shelter there. I took *Pytheas II* and the reefing sail and quickly had to remove first one reef then the other as the wind freshened to about force 7. For several hours I went flat out on a close reach, taking some acrobatic tumbles but largely relishing the stiff conditions. The air was moist with a patchy Scotch mist and I experienced the curious sensation of sailing into pockets of warm air. At one point I thought I caught a whiff of manure. Then it became unmistakable: there was a strong smell of cow dung in the air. Almost in the same instant the mist cleared ahead to reveal a dark mountainous mass which had to be the Mull of Kintyre.

After hours in sightless fog it was a hugely inspiring vision which triggered off some tuneful humming of the eponymous song. I stopped for a coffee break to collect my strength before the mull itself, and prayed that the tide-race would be kind to me. Chris and Charlie were humming the same ballad – it was catching – and seemed full of beans, evidently looking forward as much as I to being among the Western Isles. I looked at the Ordnance Survey map of the mull to see if I could work out where the fruity Highland cattle smell was emanating from. By coincidence, the little village at the tip of the Kintyre peninsula was called Southend. I chuckled and thought of its namesake still some thousand miles around the corner, and wondered if I would make it.

I had a helter-skelter ride round the mull, whistled along by the breeze and a strong following tide. I must have been making a good eighteen to twenty knots over the water, which, added to five knots of tide, meant about twenty-five over the ground! *Bumble* had a hair-raising job trying to keep up and at one point took off on a steep wave, almost being flipped upside down by the wind. The force of the landing snapped a steel pole that we used for the radio aerial and broke one of the oars lying in its sleeve along the boat's hull.

At about 8pm I stopped and radioed Paul for a brief discussion about where we were headed that night. 'Port Ellen's only twelve miles to the north-west. We're making such fast miles, we should be there in an hour,' he said. 'No problem,' I thought, charging off eagerly. Ten minutes later the wind dropped to nothing, low clouds enveloped us and it began to drizzle. We sat for ten minutes waiting and then quit for the day, forty-three miles sailed. 'Every time we seem to make a plan, the wind changes and foils us. Let's take it as it comes in the future – no plans!' I said to Paul, once back on *Morningtown*.

We motored to Port Ellen on Islay, arriving at about 10.15pm. The sun was just on its way to bed – the days were growing significantly longer as we progressed north. Liz and Paul stayed on board and the rest of us went ashore and discovered a Masonic lodge that doubled as a bar, selling a delicious thick beer called Tennent's Light.

In the morning of 6 June we were able to see Islay in all its glory. Port Ellen sits on the edge of a deep, half-moon bay on the south-east corner of the island. A line of grain-driers on the quayside dominates the town and provides a strong clue to the industry which supports the island's four thousand inhabitants – *uisegebaugh*, the water-of-life, whisky – what, by virtue of its unsurpassed peat streams, Islay has been famous for since the Middle Ages.

We were not leaving till the afternoon and I went for a wander ashore, ending up in the Victoria Inn, where my attention was evenly divided between hops, pints of the excellent Tennent's Light, and the jukebox on which I repeatedly played an old favourite, '99 Red Balloons', by Nena. In approachable, contented mood I was soon surrounded by a trio of inquisitive Scotsmen who gave me a good talking to about a hazard lying in wait a few miles up ahead – the Gulf of Corrievrechan, Europe's largest whirlpool. 'You could nay come through it, laddie,' said one. 'You'd be a fool to try,' said another.

The first man had passed through the gulf in a naval minesweeper, a ship of unusual power. 'Even with four thousand horses to help us, we were lucky to escape, aye, admitted it was a foul night.' The second man, a crew member of the Port Askaig (Islay) lifeboat, had been through once in the lifeboat and said he would rather not go back. 'You'd nay be safe even with us right there. It'd make no difference.' The third Scotsman then chimed in with the recollection of a recent incident, that was greeted with vigorous nods of approbation from the other two. 'One rough day a MacBrayne's ferry took a short cut through the gulf and was caught by the whirlpool. They had to jettison their cargo of cattle to avoid being dragged down!' 'Will you nay change your mind, laddie?' they practically chorused at the end.

I almost laughed, the scene reminded me so strongly of a Tintin book, *Black Island*, in which Tintin is warned by a wise, kilt-clad, old Scotsman on a quay, 'If you value you life, laddie, nay go near Black Island!' (Tintin, of course, ignored the advice and survived to star in the next adventure!) I did not have the heart to tell my counsellors that the Corrievrechan actually lay just off my route and that I had only considered going through it as a sort of dare.

(*above*) 'See, I can still box!' Mark in Golspie hospital; (*below*) Through the
Pentland Firth

(*above*) Paul throws in a fresh rig; (*below*) A good-humoured Chris passes the old rig up to Haydn

We left Port Ellen at just after 2pm. Turning out of the bay, *Morningtown*'s engine cut out suddenly and, carried by her own momentum, she drifted towards the lighthouse on the southern headland of the Mull of Oa. The engine would not restart immediately but Paul hoisted the yankee in seconds and we sailed out of trouble. Then the motor began to chug confidently again, though refusing to divulge what had been the matter.

There was negligible wind when we reached our starting point at 4.15 and we amused ourselves by taking hostage another giant jelly-fish. In an attempt at domestication, I wedged the creature on my board against the mast foot and sailed off! But jellyfish must have a close understanding with the elements as a breeze very suddenly sprang up. My subsequent burst of speed caused waves to wash over the board, allowing the great, wobbling animal to slither away to freedom.

I headed north to Jura, covering twenty-four miles in six long hours. It was a dreary, misty evening and the sailing was tedious – by fits and starts into a fickle headwind. At times I was overpowered with the 8m sail, struggling to hold my line to the wind, and at other times had too little breeze to make decent progress and clawed emptily at the air. The session was only memorable for my mastering the (not particularly difficult!) art of drinking orange juice from a bottle while sailing along, and for a silly friction developing between Chris, Charlie and myself and the others on *Morningtown*.

Encouraged by the broken progress and monotonous quality of the day, I had evidently bothered Paul (via *Bumble*) once too often for a mileage report; Chris and Charlie had likewise made one too many demands on the galley for fresh coffee and biscuits. By the time we closed the shore of Jura at the end of the evening and stopped, the vibes we were getting on the airwaves had become sufficiently frosty to warrant some sort of demonstration. The three of us in *Bumble* splintered off, overtaking *Morningtown* on the way into Craighouse Bay (the anchorage for the night) and headed for the shore, intending a few quiet drinks before closing time (it was 10.20pm).

Things did not go smoothly, however. We eventually found the one hotel on the island, but only after Chris had fallen into the bay looking for a place to land in the dark. He had been plumbing the depth in front of us with *Bumble*'s oar and, when the oar became stuck, had stayed with it while we motored forward. Our brief stay in the crowded bar was marred by Chris's great pool of water which the barman ostentatiously launched into with a mop. Returning to *Morningtown* to cold supper and dagger looks from the others we immediately regretted the whole escapade and went to bed feeling thoroughly chastened.

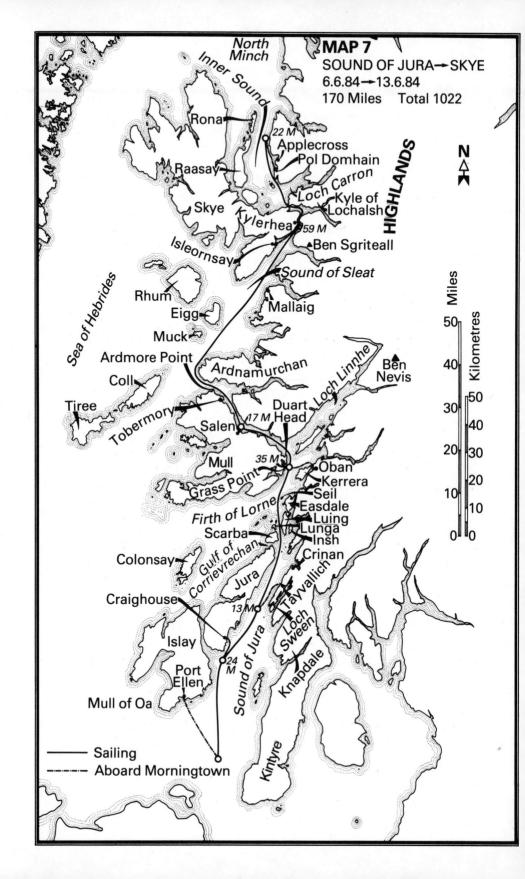

MAP 7
SOUND OF JURA → SKYE
6.6.84 → 13.6.84
170 Miles   Total 1022

North Minch
Inner Sound
Rona
22 M
Applecross
Pol Domhain
Loch Carron
Kyle of Lochalsh
Raasay
Skye
Kylerhea
59 M
Isleornsay
Ben Sgriteall
Sound of Sleat
Sea of Hebrides
Rhum
Eigg
Muck
Mallaig
Ardmore Point
Ardnamurchan
Loch Linnhe
Ben Nevis
Coll
Tiree
Tobermory
Salen
17 M
Duart Head
Oban
Kerrera
Mull
35 M
Seil
Easdale
Luing
Grass Point
Firth of Lorne
Lunga
Insh
Scarba
Crinan
Colonsay
Gulf of Corrievrechan
Jura
Tayvallich
Craighouse
13 M
Loch Sween
Islay
Port Ellen
24 M
Sound of Jura
Knapdale
Mull of Oa

HIGHLANDS

N

Miles
Kilometres
50
40
30
20
10
0

50
40
30
20
10
0

Kintyre

——— Sailing
—·—·— Aboard Morningtown

Any remaining tension evaporated the next day. It was a crisp sunny morning and, anchored off beautiful, deserted Jura, we had a taste of the Scottish isles at their magical best: crystal water, golden sand, dark green forests, purple mountains and clear blue sky. The tide ran north late in the afternoon so we had a half-day off to enjoy the island: on that morning I think everyone would have liked to stay forever. Paul and Liz went ashore to look for deer while Chris and Charlie had one of their famous windsurf races round the bay. The sea was so inviting, an aquarium of great seaweed fronds and darting fish, that for the first time on the trip I was tempted to go sailing just for the fun of it.

Later, I decided that it was time to add up the miles travelled. To my surprise and delight, I found that we had covered 850, less than a hundred miles short of half-way. Until then, I had somehow assumed that half-way was at the top of Scotland, but now it had suddenly crept up on me. Perhaps for the first time I thought to myself, 'I can really do this – it's not so impossible after all.' Everyone else was excited by the news and, I think, as surprised as me. We planned a celebration barbecue on the beach at the half-way stage itself, Tobermory, on Mull.

I would be arriving in Tobermory after about thirty-nine days at sea, just a week longer than the target set in planning. At this rate the trip would be over in a total of eleven weeks, a fortnight longer than predicted. Of course, anything could happen between here and Southend: I could be delayed down the east coast by fog and light headwinds, or I could come unstuck at the formidable hurdles of Cape Wrath and the Pentland Firth; on the other hand, I might at last get the strong reaching winds that would give me the much greater mileages that I had hoped for.

At five o'clock it was time to leave and we weighed anchor, or rather tried to, and found about a ton of seaweed festooned around anchor and chain. This lovely little bay did not want us to go! It was a perfect evening for sailing – a moderate breeze and flat water, warm and balmy. For the first time I wore light sailing gloves rather than my rubber dry-gloves. With the *Log* and 8m sail I was on a close reach up the Sound of Jura, the island's three conical mountains, the Paps, to my left and the mainland to my right. Again, it was comforting to see land both sides and not to feel vulnerable in the middle of the ocean.

The breeze, lively and consistent, was ideal for the large sail and I got up a cracking pace, taking pleasure in sailing as precisely and efficiently as I could. The flat water was a great advantage as I could concentrate on the behaviour of the sail without worrying about the board suddenly being thrown off line by a wave. The breeze freshened further and I leant out in the harness, feet on the edge of the board, my back practically touching the water, my hands sliding further and further down the boom as the centre of effort of the sail shifted with the increasing wind. My right hand reached the end of the grip on the boom and I found myself sailing at the absolute limit with this sail. I skimmed along – glorious, proud, smooth white wake behind me, unblemished blue sea ahead, the wind on my face, the sun on my back, the water inches from my shoulder. This was worth coming nearly a thousand miles for.

Perched on a rock up ahead was the Skerrivule lighthouse. As I approached I caught sight of what looked like an otter lolloping off the flat rock into the water, then several otters. At closer sight I realised they were not otters at all but seals, dozens of them. They were basking on the rock in the late sun or lurking in the cool waters nearby with just their heads poking out, looking for all the world like dowagers in bathing caps. I shouted a greeting as I cruised past, wanting to share the lovely evening with them. They merely oinked.

As the sun went down behind Jura the breeze died and all became still. Having covered just over twelve miles in two glorious hours' sailing I stopped. We were in the luxurious position of having a choice of four or five anchorages for the night, all recommended as excellent by the *Clyde Cruising Association Handbook*. We opted for Carsaig Bay, an oval dent in the coast some four miles further up the sound, and in the shelter of Carsaig Island we dropped our anchor next to a lump of granite appropriately called Seal Rock.

By good luck we managed to reach Mark, who had been roaming the wilds of Knapdale all day looking for us, on the radio. We badly needed petrol and a shore party was despatched before dinner to meet up with him. His news was twofold: he had scraped the truck backing into a tree-stump and we had attracted some vitriolic comment in the yachting press – namely from John Chamier in *Yachts and Yachting*. He had called the trip a worthless stunt and censured the RNLI for being involved in a fund-raising event which was more than likely to require their professional assistance. He compared the absurdity of trying to windsurf around Britain with that of attempting to climb Everest in gym shoes! My blood boiled as I read on but, after half-composing a hotly indignant reply, I decided that completing the journey successfully was the best way to counter attack. After the event finished, *Yachts and Yachting* carried a very different piece starting with the words, 'Contrary to an earlier opinion expressed by a fellow columnist . . .'

Looking for petrol ashore we came across the village of Tayvallich on Loch Sween that runs parallel to the Sound of Jura. I was surprised by the number of yachts at the end of the loch; it was not a large place but seemed like Sydney harbour in comparison to our deserted little bay not a mile the other side of the peninsula. While we stopped to telephone at an hotel, some guests noticed the signwriting on the camper and approached us. I had a long chat with a retired colonel who was 'mad about the RNLI'. He told me he had just given them a new lifeboat and something about the way he said he was going to make a donation to our appeal made my eyes pop out in anticipation. I only hope I did not look disappointed when he slipped me £10.

On the way back to the boat, I bumped into a lad who spent time canoeing among the islands and had more to tell me about the indomitable Corrievrechan. Everyone up here seemed to know it intimately. 'On a stormy night you can hear the moaning of the whirlpool for miles around,' he said. 'A new hotel has been built at Crinan, ten miles across the sound so that people can listen on wild evenings and even see the eerie green light hanging over the area. Some say the gulf is haunted by the spirits of all the dead at the bottom,' he repeated matter-of-factly, pausing for breath before launching into a detailed explanation. 'The whirlpool occurs due to a combination of the strong tides ripping through the channel and the unusual shape of the sea bed, which drops suddenly from 90 to 450ft forming an underwater canyon with sheer 400ft walls. On the ebb, water drains from the Sound of Jura through the Corrievrechan and out into the Atlantic. With a westerly gale against a spring ebb the whirlpool is at its worst and a ferocious tide-race extends five miles westwards towards Colonsay. When the tide turns, you've got precisely fifteen minutes of slack water before the whirlpool starts spinning the other way.'

I was more eager than ever to see this phenomenon, but probably from a helicopter or, failing that, the bridge of HMS *Hermes*! But the lad had not quite finished: 'If you have not had enough of whirlpools with the Corrievrechan, there are some more a little further on, between Lunga and Scarba, the Nine Grey Dogs. You're in for some of the most interesting sailing in Scotland tomorrow,' he concluded cheerfully. 'Good luck!' I was definitely going to wear an extra lifejacket.

Ambling back to *Bumble*, something bit me. It was a midge, my first of the season. Soon I was being attacked from all sides and ran the rest of the way to the boat. Retreating onto the water from Scottish mosquitoes reminded me of an outward-bound course (care of John Ridgway, whom I was soon to visit) in 1976 near Cape Wrath. On a survival course in the open I had been so pestered by the midges, which covered any exposed flesh with a black mat, that I had spent the best part of two days lying immersed in a stream!

On the next day, 8 June, I was up soon after six o'clock for the forecast. Although light winds were predicted, it was beautifully still here and I postponed starting for a while. Sitting on deck with a mug of tea I enjoyed the most peaceful morning that I can remember, the sun climbing slowly above the hills, its warm rays waking two fat seals lying on their namesake rock nearby. After about an hour a gentle breeze began to tease the surface of the loch. Time for action.

Leaving our anchorage there was a minor disaster with *Bumble*. In the calm conditions we relaxed our guard and steamed off without noticing that she was tangled up with the buoy of a wayward lobster pot. There was a swift tearing sound and we were left towing just a painter line attached to a couple of rubber patches. Fortunately, we were able to improvise another towing line, but we had learnt a lesson about lobster pots – they are not easy to shift off the sea bed!

On the way down the sound we breakfasted off porridge and treacle, a habit since entering Scottish waters, and started sailing at 8.30am. In the light airs I took the Division II and 8m sail and began to work my way up the sound, crossing from patch of wind to patch of wind, heading for wherever there was a darkening of the water's surface and tacking whenever I ran out of breeze. *Morningtown* was also under sail power and, finding myself a little way ahead after a quarter of an hour, I challenged them to a race up the sound, a distance of about fifteen miles. They readily agreed. The Division II was ideally suited to the calm conditions, its high volume prolonging the momentum from any thrust of wind, and I crept further and further away from *Morningtown*, staying in the middle of the channel where the wind seemed to be most in evidence. It was a breathtaking day and place. As I sailed the bow of the board gently parted the blue water, sending out tiny ripples that sparkled in the sunshine. Behind me the board's wake, like the deliberate trace of a snail, stretched for yards across the still surface of the sea. The sound narrowed towards its head and the stunning scenery both sides came close into view. Looking up at the Jura Paps in the clear air I could even make out the course of a stream snaking its way down the mountainside.

After a beautiful, lazy three-hour sail I was but a mile from the finish and *Morningtown* a good two miles behind, when I became totally becalmed. Under normal circumstances this would have been a perfect excuse to sit and idly enjoy the surroundings but, for the sake of the race, I began to pump laboriously towards a patch of dark water some three hundred yards distant. It was while thus engaged that I noticed that *Morningtown*, way off west near the Jura shore, suddenly appeared to be moving at some considerable speed up the sound. I closed my eyes, hoping that it was an illusion, but when I opened them, the ketch was unmistakably flashing past the land – at eight knots, maybe more. I knew I had been outsmarted. Paul, in wily fashion, had closed the shore, hoping for the beginnings of a sea breeze, and that was what he was fizzing along in. I pumped harder but to no avail; the patch of dark blue was if anything retreating before me. *Morningtown* kept going steadily. I had lost just when I had been counting my victory. By the time I was back in the breeze *Morningtown* was well in front. In a last burst of speed I pulled back several hundred yards but it was not enough. It was my round that night.

Reaching the end of Jura I saw, with a surge of excitement, that I was approaching the entrance to the Gulf of Corrievrechan. It looked harmless enough from here, just a blue channel between two islands. Half-way across the channel and heading towards the Sound of Luing, I was hit by a sudden blast of wind from the west. My board keeled over and capsized so quickly that the daggerboard (with me kneeling on top!) hammered into the boom, snapping off a corner of itself in the process. I righted the board and, the mysterious wind having disappeared as fast as it came, I set off again. A hundred yards later the same thing happened: a sudden whoosh of wind, and again I capsized and chipped the daggerboard. At this rate I soon would not have any keel left. A little further on I was in even weirder conditions. The board was gripped by a powerful current, pulled steadily backwards and then swung round in two complete circles while I stood helpless in the middle. Then I was spat out, fortunately in the direction of Luing, and caught a segment of tide that carried me, feeling distinctly dizzy, about a mile up the Sound of Luing. That was as far as I could sail for a while as before long the tide turned solidly across the sound and I began to drift backwards again. I stopped, unrigged and made my way in *Bumble* to a little bay on Scarba where *Morningtown* had anchored to wait out the foul tide.

Scarba is rocky and choked with thorny vegetation and we were not inclined to much exploration on land. Paul paddled off on a board to investigate a colony of seals nearby and was soon immersed in playing with them. Alice, Liz and Haydn sat on deck in the sun but Chris, Charlie and I had other ideas. We decided that the lure of the Corrievrechan was too much to resist, and set off to explore it in *Bumble*. We took various precautions, putting on lifejackets, checking fuel leads and generally psyching ourselves up. We were all excited at what we might find, confident, though, that *Bumble*, being light and powerful, would be able to pull us out of any problems we met.

On entering the gulf, we were carried quickly by the tide towards the western end, where most of the troubled water lies. We strained our eyes to see what lay ahead. There was an area of disturbed water, foaming white, perhaps covering an acre or more. In the middle was a circle of water some thirty yards across, ringed by angry waves that sequentially stood up proud, then collapsed and disappeared as if a trap door had suddenly been opened beneath them. Inside the circle was an area of silky smooth water and at the very centre a sizeable depression, a vortex of swirling water. There really was a whirlpool.

We motored carefully round the edge for a minute or so, then broke the circle and cut our engine. Gradually, *Bumble* was drawn into the centre and started to spin round and round. It was rather like being on a children's roundabout. Altogether the whole thing was an anticlimax – at no stage did we look like being sucked to the sea bed – no water even broke into the boat. As we motored away back to Scarba we all felt rather let down. There had been only a lazy hint of the power we had heard described and a pact was made to reunite there one stormy winter's night!

Our target was to reach Oban by nightfall, but a hefty eighteen miles still remained to be covered. Looking ahead up the Sound of Luing from Scarba we could see that a healthy sea breeze was blowing from the west, ideal for sailing. But we were in a dead patch in the lee of mountainous Scarba and faced a frustrating wait till 5.30 or so when the tide would turn to carry us north.

By 4.30 I could contain myself no longer and set off to try and clear the dead half-mile using back eddies and general guile. With the Division II and 8m sail I pumped a few yards into the main channel and, catching a friendly gust of wind, slid my way up a swathe of ruffled water that I knew to be tide going the right way. But the eddy would not drop me off at the top and I had the irritating experience of coming back down to where I started in an opposite moving stream of water. It was like using an escalator but being unable to step off at the top. This happened several times over the next half an hour and I began to yearn for a little motor or even a paddle, just for a few minutes.

At last a deep breath of wind came my way, blowing me into the sea breeze proper, and I reached happily up the sound between Lunga and Luing, passing the Grey Dogs without a backward glance. The strength of the sea breeze took me by surprise. It had been a hot day and the thermal activity over Luing was generating a solid force 5. Soon I was well overpowered and hurtling along at terrific speed. It felt quite the fastest I had yet travelled during the trip, about twenty-five knots, and on a Division II board with a large daggerboard! My wake was like that of a speedboat, a plume rising some ten yards behind. The board accelerated to almost terminal velocity, planing on the daggerboard and writhing under me like a snake trapped on burning stubble. I was frightened. I must stop before I knocked myself out or broke something. I let go and exploded into the sound.

After a lightning change to the more stable *Log* with its retractable daggerboard and the 6.5m reefing sail, I was away again. I was still overpowered, the wind attacking the sail as if meaning to carry it away, but the *Log* was easier to keep flat on the water and I sped confidently up past Ormsa and Fladda and on towards Easdale Island. The reefing sail, I could not help noticing, compared badly with my beloved 8m in both performance and handling, being heavier, lower in the clew and generally more uncomfortable. It was going out of favour.

I met hefty waves in the Sound of Insh between Insh Island and Seil but the *Log*, experienced now at taking large waves on the run, treated them with disdain. The breeze eased off and Paul suggested a change back to the 8m. I was always reluctant to change up after a recent change down, memories of the fight still strong, and hesitated out of respect for the wind, I suppose. But this time pragmatism prevailed, and up went the 8m like a kite.

There began a purposeful trudge up the Firth of Lorne past Loch Spelve towards Kerrera Island and Oban. Most unforgettable about the Firth of Lorne were the armies of jellyfish infesting the water like a plague. There were two types: small, purple ones that do not sting and large orange ones that looked a lot nastier and sting viciously. They were so dense that I sailed for a mile or more thinking, 'I still haven't found a spot where it would be safe to fall in!' I saw thousands of these creatures on my journey and wondered at their role in the oceans. To me they seemed like a strange police force – guardians of the surface waters – as they pulsated resolutely by.

At 9pm we eventually drew level with Oban and I stopped at Grass Point on the Island of Mull. We motored across to the harbour, escorted the last few miles by the Oban lifeboat. It had been a long haul of eleven hours for the thirty-five miles. Rodney Hill was to be rejoining us in Oban for the next leg through to the Pentland Firth. The prospect had been something of a cloud on the horizon and much of the day was spent debating whether or not he would be there as planned. As we motored into harbour Rodney was waiting on the quayside and with him were Jill and a friend, who were exploring the west coast.

9 June, our thirty-ninth day since leaving Southend, was a lay day. We took on diesel and water in the morning and everyone took off into the countryside to find a pub for lunch. Alice, Haydn and I stayed behind and ate an excellent sardine mousse on *Morningtown*. In the afternoon I explored Oban, a town of character dominated by an extraordinary monument – a Roman-style coliseum built about a

century ago by a philanthropic Victorian to provide employment for local masons. I collected the epoxy resin sent to Oban by Tris and was invited to supper by Anne and Harry, relatives of Tris's manager in Cornwall. Pat Maclean, the Oban coxswain/mechanic was very helpful and lent us the lifeboat shed for epoxy repairs to the nose, tail and underside of the *Log*. Paul laid the glass and we left it to cure overnight under an electric heater before sanding it down in the morning. The result was incredibly tough, armour-plated almost.

During the afternoon Alice had an unfortunate accident: she fell backwards when starting the outboard motor in *Bumble* and landed on the radar reflector. Sitting down was a bit difficult for the rest of the day but, fortified by one or two drinks, she was able to go out to dinner. We had an excellent Thailand curry and, more important, a short break from life on board ship.

10 June started cold and grey. I finished repairing my board and gave Pat a bottle of Charles Heidsieck as a thank you. A quick turn on the *Log* across Oban Bay for some photographers and we were off. It was a full boat with several extras: Dina and Sarah, friend and sister of Chris, plus Mark, who was joining us for several days (leaving the camper parked in Oban). Chris went on ahead to Mull by ferry to take some photos of us from land as we advanced up the Sound of Mull.

There was no wind at all and I braved jeers of 'cheat' by grabbing a paddle from *Bumble* and propelling myself the first few yards of the day! Beginning at eleven o'clock with the *Log* and 8m sail it took me all of an hour to cover the mile from Grass Point to Duart Head. Mark dared a ride in *Bumble* and, cutting the engine, they drifted alongside, Mark entertaining me with extracts from the Sunday papers. Duart Head was a fork: to my right lay Loch Linnhe leading to the Caledonian Canal and Loch Ness, the short cut to the east coast; to my left stretched the Sound of Mull leading to the exposed north coast. I took the left fork but did not start on this 'high road' with much panache. At the mouth of the sound we ran into some wind and I challenged *Morningtown* to another race.

They tacked off on port towards the mainland and, thinking I would be different, I went off on starboard. Consequently, I sailed out of the fair tide into a back eddy and was trapped in Duart Bay for about forty minutes. *Morningtown*, now miles ahead, declared herself the winner and came back for me. Out of the wind entirely, I sat waiting on *Morningtown* feeling rather dumb while the fair tide ran out on the far side of the sound. Paul took advantage of the lull and, in true school-bully fashion, proposed that Mark should be baptised on his first day at sea. Everyone endorsed this as a thoroughly good idea and, taking him by surprise, we tossed Mark overboard. He came up spluttering, fortunately smiling, and shouted, 'How the hell did you know I could swim?'

Finally able to start sailing again at about 3.15pm, I found myself beating up the winding Sound of Mull against the tide. I was paying for the morning's error with the slowest progress imaginable. I tacked backwards and forwards across the sound trying to creep up the shore where the adverse tide was weakest. Losing ground fast at one point, I made a tack across a shallow reef in Scallastle Bay and two seals popped up behind me, as if to say, 'What on earth are you playing at?' I did not dare stop for a rest on *Bumble* as we would have been carried so fast down with the tide, but we rested on shore a couple of times, which made a pleasant change. Charlie had smuggled a can of barbecued beans out of the galley which we ate with boy scout relish and we made the most of our latest acquisition, an indestructible stainless-steel Thermos (we had now broken three glass ones) which kept the coffee piping hot. Coffee breaks now held a significantly greater attraction.

It was a grey dusk at 9pm when I eventually called it a day, having just passed a little rock called Einan Glasa, and still eight miles short of Tobermory. The half-way celebrations went ahead as planned, but at the beginning of the evening I was in philosophical rather than joyous mood with only seventeen miles to show for eight tough hours. Mark still complained that everything was going too smoothly and press coverage was suffering. 'Can't you break something or perhaps get lost at sea?' he suggested. Then he had a better idea, recalling an Amazon adventurer called Benedict who had shot to fame after eating his dog in the jungle. 'A pet jellyfish would qualify,' Mark assured me. Chris and the others lit a roaring driftwood fire on the beach at Salen over which we barbecued sausages and chops and, in the absence of marshmallows, toasted meringues. Later we piled seaweed on the flames to smoke out the hordes of midges and played a riotous game of Wink Murder – at which Liz and Alice inexplicably excelled.

I woke in the morning with a stiffness in my finger joints, a legacy of the hard gripping of the boom and the cold damp of the day before. After exercise the discomfort eased. The tide ran fair at 11am but there was too little wind for it to be worth starting and I sat on deck and read love-story comics. Half an hour had elapsed when a puff of breeze came up the sound from the south. 'Quick, get going!' said Paul. 'There's a good mile in that gust.' I doubted this but jumped on the board anyway. It turned out that the gust was worth fifty-nine miles – a new record!

With the *Log*, the 8m sail and a good breeze on my back I coasted up the half-mile-wide sound, flanked by green hillsides of woods and fields that sloped down to the water on both sides, a perfect valley for the wind to funnel through. I cruised past the pretty sheltered harbour of Tobermory, the official half-way mark, and peered into the water hoping for a glimpse of the wrecked *San Juan Bautista*, a relic of the Spanish Armada. Still moving at fine speed, I passed Bloody Bay and Ardmore Point and was out into the open water of the Sea of Hebrides. At Ardnamurchan, 'point of the great ocean', I was the furthest west that I would be during the trip (twenty-three miles further west than Land's End). Looking for a short cut, I sailed in too close to the cliffs and ran into a sloppy tidal race which slowed me down for a while. Fortified by a lunch of soup and sandwiches, I scraped round the headland and, still running before the wind, pressed on towards the well-known small isles, Muck, Eigg and Rhum.

Ambling along about an hour and a half later I suddenly noticed some dark shapes up ahead near *Morningtown*. 'Shark?' I wondered for a moment before shouting 'Dolphins!' at the top of my voice. Then they were all around me, forty or more of them, leaping and diving, clicking their tongues and grinning away happily. One baby dolphin caught my eye, swimming so close to its parent that they seemed glued together. By chance the wind freshened and, temporarily out of control, I surged forward into the school, worried about bumping one of them with my fin – those sharp white teeth looked as if they could give you a nasty nip! There was no question of collision; the dolphins matched my speed and continued to cavort in masterly, controlled fashion, jumping around and over my board without even a scrape. All too quickly they were gone, the last tail having splashed out of sight. The sea suddenly seemed still and lifeless: I had had my treat for the day.

An hour or so later I was trundling along off the north-east tip of Eigg, probably still dreaming about being a dolphin when I heard a cacophony of seagull shrieks and 'khaas'. I traced the noise to a fishing boat some two hundred yards away and as I watched, realised we were on a collision course. 'He must turn to avoid me,' I thought, steam giving way to sail and all that. Then I noticed he was trawling and appeared to have no intention of altering course or speed. I did not want to go behind him for fear of being tangled in his nets and ending up as a fish finger, so I gybed and tried to pile on the speed to pass in front. Piling on the speed on a sailboard is much less reliable than opening the throttle in a speed-boat, but I managed to shave in front of the boat with a few confident yards to spare. Subduing my jangling nerves, I turned and squinted at the crew of the trawler, wondering if they would be looking angry or apologetic, and unsure which tactic to adopt myself. To my surprise they looked unconcerned, as if they ran over sailboards every day!

Our original intention was to spend the night in the harbour of Mallaig on the mainland but in the late afternoon, as we were entering the Sound of Sleat, a bulletin came over the radio forecasting severe gales within twelve hours. Rodney thought that in bad weather Mallaig might become badly congested with fishing boats, and we changed plans accordingly and carried on towards the anchorage of Isleornsay on Skye. We reached Skye at 8.30pm and *Morningtown* peeled off into the bay to anchor. In the decent breeze I saw two good hours' progress left before dark and obtained leave to carry on alone with *Bumble*.

Fifteen minutes later came another radio bulletin: 'Sea area Hebrides, south-westerly gale force 8 now imminent.' I hoped that the front of the trough with perhaps force 4–5 would come through this evening so that I could race up to the Kyle of Lochalsh but, though the sky darkened ominously, the wind did not arrive for a couple of hours. All was strangely quiet as we plodded up the winding sound, not a boat in sight or other sign of life save a lone seal, head almost invisible against the black water. With tall mountains like walls on both sides, we were sailing down a dark, narrowing trench, and my imagination began to speculate about what lay round the next corner. The wind gathering its forces behind was Tolkien's Nazgul, herding me towards the entrance to the mines of Moria!

At 10.45pm we were several miles past the Sandaigh Islands when Rodney requested that we halt before the light faded completely. We took bearings as best we could from Sandaigh lighthouse and the closest mountain top, Benn Sgriteall, and then started back. The wind was now steadily freshening and the return ride, at full speed, was exhilaratingly wet. By the time we reached Ornsay Bay it was pitch-black and Rodney flashed a searchlight to guide us in to *Morningtown*. We sat down to a welcome meal of chilli con carne followed by baked apples. With the wind rising furiously now, tomorrow might be out as a sailing day, but today I had covered fifty-nine miles, five more than my previous best. I celebrated with a glass of beer before bed and wondered whether my stamina or capabilities were increasing. What might I be able to achieve with the right winds: a hundred miles perhaps?

A force 9 gale blew itself out during the night, but we woke in the morning to a fresh gale warning and once again rapidly rising winds. The storm turned into a real Scottish 'hoolie' and even made the national news: 'Summer gales of unusual severity in the Western Isles,' which caused concern among one or two relatives who thought we might have been caught out in it. Our anchorage was excellent and sheltered from all directions, especially south-westerly, but two other yachts got into trouble putting their anchors down, being blown repeatedly across the bay before the anchors could bite. *Bumble*, manned by Rodney and Charlie, was launched in an undercover RNLI capacity to lend assistance.

Little else to do but watch the white-caps, we went ashore to the pub for a huge Sunday-type roast lunch (even though it was Tuesday), getting absolutely soaked on the way. No one could understand why I minded: 'Surely you're used to it?' they protested. Afterwards most of us returned to the boat but Mark, Charlie and Chris stayed ashore to play board games borrowed from the publican. Chris had his head bitten off by Rodney when he radioed up: '*Morningtown*. This is *Boardwatch 2*. Anyone fancy a game of Monopoly, over?' 'Restrict radio use to marine business, out,' came the curt reply. It was the portent of a much bigger clash the next day.

I spent the afternoon writing up my log. A delay like today's somehow seemed to sap my incentive and enthusiasm whereas covering many miles was by contrast a great spur to do more. I knew, for example, that the initial fifty miles the day before was what had driven me on a further two hours. I told myself to try and disregard these fragile material incentives, to relax and take things as they came – delays or achievements. That way I was sure eventually to get to the end.

By the next day, the violent winds had passed over but we did not leave till 2pm when the tide turned fair. The morning was spent finding petrol for *Bumble* and on other mundane jobs. Chris and Charlie came back on board wearing Scottish berets, souvenirs of Skye, which made them look like Thompson and Thomson. All we needed now was a little white dog and we would have the entire Tintin team!

The afternoon's sailing began in great style with a fast scenic burst through to Loch Alsh but went steadily downhill from there. I set sail with the *Log* and 8m in a lively following breeze and headed round the south-east corner of Skye towards the exceedingly narrow Kyle Rhea. As I approached the tide built and by the time I reached the gap it was boiling along like a river, sweeping me with it. At the narrowest point (about three hundred yards) there was a grassy plateau to the left with a scattering of houses, the little village of Kylerhea. Bubbling next to the bank, I went so close that I practically touched a farmer walking out of his farmhouse. Further on we met a small square ferry manoeuvring skilfully in the rushing stream and wondered how Skye farmers here used to drive their cattle across to the mainland.

When I was through and slowing down in the wider waters of

Loch Alsh, the wind, looking so promising at first, eased off and backed to the north so that it was now on the nose. Alice took advantage of the lull and went ashore to Kyle of Lochalsh to stock up with provisions – we would not see another large town for the next 150 miles. I eventually reached the head of the loch where it narrows again to another small channel, Kyleakin, between Skye and the Kyle of Lochalsh, and was into the path of the ferries plying across the four-hundred-yard gap. One approached within a few yards of me and I saw that it was literally choked with passengers. This was the first time (since Tower Bridge) that I had sailed in sight of large numbers of people and I was excited, expecting them to know all about the event and perhaps cheer or clap as they passed. The ferry forged by in front of me and I looked up at the crowded decks – every single person was looking the other way!

Beyond the ferries lay yet another narrow channel to negotiate, some two hundred yards wide, between Skye and Eilan Ban lighthouse, which was covered in scaffolding and evidently having a facelift. This gap was far trickier than the previous two because the tide was flowing unpredictably against me, at about two knots; according to *Reed's Almanac* it should have been going briskly in the opposite direction. After half an hour and, having tacked three times on almost the same spot, I scraped through at last to the open waters of Loch Carron. I had not gone two miles, however, when the wind became a real headache. Beating my way past the Black Islands the wind freshened so much that I still needed a sail change but, as I waited for the smaller sail, the wind died away and I was left with too little breeze even for my biggest sail. I continued as best I could, in the blackest of moods. An hour later, near the Crowlin Islands, the wind was so frustratingly light that I only kept myself sane by sailing backwards, standing the wrong side of the sail, and by convincing myself that I would one day own the idyllic house jutting out at me from the forested hillside opposite.

Two hours and five miles later the drama of the week occurred just off a remote little bay called Applecross, where reputedly an excellent salmon river runs into the sea. *Bumble* motored over to me piled high with luggage. Before I had time to take in the significance of this, Chris was saying, 'I'm just off, Tim, I came to say goodbye. Mark and Charlie are dropping me on the shore.' Chris looked nervous but determined, Charlie and Mark nonplussed. 'Oh, no, you don't,' I said. 'Stop a second and let's chat this over.' I thought quickly while they came and grabbed the board: no photographer, no crew for *Bumble* and no Chris, just as we were coming up to the most exposed stretch. No way. Chris could be hot-headed. I had been stroppy with all three of them earlier on because they had disappeared to explore some island without telling me; maybe that was the reason?

I sat in *Bumble* and talked to Chris, who was reluctant to give me the whole story, sensing, I think, that the longer he stayed now, the less chance he had of getting away. The facts gradually emerged – there had been a row with Rodney. Rodney had been testing the radio-direction finder and asked Chris, radio man in *Bumble*, to talk into the radio so that he could get a fix. At first Chris had counted to ten over and over again as instructed but, growing bored with this (it was a slow afternoon) he had started to sing, 'Daisy, Daisy, give me your answer, do. I'm half-crazy – all for the love of you!' This was followed by a recitation of 'The Walrus and the Carpenter'. Anything more likely to cause Rodney to blow a fuse has yet to be conceived. He prides himself on radio correctness and woe-betide anyone on his ship who jokes on the air or uses the radio irresponsibly. At first Rodney could not believe what he was hearing, thinking that there was interference from another frequency. As soon as he realised, he bawled, 'Off the radio! Chris, you're banned from using it from now on!'

That was the story. Not as bad as all that, but Chris decided that he had had enough and, returning to *Morningtown*, packed his bags for the off. Fortunately, I managed to persuade him to stay, first for a couple more days to see how things worked out, then for the rest of the trip. Chris would have been an irreplaceable loss to the team, but I could understand his feelings. Everyone – including me – had moments of wishing they were anywhere but half-way round Britain on a crazy windsurfing adventure, but I thought it was important for all of us to finish what we had started and get back to Southend – or perish on the way, of course!

The team still intact then, we continued north up the Inner Sound. At 9pm *Morningtown* left us to find an anchorage for the night, but *Bumble* and I carried on for an extra hour stopping eventually on a deserted sandy beach; my lower back was sore and I hoped the invaluable back-supporting harness was not going to let me down after all. We rejoined *Morningtown* in a very deep, sheltered anchorage behind a large rock at Pol Domhain and ate a scrumptious dinner of roast pork, bought that day in Lochalsh. The earlier flare-up had left tension on board; Chris and Rodney were not talking to each other and the latter sat up till late watching the glow of the northern lights, looking sad and lonely. I went to bed tired after the eight hours of upwind effort, and philosophical about the meagre reward of twenty-two miles. Getting half-way certainly did not make the miles any easier. In the morning we would be venturing out into the North Minch and the most exposed section of the trip. I hoped the headwinds would not continue for this stretch.

(*above*) Silvery surf across the Moray Firth; (*below*) Sitting down past Bamburgh Castle

(*above*) Tyne Tees film breakfast on the River Coquet; (*below*) Not all plain sailing! Waiting for Wimbledon to end, West Mersea – Matthew, Martin, myself and Charlie

9 NORTH MINCH TO PENTLAND FIRTH

Rodney woke me at about 9am and sounded excited: 'Wind, there's wind. You'll make miles today.' Whatever breeze there had been earlier obviously found better things to do because when I went out on deck there was nothing, not even a whisper. But there was no point in waiting – conditions can vary so much in a short distance – so we breakfasted and set off. *Bumble* and I returned to the sandy beach where, watched by a couple of inquisitive seals and a dolphin, I rigged the 8m sail. Charlie was having difficulty changing the radio battery in *Bumble*'s cockpit and was swearing under his breath. Chris was taking photographs and still needed jollying along after yesterday's fiasco.

I had to pump vigorously to escape through the breakers on the beach as there was still no wind to speak of. Once I had crept about four hundred yards off the coast a paltry breeze filled in, but a bad chop made sailing uncomfortable for an hour or more. I tacked for a couple of hours up to Loch Torridon and was then past the northern tip of Rona and out into North Minch proper. I had expected it to feel different out here in the exposed sea but noticed only a drop in temperature. After a mildly sunny start, the sky had filled up with clouds, purple-black ones, that gave the land a forbidding, cruel look and a cold wind blew under the dark shapes. Water had seeped through holes worn in the knees of my drysuit and my legs began to shiver. After sneezing a couple of times I put on a pair of dry gloves and a rubber hat which warmed me up, and Alice sent hot Bovril from the galley.

At Loch Torridon the wind backed round to the west, for which I was grateful, shifting from close-hauled to a close-reach and I was able easily now to lay the eastern tip of Longa Island which guards the entrance to Loch Gairloch. After the next headland, Rubha Reidh, my course swung eastwards 30° or 40° and with a further wind-shift to the west was now a dead run. After all the miles of practice and with the advantage of such a wide, stable board, I found running every bit as comfortable as reaching by now. In light airs it was, if anything, more relaxing with little weight put on the arms and a clear view forward through the window of the sail. I could switch off almost completely from the sailing.

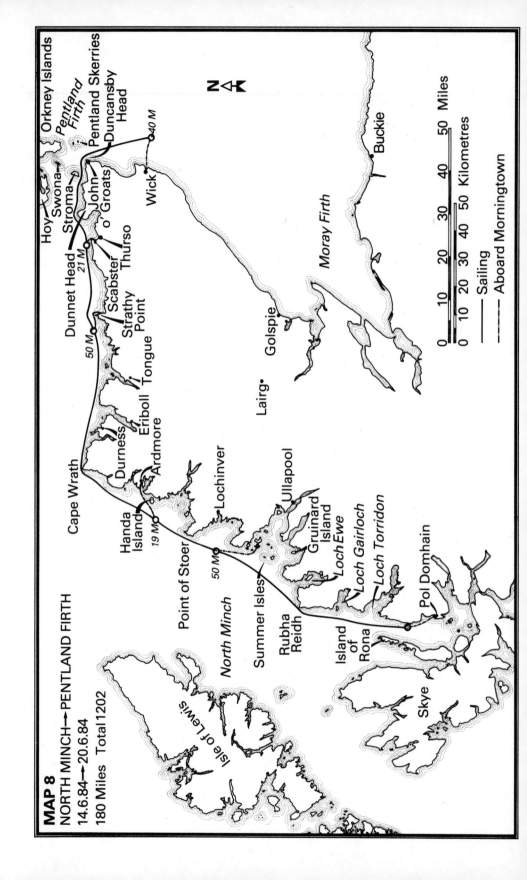

MAP 8
NORTH MINCH→PENTLAND FIRTH
14.6.84 → 20.6.84
180 Miles Total 1202

Orkney Islands

Pentland Firth

Pentland Skerries
Duncansby Head

Hoy
Swona
Stroma
Dunnet Head
John o' Groats
Thurso
Scrabster
Strathy Point

40 M
21 M
50 M

Wick

N

Buckie

Moray Firth

Golspie

Lairg

Cape Wrath

Durness
Eriboll
Tongue
Ardmore

Handa Island
19 M
Point of Stoer

Lochinver

50 M

Ullapool

Summer Isles

North Minch

Rubha Reidh

Gruinard Island
Loch Ewe
Loch Gairloch
Loch Torridon

Island of Rona

Pol Domhain

Skye

Isle of Lewis

0   10   20   30   40   50   Miles
0 10 20 30 40 50 Kilometres

——— Sailing
- - - - Aboard Morningtown

The breeze freshened towards late afternoon and I clipped past Loch Ewe where lies the Isle of Ewe, famous for the 'Try whispering Isle of Ewe to your sweetheart' slogan of the Scottish Tourist Board! Then the land fell away to my right as I crossed a large bay fringed with sea lochs and full of islands. One of the islands is Gruinard Island, still out-of-bounds to humans after being contaminated during World War II by anthrax in germ-warfare experiments.

Towards evening I had unexpected visitors. I heard a squawking above my head and saw a tern sitting on top of the mast, and another fluttering excitedly, contemplating landing. They must have been on a long flight – perhaps migratory – and my mast was the nearest perch for miles around. I enjoyed their company which was the high spot of an otherwise monotonous day's sailing. I had once contemplated taking a parrot or cat along with me, so why not a pair of arctic terns? But they had other ideas, perhaps finding the perch too unstable, as they flew off before I even had a chance to broach the subject of 'house rules'.

By 8pm the day seemed very long. I listened to my music pack for the first time since Cornwall but the reggae beat clashed with the slow rhythm of the sea. On the whole, music was distracting. I preferred just the noise of the wind and waves which let time pass more gently.

At about 9.15pm Rodney announced that he wanted to stop and anchor because there would not be enough daylight to reach Lochinver. We were approaching the longest day of the year, night not falling till 11.00 or even later, and I wanted to carry on sailing. We had a comic argument, me talking from the board with *Morningtown* bowling along beside, which reached a stalemate until Paul intervened with a compromise. *Morningtown* would anchor now while I proceeded with *Bumble* for a maximum of one hour. Half an hour later I had to stop to rest my back. It had been bothering me recently and the long day had aggravated the pain. Stretched out in *Bumble*, I drank part of a can of beer that Chris had smuggled off *Morningtown*.

Our position felt quite exposed. On the horizon to the west we could just see the tops of the high mountains on the Island of Lewis, the furthest north of the Outer Hebrides. From this distance the peaks looked like five volcanic islands rising out of the sea. A large swell was rolling in from the north-west – presumably from a distant storm. It must be rare not to have a big swell in this part of the world and I mentioned my fears of being caught in a gale up here to Chris and Charlie, little realising that within a few days we would be.

I wanted to keep going for a little while longer to set a personal record of twelve hours at a stretch on the board. For twenty minutes

I hung on, blacking out the discomfort and counting the seconds until Chris announced the time of 10.30pm – a magical moment – and I quit. We sat in *Bumble* for a few moments and opened another can of beer to celebrate the twelve-hour stint. Charlie gunned the Mariner 40 into life and we motored back to *Morningtown*, surfing down the large swells at high speed. *Morningtown* was sheltering in a tiny inlet behind Isle Ristol, one of the Summer Isles; using the radio as a homing device, we talked our way towards her in the semi-darkness, weaving a path through the other islands.

After feasting on roast lamb, we turned in to bed. I was pleased with the day but more than a little tired. My body was so stiff and aching as I lay down that I wondered if it was tempting fate to subject myself to such long, gruelling sessions.

We raised anchor at 7am next morning, 15 June, and motored towards Lochinver. We needed supplies of water and diesel to take us round the remote coastline of northern Scotland and I had to pick up the replacement equipment – drysuits and sails – which had been forwarded there. I lingered in bed, eager to snatch the extra hour and a half's rest, until we arrived in port. The weather was vile – wet and windy – and, as we tied up at the quayside, the place seemed deserted of people although the harbour was crammed with trawlers. It turned out that half the east-coast fishing fleet had gone west, following the migrating shoals of fish.

I discovered ashore that none of my gear had arrived. The sails were still unfinished in Ireland, while the drysuits were sitting in Lairg, the nearest large town and a couple of hours' run over hill and valley by post van. By good fortune a friendly local coastguard offered to drive them north to our next stopping place, which looked like being Ardmore, near Laxford Bridge.

Returning to *Morningtown*, I learnt that she had narrowly escaped being sunk by a trawler. Chris had saved the day by leaping into *Bumble* and wedging her between *Morningtown* and the crunching steel prow of the approaching fishing smack. Such hazards, it seems, are to be expected in a crowded fishing port, although the incident says more about some fishermen's regard for 'yachties'. In complete contrast, the skipper we moored next to after this near-disaster could not have been more accommodating and presented us with several haddock for supper.

The lifeboat coxswain came on board for coffee and we quizzed him about the impending obstacle of Cape Wrath. To our surprise, he had passed by there only once and could give us little first-hand information – we began to feel that we were heading for uncharted waters. Before leaving, we said goodbye to Mark who was returning to Oban to rejoin the camper. He was in the care of a local fish-buyer, trying to decide whether to hold his nose all the way back to Inverness or risk hitching another lift in the pouring rain!

A good force 4–5 was blowing from the south-west as we motored out of Lochinver. We lunched on the way and I began to feel seasick. It must have been nerves at the prospect of heavy wind-surfing to come as much as the boat's motion – the sea was hardly rough. I set off just after 2pm, sailing on a run with the *Log* and reef-ing sail, minus a reef. At first, with the stiff breeze there was an out-side chance of rounding the cape that afternoon, but we soon had to forget the idea. Suffering from the effects of the previous day, I had a bad time of the sailing, frequently making mistakes, falling in repeatedly and tiring myself out. My discomfort reached a peak in the overfalls round the Point of Stoer: while wrestling with the sail to keep control, I wrenched my right shoulder. I was forced to transfer most of the effort to my left and weaker arm which consequently suffered from the strain.

Fortunately, the wind took off for the rest of the afternoon allowing me to continue for a total of six hours. I stuck with a small sail to rest my arms and finished the day's sailing with only nineteen miles to show for my efforts. We stopped at about 8pm some half an hour's motoring from Loch Laxford and Ardmore, home of John Ridgway's School of Adventure, where we decided to head for the night. The school is run on the Gordonstounian principles of strenuous exercise and fresh air, featuring climbing, early runs, canoeing, and assault and survival courses. Having been on one of these courses at the age of seventeen, I was excited to be returning and looked forward to meeting John Ridgway again. He had advance warning of our arrival having intercepted some of the radio conversation between *Morningtown* and *Bumble*: 'Boardwatch 2, this is Boardwatch 1, over.' His perplexed voice came through the crackle: 'What is this Boardwatch operation?'

My anticipation mounted as we motored down Loch Laxford and neared the school. The landscape is barren and windswept but tinged with unusual colours – pink rock and luscious green bracken fringe the loch's clear waters. Some crofters' cottages came into view and then a scattering of wooden huts that comprise the school itself. We dropped anchor and, scanning the shores of the loch for familiar landmarks, I noticed that the large window of the main building was crowded with people waving to us. An invitation to come ashore for a drink soon followed on the radio.

We were met by Keith, one of John's small army of young instructors, who escorted us up the hill to the main hut. He pushed me through the doorway to a chorus of 'For he's a jolly good fellow' from about thirty women seated at the large table. As I blushed and tried to edge back through the door, John Ridgway, the orchestrator of this welcome, emerged grinning from the kitchen. His smile broadened further when I introduced myself as a former inmate of his camp. We all sat down and joined the congregation of women who were celebrating the last day of their course, which perhaps accounted for the very high spirits!

Ridgway is a dedicated adventurer, best known for having rowed across the Atlantic with Chay Blyth in the sixties. Though he does not number windsurfing among his many accomplishments, he was full of interest in the trip. Talking to him I could not help remembering the last time I had been here, able only to dream of one day organising my own expedition.

We had a peaceful night and rose late. I was glad to have a rest day – a chance to unwind and recover from the wrench the day before. The day was marred, however, by a problem aboard *Morningtown*. Liz had noticed that the forestay, which supports the mast for'ard, was gradually lifting up the teak decking and in danger of coming adrift. It turned out that the forestay had not been coupled to the prow plate, which left the mast in a vulnerable state, particularly in strong winds. Any future catastrophe was averted by Paul and Rodney that afternoon. They inserted a large block of hardwood under the decking to spread the load and strengthen the forestay. We went ashore to eat lunch with the Ridgways.

Lunch was a delicious meal of bread and cheese, called a 'crofter's' lunch in this part of the world and not to be confused with a 'ploughman's'. It was a perfect sunny day and we sat outside with John and his wife, Marie Christine, on the bank of a hill with a peaceful view over the loch. Ridgway was in reflective mood and confessed he was tired of the sea and felt his next project should be to walk up Everest. The wine had relaxed me so much that I found myself volunteering to join him (in gym shoes, of course!). 'You had better make sure you finish this one first,' said John, reminding me that the toughest stretch of the trip around Cape Wrath and the Pentland Firth was yet to come.

During lunch a helicopter flew over and landed on a flat area of grass next to the loch. There were two passengers, Ivor and Colin, the first of the next batch of would-be adventurers on the businessmen's course (significantly the most popular), who joined us for lunch. Ivor was a sharp, red-headed corporate lawyer. He arrived with a box of chocolates for Marie Christine and showed off his neat Swiss army knife and new orienteering compass to John. There followed a highly technical conversation about the difference between true and magnetic north which everyone else felt too contented to become involved in.

When the other recruits for the course arrived, the reason for Ivor's premature helicopter descent became clear. The men appeared around the corner of the loch gamely paddling canoes. As they neared the shore they were instructed to tip their canoes over in the icy water, crawl out and swim to the shore. John explained away this spartan baptism with a smile: 'It's a chance for them to cool down after their long journey!'

Mournful cries of chilled managing directors echoed up the hill to us and Ivor watched the discomfort of his fellows with a mixture of relish and relief. He strolled down the hill to the accommodation buildings to execute his master stroke – changing around the names on the doors to convert his three-man dormitory into a single suite. As penance for this crime or to impress John (or both) he set off quickly for a jog over the hill. Ivor's ginger and white body passed below us and a whiff of his patent midge repellant, Eau Sauvage, wafted up; he had thought of everything.

The telephone rang in the house. It was for me. I wondered who could have possibly tracked us down in this far-flung corner of Britain. It was Radio Scotland, wanting an interview. The phone rang again. This time it was Mark; he was at Inverness and wanted to join up with us. Marie Christine gave him directions and we expected him for supper.

Later that afternoon, while the businessmen thawed out and gritted their teeth before the next ordeal, we explored the bird sanctuary on Handa. Paul, Liz, Chris and I set off in *Bumble* into the open sea three miles south to the small island. The island itself is barren, just scruffy turf and a few rabbits. But the cliffs on its northern side are stupendous with every ledge of the three-hundred-foot rock-face lined with birds; there were tens of thousands, of all different species: the familiar guillemots, perched like penguins; shags, solitary and black, sitting hunched like vultures; fulmars, stocky grey birds and excellent fliers; our old friends the puffins; and gannets, majestic birds with a six-foot wing-span, yellow head and black wing-tips. We drifted around under the infested granite walls, marvelling at the sheer numbers living on this windswept island. I wondered how they fared in the all-too-frequent storms.

As we left, Paul pointed to a dark mass of clouds way off to the west. 'Bad weather on its way,' he said, 'but we ought to be able to round the cape tomorrow before it hits us.' With this in mind, we chugged slowly back to *Morningtown*. Waiting for us on deck was Haydn, looking worried: 'Bad news. Mark has rolled the camper into a ditch and broken his arm. He's in hospital.'

My heart sank – just when things were going so smoothly this had to happen. I thought of Mark on his way here, looking forward to a reunion; now he was in hospital and I hoped he was all right. From the sound of it, he would be out of action for the rest of the trip; the truck would be off the road and perhaps equipment ruined, which left us with no PR man, no back-up for fuel and no co-ordination with the shore. Mark was a vital link in the whole operation and the future of the appeal and of the publicity Charles Heidsieck expected looked bleak. After bolting down some food, I took a deep breath and went ashore to the pay-phone.

I got through to the police who had arranged for the truck to be righted and taken to a garage in Lairg; they were vague about the extent of the damage. I succeeded in reaching Mark in hospital. He had just been given his premedication prior to an operation on one of his arms and gradually faded away as I talked to him. The news did not improve. Mark had broken not one but both his arms. When he told me the story I could not help laughing, it was such Laurel-and-Hardy bad luck. He had been hurtling along a narrow Highland road and, on finishing a banana, tried to throw the skin out of the window, whereupon it was caught by the slipstream and forced back in. Trying to flick the skin out of his way, Mark momentarily lost concentration and found himself mounting the grass verge on the other side of the road. He flung the wheel hard over, ricocheted off the other verge and the truck turned over. He was dazed but uninjured thanks to his seatbelt and as he climbed out of the cab quietly rejoiced at his lucky escape. He pulled himself onto the main body of the vehicle and accidentally put his left hand on the rear wheel which was still spinning. This promptly broke one arm and he fell onto the road, landing on his right hand, breaking that arm, too. He had to sit for half an hour on the lonely road with two throbbing arms till the first car came along. To add insult to injury, he had been charging along the wrong road, having missed the Ardmore turning. By the time Mark had told me the basic facts he was slipping into unconsciousness and, wishing him luck, I rang off.

After a couple more phone calls – one home to check on insurance for the camper and one to Oliver Moore of Charles Heidsieck – I decided to take the next day off to visit Mark and somehow sort out all the problems. The RNLI and my sponsors were depending on good press coverage at the Pentland Firth. I only hoped the weather

(*opposite above left*) Alice and the vanishing souffle! (*above right*) The Anstruther coxswain, Paul, myself; (*below*) A perfect offshore wind makes for fast sailing down the Angus coast
(*overleaf: left above*) A shepherding Atlantic 21 lifeboat, Yorkshire; (*left below*) Welcoming sailboards, *Morningtown* and the 10m sail off Flamborough Head; (*right*) Passing Maplin on the last evening

would hold off one more day for the sake of a safe passage round Cape Wrath. I returned in *Bumble* to a sleeping ship for a short night's rest and lay awake for a while rehearsing what had to be done the next day. How ironic for disaster to strike first on land.

The first problem in the morning was to find transport across the countryside from Ardmore to Lairg, where the truck was, and on to Golspie where Mark lay in hospital. John Ridgway came to the rescue and gave Angela, one of his instructors, a day off so she could drive me down in her car. Charlie and Chris came along for the ride and off we went, Angela smoking as if she had not seen a cigarette for months. I sank back in my seat and unexpectedly enjoyed the drive. We passed through superb countryside of forests and heather, salmon rivers and lochs and at one point we caught sight of a golden eagle hovering over the woods. It was good to be away from the sea for once.

Arriving at Lairg, I went straight to the police station and found the policeman deep in conversation with a couple of men. He asked if I would mind waiting, but after twenty minutes I began to grow impatient. Thankfully, I resisted the impulse to butt in and say I was in a hurry: I was still adjusting to the pace of life in the Highlands. Constable Mark could not have been more friendly and helpful, seeming to know everyone and everything. He told me that the two visitors were newspapermen up from Fleet Street; the area was crawling with journalists and photographers hunting pictures of the latest news – the surrogate mother in Lairg!

PC Mark took me along to see the truck, still attached to its 1950s rescue vehicle at a garage. I was astonished at how little damage there was to the outside; the grass verge had cushioned most of the blow. The inside, however, was a terrible mess: a jumble of papers, bottles of champagne (unbroken fortunately), food (mainly rice and spaghetti) and all Mark's possessions. We set about clearing up and the policeman became quite excited when he found half a banana skin in the driver's cab: 'Evidence!' he declared triumphantly. Before leaving we received excellent news from the mechanic who, like PC Mark, was unbelievably helpful: subject to clearing up insurance, he could patch up the truck to be back on the road within a week. Things were certainly looking up.

We found Mark in Golspie hospital with both arms in plaster. He was in moderate pain but still smiling. In die-hard fashion he had already commandeered the trolley pay-phone and was carrying on his PR duties from the bedside. Mark had arranged for an old school-

(*above*) Thames barges racing off Harwich; (*below*) The finish party – something for the bath! From l to r: Oliver Moore, Alice, myself, Chris Longman

friend of his, Chris Longman, to come up and join the team at the end of the week, which seemed to tie in well with the camper's rebirth. We had all expected Mark to be returning home as soon as he was fit to travel, but he had no such plans, wanting instead to carry on. 'If I went home I'd only sit around being bored and wondering what you were all doing.' Chris would drive the camper while Mark lay in the back directing operations.

In high spirits now, we decided to make some profit out of our setback by seducing the national press, rather reluctant so far to give the expedition, and particularly the appeal, much coverage. Just as we began a round of phone calls, a local freelance reporter, Jim Henderson, turned up. He had been alerted by PC Mark and was exactly the energetic man we needed. He took over. Soon a photographer arrived and a story with photos was wired off to London. In the end, despite all Jim's enthusiastic efforts, the story only caught on locally and the surrogate mother remained the Highlands' contribution to the week's national news. If I had broken both my arms, and better still, carried on windsurfing, it might have hit the headlines, but there was a limit to what I would do for publicity! Jim Henderson carried on being most helpful, putting Mark up for a few days when he came out of hospital and allowing him the use of his offices.

When the police arrived to interview Mark, the ward became overcrowded and we took our leave, Mark urging us to hurry round the north of Scotland so he could see us sail past his window, which looked out over the Moray Firth. Later, we languidly ate fish-and-chips sitting on a stone wall, gazing out over the rugged Scottish countryside. The interlude was over; it was time to return to the confinement of *Morningtown* and start our most hazardous stretch. Weather prospects were not great: a fresh breeze was blowing with periodic showers, and the sky to the west looked dark and unsettled. We could only hope.

By the time we reached Ardmore it was dark. The others had spent an active day, too: Rodney and Haydn had walked twelve miles towards the nearest pub. They stopped at 2.30, still five miles short and turned to come home. Meanwhile, Alice, Paul and Liz had gathered mussels from the shore of the loch.

I woke at about 8am on 18 June to the now familiar noise of wind soughing in the rigging. Out on deck it was a fiercely windy morning and I thought immediately of Cape Wrath. What on earth would the waves be like today? Paul went ashore and surveyed the sea from a hilltop. 'A lot of white among the greeny blue!' he reported.

Paul, Rodney and I held a quick conference. It was blowing a force 6 and presumably more outside: the cape might well be impassable.

Was it worth a try? The decision was given to me. I did not feel one hundred per cent even after two days off, but there seemed little point in waiting another day for the weather to improve as it could just as easily deteriorate further. I decided that there was no harm in having a go and we hurriedly prepared the ship for departure and bad weather, stowing everything that was likely to fly around. We hoped to reach the cape before 3pm when the tide would turn heavily against us.

Just before leaving Ardmore, John Ridgway came through on the radio to say goodbye and to wish me luck for the rest of the journey. I was touched and felt more than ever determined to succeed today. I did not fancy slinking back to Ardmore in a few hours with my tail between my legs.

Steaming out of the loch towards the open sea, we passed *English Rose IV*, one of Ridgway's yachts. It was manned by Keith, chief instructor, and Bruce, Ridgway's round-the-world sailing partner, who were having an exciting sail beating backwards and forwards across the loch, well heeled over with two reefs out. They gave us the thumbs-up as we passed and I wondered if they suspected I was crazy attempting to windsurf round Cape Wrath on a day like this. I waved enthusiastically back, but would happily have changed places with them.

Once out beyond Handa Island we met the full force of wind and sea, and tension grew on board as spray began to crash over the decks. I was sitting up on deck already in my gear as I knew these were prime seasickness conditions and dare not risk being below. I was trembling a little with nervousness and limbered up with some exercises to occupy my mind.

The south-westerly wind direction meant a run once again but I was not unhappy about this since it meant using the *Log*, which would have the best chance of coping with the wild sea conditions round the cape. I set off with the reefing sail, minus one reef, but the wind freshened quickly and I soon removed the last reef. It was demanding sailing and I had barely acclimatised when the visibility deteriorated from about a mile to less than a hundred yards: we were in thick fog and still the wind continued at a solid 6–7. We closed up our flotilla so that I was within thirty yards of *Morningtown*'s stern and *Bumble* level with me but, despite two watches being posted on the afterdeck, it was extremely difficult for our three vessels to stay together.

In the blustery conditions my speed kept fluctuating. One moment I would run right up under *Morningtown*'s stern and the next I would drop back almost out of sight. Inevitably, I fell in once or twice and *Morningtown* nearly lost me in the time it took them to heave to and stop. On one such occasion, Rodney came over the radio and warned that conditions were so marginal that he might have to call a halt any moment. 'We can't risk getting separated,' he insisted. If we were I could be swept onto the lee shore of the eight-hundred-foot cliffs south of the cape long before any rescue party would find me; but I could not face the prospect of returning, beaten, to Ardmore and urged Rodney to carry on. 'It surely can't get any worse,' I said unwittingly.

We hurried on in our tight formation. I was surfing down the waves, fully stretched by the wind. My arms began to feel as if I were carrying heavy suitcases down an endless airport corridor. I wondered how long I could continue and hoped that if only we rounded the cape things would improve. Then I leapt with fright as an unearthly booming sounded ahead. At first I took it to be the fog-horn of a huge tanker bearing down on me in the mist. The noise repeated itself – an appalling, mournful sound. I clung on, terrified, wondering what was going on, when the fog peeled back in front of me to reveal the cape itself – towering black cliffs hundreds of feet high. I had no idea we were heading in this close, so close that I could make out the top of the lighthouse perched on the cliffs. Rodney had been worried about outlying rocks and to avoid them was steering in to the cliffs using the radar.

I was so awed by the sight of the cliffs and the seething mill-race ahead below the thinning fog that I lost my balance and, in the time it took me to get moving again, slipped back several hundred yards. The tide was supposed to be still in our favour and I found this loss of ground hard to account for. It was only later that we found out that by some curious anomaly the tide always runs west close to the cape, never east.

Underway once more, the wind had freshened to about force 8 and I found the small sail an increasing handful. My arms lengthened as every sinew strained to hang on and I toboganned down the waves at incredible speeds, too fast in fact. I bent my knees and gradually sank lower and lower onto the board to reduce the surface area of the sail until I found myself sitting down. For the first time in the voyage I was no longer standing up to do battle with the wind and it felt strange. The wind continued to wrench at my sail as if wanting to carry it off as some sort of trophy and I knew I could not hold on much longer. Every muscle screamed for me to stop and I told myself it was getting ridiculous; I was physically frightened by the strength of what I was wrestling with, something that had not happened since my unfortunate experience in the Scillies. A few moments later the sea put an end to my deliberations. In the fearsome overfalls created by the gale raging against a strong tide my board had been bucking like a bronco. As I surfed down one large breaker, the nose speared the back of a toppling wave in front, and board, sail and I went head over heels in the maelstrom. After a winded pause I crawled back onto my board, thinking, 'No way. I'm risking everything like this.' I gestured to *Bumble* and requested a smaller sail, the 3m, my smallest and one I had never needed before.

The initial response from *Morningtown* was: 'Negative. Absolutely negative . . . to make a sail change now would jeopardise the safety of the ship and crew . . . you will have to make do with what you have.' The unseen rocks that we were being swept towards in the fog were Rodney's fear and that of most of the crew. Allying that worry to the wild conditions put us in the worst place so far. Unable to see much of *Morningtown*, I learnt later of the bitten lips and white faces on board.

Taking in the import of the radio message, I turned to look south-west towards the heart of the wind for any sign of abatement. It must be blowing a good 8–9 now; heavy froth tumbled down every wave face and a curtain of water had lifted off the sea, whipping along independently over the surface. I wiped my face as the wind spat at me as if to say, 'Don't expect mercy – you come here at your peril.'

Shrugging with resignation, I decided on one last attempt. I tried waterstarting but the confusion of sea kept catching the long boom of the sail. Attempting instead to uphaul, I clambered to my feet and began a precarious balancing act, tugging hard on the sail for support. Try as I might, there was no way the sail would lift more than a few inches off the surface – the force of the wind kept it sheeted hard down on the water. Finally, I gave a desperate heave and next thing I knew I was on my back in the sea with the sail on top of me and the board drifting off in the race. I could not believe what had happened: the universal joint, the knuckle between mast and board, had snapped with the strain. Quickly I swam after the board, knowing which half I would rather be left with and radioed *Morningtown* that, like it or not, they would have to give me a new rig.

Somehow Paul and Haydn managed to rig the sail on *Morning-town*'s pitching foredeck in the appalling conditions and quickly, too. We were lucky to have had the chance to practise. If similar conditions had arisen in the first few days we would not have been able to cope.

As I sat on my board being swept back towards the rocks, my heart beat fast with an excitement tinged by fear. Would I be able to manage even with the fresh sail? If I failed now would I ever get past Cape Wrath? The sail arrived and by a stroke of good fortune we missed the rocks, passing some few hundred yards north of them.

The 3m sail looked no larger than a pocket handkerchief but was easily large enough to lift me out of the water. The rig felt as light as a feather in comparison to the heavy reefing sail and was a joy to handle. I never used the reefing sail again.

I sailed much more effectively now and was soon in sight of land again. 'I must be making good progress at last,' I thought, before recognising the unmistakable features of the cape; I had drifted so far back that I was now passing the cape for the second time. If it had gone to a third round I am sure I would have given up. My determination nearly snapped but I hung on, desperate to put the treacherous rocks behind me for good, and eventually the conditions eased. I turned the corner and sanity was restored. Cape Wrath had certainly earned its name.

The fog lifted to reveal a severe rocky coastline to my right. To my left, the white-flecked turquoise sea stretched away over the horizon – only a few storm-washed rocks lying between here and Iceland. There was an eerie feel to this northern stretch where the light is strangely disquieting, where you tread carefully for fear of disturbing the elements. I had no doubts that what we had just gone through was only a taste of the savagery this place was capable of.

It had taken me an hour and a half to sail round Cape Wrath and it was 4pm when I emerged. There was still plenty of daylight left and, with the strong westerly breeze behind me, I made solid miles along this back straight. The coast consists in the main of inhospitable-looking rocks and cliffs interspersed with wintry beaches. The most distinctive features are three deep glacial cuts into the land – the Kyle of Durness, Loch Eriboll and the Kyle of Tongue – providing safe anchorage in winds from points west through south to east, though untenable in weather from the north. There is no shelter from a northerly blow on this coast and we all prayed against this.

Gannets live in huge numbers in this isolated spot – a handsome species of bird which I had grown much attached to. Sailing through their feeding grounds I admired their brazen confidence as they wheeled in close to take a look at the intruder. Seeing that this ungainly creature with its clumsy yellow wing could prove no territorial threat, they would sheer away and, with a few powerful wing-beats, climb gracefully to a dizzy height. Scanning the depths with beady yellow eyes for a likely morsel, they then fold their wings and plunge oceanwards splashing into the water with an exact precision. I wondered what made the gannets congregate in such numbers in this distant refuge. Perhaps it offered a retreat from interfering mankind, though I suspect the reason is less romantic, having to do with richness of fish in the area.

By 6pm the wind had subsided to about force 4 and I had changed up sails from 3m through to 6m. I still kept the sail size small to rest my arms and back after the struggles of the cape and I sailed well within myself, using the large swell underneath to good advantage. Though somewhat shell-shocked and aching, I was in amazingly good spirits. I was delighted to have made it to this northern coast, the battle on the way making it even more satisfying. Through all those months earlier when the trip was just an idea, the possibility of reaching or even being on my board in the waters of northern Scotland had seemed so remote as to be scarcely credible. Now I had proved these seas navigable by sailboard; I was round one corner and if my luck held would soon be round the next and looking south to home.

Celebrating with big grins at my gannet companions, I plugged on till fatigue called a halt at 8.30pm. After eight and a half hours on the board I was rewarded by fifty miles behind me. We were all well aware that had our touch-and-go tussle in the middle of the day gone the other way, today's mileage would have been more than halved and all would be still to do.

Rejecting the closer anchorage of Armadale Bay because the swell was curling round and stirring up the shallow north-facing scoop in the coast, we anchored instead behind the rugged finger of Strathy Point that pricks the harsh north Atlantic midway along the Sutherland coast. Out of respect for the unpredictable sea, Rodney put *Morningtown*'s engines into hard reverse, giving such a bite to the anchor on the sea bed that the winch nearly sprang off the foredeck!

After supper, Paul, Charlie and I went in search of a phone box, marked on the Ordnance Survey map as lying somewhere in the middle of Strathy promontory. We beached *Bumble* on a narrow strip of shingle where several fishing boats lay hauled on metal hawsers well out of reach of the surging ocean. Ahead of us were three-hundred-foot cliffs and before starting our long climb we marvelled at the ingenious rig that bridged the walls of the chasm, enabling great chests of fish to be lifted effortlessly up to the top. We found the phone box among a nameless collection of houses, one of which appeared to have no windows. Perhaps the extremity of the weather had something to do with this and certainly accounted for the lack of trees. Although past midnight, there was still plenty of light and looking round I noticed that, while the sky above was clear, we were fringed at some distance by a complete circle of dense, indigo clouds. I was sure this implied heavy weather before long. Shivering at the prospect, I regretted being unable to enjoy this spectacular phenomenon free from concern at what it portended for our passage through the Pentland Firth.

In the morning, as if a forerunner of what was to come from the west, *Morningtown* was struck by a freak wave on the way back to our spot. Most of us were on deck at the time and saw this monster lolloping towards us like a rogue elephant. There was no time to take evasive action. *Morningtown*'s foredeck was momentarily smothered as she nosed into the obstacle, but as she surged up again the water ran harmlessly off the decks and back into the sea – or so we thought. Suddenly Alice realised that we had forgotten to fasten our hatch cover. Going below we found to our dismay that the cabin was awash – clothes, towels, bedding, everything soaked. I looked at the impudent sea water washing among my books, happy to have penetrated at last a sacred dry area. Everything that could be washed would have to be. Once something gets wet with salt water it remains forever damp; one of the least appealing features of life at sea.

It was a frustrating sailing session. I worked for four hours in a large swell and for most of the time had to hitch rides on the waves to keep myself moving in the fitful breeze. A large proportion of my twenty-one miles was thanks to a strong tidal pull as we approached the narrows of the Pentland Firth between John o'Groats and the Orkneys. The myth and legend of this incredible place conjured up the image of a force drawing us inexorably forward, a force not so much tidal as pure gravity – perhaps the earth really was flat and here was the edge where the sea plunged over into a bottomless gulf.

Rodney wanted to test out these theories today and was in favour of pressing on through the Firth towards Wick. I was against this for several reasons: *Bumble* was short of petrol, there was barely enough time and I had no desire to rush this most hazardous of sections. I was still stiff and tired from Cape Wrath and decided to tackle Pentland when fresh and rested in the morning. We motored the few miles in to Scrabster, the small lifeboat town on Thurso Bay, and on the way Rodney mentioned that he was leaving the ship to attend to his business. He had wanted to see us through the Pentland Firth before departing but could not afford any more time.

As soon as we touched the quay in Scrabster I dashed ashore to telephone Mark about the state of media relations, and Lairg and London to clear up insurance details on the truck. Leaving the call box I met Haydn who told me that Rodney was in a crusty mood about missing the Pentland Firth and seemed to be spoiling for a fight; he added that Rodney had packed the ship's log to take back with him to Mersea. I hurried back to *Morningtown* perplexed, but determined that the ship's log – recording all my hours of sweat and tears – should stay with the ship till the end.

Rodney was sipping whisky in the saloon and, noting that the log had indeed vanished from the chart table, I asked him if he knew where it was.

(*above*) The expedition trio at Whitby; (*below*) Myself and Paul looking at charts in Spurn lifeboat with Brian Bevan

(*above*) A friendly reception on Bridlington beach; (*below left*) 20 miles offshore at Inner Dowsing light vessel; (*below right*) Uphauling

'It's in my suitcase,' replied Rodney, casually.

I asked the obvious question as to why it was there.

'Because I'm master of this vessel and as such this is my ship's log and I'll do what I like with it!' he said, flaring up suddenly.

'Don't logs normally remain with a ship till the end of a voyage?' I enquired.

'Maybe,' he said defiantly, 'but not on this occasion. I'm taking the log and you just try and stop me.'

I commented that this struck me as bizarre behaviour, which provoked Rodney to say that it was not as bizarre as mine. The argument then degenerated into a furious slanging match, climaxing with Rodney declaring that I knew nothing at all about boats or the sea, to which I said, 'Bollocks to you!'

'Bollocks to you, too!' he replied, adding, 'I want nothing further to do with you – get off my ship!'

Ill-considering that this might be the end of the line, I said, 'That suits me fine. I want nothing more to do with you.'

Rodney disappeared on deck and began pacing around while I stood looking rather foolish in the cabin, wondering what had hit me. How on earth was I going to get out of this? I began to go through the possibilities in my mind – whether I could charter another boat at short notice, whether *Bumble* was mine to carry on with and whether I could rely on Paul, Liz and Haydn to stick with us without *Morningtown*.

Having also had time to think, Rodney came below to fire off another salvo. 'You and your team [Alice, Chris and Charlie] will leave immediately, taking only one bag each. All the other kit, including your windsurfers, will stay on board until all bills are paid.' He turned to Paul who had come into the cabin: 'You and Liz will sail *Morningtown* back to Mersea.' So that was that.

When Rodney had left the saloon again, I turned to Paul, who with Liz and Alice had listened dumbfounded to the whole scene from the aft cabin.

'What the hell am I going to do now?' I asked.

'You've got to make the peace,' said Paul, gravely.

I found Rodney on deck and suggested that a discussion on the quayside was called for and we clambered ashore. Paul sat in the cabin, waiting for the splash that he was sure would come as one or both of us hit the water, but we cooled down and came to our senses. There was too much to lose if the charter folded now (what would the RNLI and Charles Heidseick have said?). Apologies were exchanged and a truce called, the ship's log returning to the chart table.

It was an unfortunate incident but I suppose the confrontation had been brewing since Rodney returned in Oban. Though we got on very well at times – especially when we first met and during the first part of the voyage – we had a deep-seated difference in attitude. I thought of the trip as my baby, my creation, and all about sailing a board around Britain with whatever back-up was necessary to ensure safety. Rodney, for right or wrong, was more of the impression that the trip was about how he and *Morningtown* shepherded a helpless windsurfer around the coast.

Almost immediately after the furore we were visited by the coxswain of the Scrabster lifeboat who took us for a guided tour of the lifeboat house and a detailed examination of the boat itself. It was a sturdy Solent Class boat and, like all lifeboats we came across, in immaculate condition. One feature of particular interest was the thick padding on the cabin ceiling which is to reduce the likelihood of injury to crew when the boat rolls. For some lifeboats this is something of a luxury item as rollings are so infrequent; for the Pentland lifeboat, where the seas are so violent, it is a must. While Rodney was examining the engine, Paul found time to whisper me a quick 'well done'. Here we were looking round a lifeboat as if nothing had happened when only an hour or so earlier the whole enterprise had seemed in ruins.

Nearby Thurso offered good shopping for the first time since Oban, and Alice replenished depleted stores and bought us salmon as a treat for supper. When we had eaten, Rodney departed for Aberdeen and West Mersea to a general sigh of relief from the ship's company. After the central role he had played in the project since February it had been a sad finale.

Later, we went ashore to meet the Scrabster coxswain and some of his crew in the pub. We wanted to hear the coxswain's experiences and stories about the Pentland Firth, where the water can rush through at up to fifteen knots, more like rapids than the sea. This tide-torn channel is a notorious graveyard for ships and its awesome standing waves are known to have bent the barrels of twenty-inch guns on a World War II battleship. Legend has it that two witches lurk in the depths between the islands of Stroma and Swona, luring ships to their doom.

The coxswain's stories were firmly rooted in fact. His first service with the Scrabster lifeboat was on a winter's night in 1969 when the Longhope (Orkney) lifeboat was lost with all hands. They had been trying to assist a stricken coaster in a storm when the lifeboat was smitten by a monstrous wave that rolled the boat upside down, drowning all the occupants. 'You don't get weather like that every day,' the coxswain told us, 'but pebbles have often been thrown on to Dunnet Head from the beach and broken the windows of the lighthouse, four hundred feet up. On one memorable occasion a chicken coop was blown all the way over from Orkney and landed on the cliffs with the chickens still alive inside!' All this was delivered with Scottish good humour, to be received with a mixture of awe and concern as we contemplated our task for the next day. Seeing our long faces, he reassured us, 'You'll be all right tomorrow. It'll be as easy as crossing Dunnet Bay – ne'er you worry!', and as if to show good faith, one of the lifeboat crew, George, offered to join us for the passage and act as pilot. I was glad to get to bed that night – it had been a long day.

When I woke the next morning, 20 June, Pentland coastguard were giving the wind forecast for Fair Isle over the radio: 'South-east force 3, then south-sou'west 4–5 becoming south-west 5–6, then west-nor'west 7–8', a classic depression beginning lightish in the south-east, backing and building steadily all the time and finally reaching gale force from the north-west. I had no wish to be caught in the Pentland Firth with that amount of wind around. Butterflies fluttered in my stomach as I leapt out of bed and began dressing. 'Paul,' I shouted through the cabin wall, exaggerating my excitement, 'let's get the hell out of here before that lot comes through.' George, our pilot, arrived with some fresh rolls for breakfast and we ate hurriedly on deck watching gusts of wind like monstrous cat's-paws scurry across the harbour. Just before we cast off our ropes the coxswain arrived to wish us well for the passage. 'What do you think of the wind?' I asked, unable to resist the question. 'Och, this is no more than a breeze. Come back in January and I'll take you out in some real weather!'

We headed out of Scrabster due north-west towards our starting point. To port we passed the iron cliffs of Holborn Head which have been hollowed out into several natural arches. George told us about the favourite sport of dare-devil fishermen who pilot their boats through these arches in conditions when a miscalculation of the swell could mean disaster. To the north we had a brief view of the Old Man of Hoy – the 450ft rock pillar sticking out from the 1,000ft cliffs on the Orkney island of Hoy – but there was not really time for sightseeing.

The wind was southerly 4 when I started so I chose the 6m sail. Almost as soon as I began crossing Thurso Bay towards the pear-shaped horn of Dunnet Head, the wind freshened to at least 5 and I was gripping hard to stay on. Typical. I knew the Pentland Firth would not let me through without a fight. I just hoped the wind would not freshen any further. Then I was at Dunnet Head itself, the most northern part of the British mainland and a full two miles closer to the Arctic Circle than the more accredited John o'Groats. I kept a respectful distance from the head itself to avoid the worst of the broken wind and overfalls. In fact, my speed made for a quick if lumpy rounding of the head and I was soon streaking across Brough Bay towards the beginning of the Pentland Firth proper. The tide had not shown itself as yet, but I was nervous and had to stop for a pee, kneeling on the board and using the dry zip, praying that a wave would not choose this moment to tip me in! I took the opportunity to radio Paul: 'All well so far. When do you think the tide'll begin to hit us?' 'Should start to pull as we near the Men of Mey rocks – no more than a few miles,' he replied.

Sure enough, three miles further on the tide took a hold of me. I was abreast of the village of Mey on my right and could identify the towers of the Queen Mother's home, the Castle of Mey, close to the shore. What a magnificent view she must have of the shipping struggling through Britain's most treacherous stretch of water. Way off to my left was the impressive blur of Britain's highest cliffs and ahead the oblong shape of Stroma, one of the two small islands in the middle of the Firth. We had opted for a passage through the Inner Sound between Stroma and the mainland. The southerly wind meant that any distance sailed to the north would have to be fought back by hard beating on turning the corner to head south.

Events were destined not to go smoothly. I was supposed to be in the quaintly named Merry Men of Mey race which would whoosh me rapidly through the sound; instead, the tide was pushing me further and further north and in a short time I was too far off course to weather Stroma. Deciding not to head north to Swona and double back later, I tacked into the fierce tidal stream which runs onto the Pentland Skerries, aiming to beat south and maintain my original course. This proved a complete failure. With the quirky tide I was now heading north-west in the opposite direction to where I wanted to go. Feeling exasperated, I tacked again and decided to let myself be taken wherever the tide wished; there seemed no particular harm at this stage as I had several hours of fair tide to play with.

On starboard tack, then, I was carried closer and closer to Stroma. The island loomed up and I could make out dozens of houses dotted around, although there was no sign of life. Stroma's few inhabitants had long ago left this isolated place in search of the creature comforts: TV, water, electricity – everything that we take for granted. Approaching the brown cliffs of the island I began to worry. Surely the tide would take me one way or the other and not dump me on the cliffs themselves? Then I must have crossed a boundary between two tides because I suddenly began to be pushed south again, and miraculously found a course passing all but the outer rocks of Mell Head on the south-west corner of Stroma. A mile to my right

Morningtown was advancing strongly in the main stream, almost beyond the island already, while I was still in a tricky position. On this tack I could weather all but the beacon, stuck on a ledge of rocks, marking the limit of the Stroma Skerries; so presumably a reef extended for most of the way back to the island. There was no evidence of it on the surface, though, and I decided to risk going straight on. In any case, I did not have much choice as the tide was still very much in control and surging under me as it had been for the last half-hour.

I was almost on top of the rocks before I spotted them – just below the surface and extending in an unmistakable jagged line right across my path. Travelling at some speed, I leapt off the board the instant that my daggerboard scraped the reef, trying to prevent any serious damage. I landed flat on the water on my bottom to avoid jarring my legs and felt a sharp stab in the upper thigh that made me wince, but I managed to lunge forward and grab the board as the next wave lifted me further among the submerged rocks. Then I was able to stand up. I had got off lightly and I glanced back at *Bumble* to see if they had registered what was happening. They had slowed right down and were peering forward as if looking for a way through. I shouted at them to retreat and a moment later they scuttled back the way they had come – one of the advantages of having a motor.

Meanwhile, I began to walk or rather lurch my board across the rocks. Waist deep in water I let out an involuntary gasp of astonishment as a black shape broke the surface ten feet in front of me. My heartbeat subsided when I recognised the familiar whiskered face of a grey seal before it ducked back below the surface. Partly for fear of treading on my hefty friend and partly because of the uneven sea bed that swallowed alternate legs, I gave up walking and tried to swim the board the rest of the way. This was distinctly unprofitable, but soon I was in deep enough water to resume sailing – a considerable relief. A minute or so later I looked back to see the beacon and again no sign of rocks. What a fearsome trap it would be in bad weather.

My sights were now on distant Duncansby Head, the north-east corner of Britain which marks the end of the Pentland Firth. Black clouds were rumbling towards us from the south-west and I wondered if the long-awaited wind had come at last to put me out of my misery and blow shreds of windsurfer all the way to Norway. Instead came a monumental downpour, the rain so thick that all was obscured by a curtain of grape-sized raindrops. This was the first major rainfall that I had encountered during the whole journey and I found it most agreeable. Being permanently wet anyway, rain was like water off a duck's back and I tipped my head back, letting it plaster my face, washing the salt out of my eyes and removing for once the salt taste from my mouth. The sea looked unrecognisable under this concerted attack, the waves cowed and flattened like dunes by the raindrops, and a diffuse mist drifted across the surface. It put me in mind of some futuristic moonscape which I was forging across like a twenty-first-century explorer, one eye closed against the driving rain.

In this refreshing manner I reached John o'Groats and so became the first person to windsurf the thousand-odd miles from Land's End – it had taken forty-nine days. Before I had time to bask in the glory of this achievement or question whether it might have been easier by British Rail, I was plunged into the familiar confusion of squabbling waves and more overfalls. I was off Duncansby Head itself. Ahead, *Morningtown* was being tossed like an ice cube in a cocktail shaker; it always astonished me how much punishment she could put up with. I hung on grimly willing myself not to fall in, knowing that this was the Pentland Firth playing its final card.

Once round the headland, the red-black cliffs that earned the name 'Iron Coast' for this inhospitable stretch to Wick came into view. Their most unforgettable feature is the Duncansby Stacks, a group of isolated rocks chiselled to fine points by the sea and waiting to rip into the bellies of any ships (or sailboards!) unwary enough to venture too close. The rainstorm had passed over and the wind was softening considerably. I tacked away from the stacks looking for more breeze and headed east towards a large northbound tanker, the first ship sighted all day.

Far from filling in, the breeze withered still further until there was little alternative but to stop and sit on my board. *Bumble* came up to pass on a message from the RNLI to the effect, so I thought, that there had been a large press conference that morning and everyone sent their congratulations. Visions of the world's press intently watching my every move by satellite and spotter plane pleasantly swelled my head for several hours until I learnt that Charlie had somehow garbled the original message over the radio; it had simply been, 'The RNLI send their congratulations – everyone is very impressed.' This was the first on-the-water message I had received from RNLI Head Office. How fussy of them to worry so much about the Pentland Firth, I thought. Here I was, not three miles past it, sitting idle in calm water.

The sun came out and warmed the stillness. I felt very much like a doze and stretched out on the board and shut my eyes. How incredibly peaceful it was – no noise of telephones or roar of cars, just the odd calling of a bird and the lapping of water against my board. I must have nodded off because, when I next looked up,

Duncansby Head had receded several miles into the haze. I was drifting south at a respectable speed with the tide.

Paul came on the radio to say that the Pentland coastguard were reporting twenty-five knots of wind just a few miles north in Orkney, so I just had to hang on and wait. Pilot George was recommending the area as a rich fishing ground so, it being a period of relaxation, I decided to try my hand at catching our supper. I put a line down at about 150ft and, attaching it to my leg so that I should be warned of a catch, awaited developments. There was no chance of my endangering the livelihood of any Scottish fishermen, not even a nibble, the only sign of activity being when I transferred the line from leg to footstrap on hearing from George that a school of piebald killer whales were regular visitors to the area. However good Chris thought it would be for photos, I had no desire to be towed back through the Pentland Firth by five tons of whale!

While I fished, those on *Bumble* and *Morningtown* engaged in a civil war, throwing water and eventually more indelible substances at each other. The battle that day culminated with Paul emptying the gash – porridge, vegetable peelings, and the like – on to Chris and Charlie as they came alongside. After this the war became a regular feature on days when the sailing was slow.

My fishing came to an end as the sea woke up with a gentle shiver to the first stirrings of the long-awaited gale. The wind stayed light till I was about five miles south-east of Wick where, having taken a good bite out of the long haul across the Moray Firth, I decided to stop. It was 7pm and I had covered forty crucial miles in the eight hours' sailing. Almost as soon as I touched the rigging to dismantle the sail, the wind took a surge in strength and by the time we were motoring back to Wick it was blowing a solid force 6 from the north-west. We had a rough hour bashing into the head sea and several of us felt sick till we got under the lee of the land.

Mark was waiting for us on the quay of the little fishing port, proudly displaying his two plaster-of-Paris arms. He could not seem to get down the ladder set into the stone quayside until Alice produced a bottle of champagne. Several others who were standing on the dockside joined us for a drink, including the lifeboat coxswain and the honorary secretary, both of whom looked so lugubrious that we kept thinking they were about to burst into tears. There were three things to celebrate: Mark rejoining us; passing unscathed through the Pentland Firth; and being on the way 'downhill' at last. Everyone was in excellent spirits and, with the help of Bacchus, we slept soundly that night.

It was a midday tide the next day, 21 June. Over breakfast at about 10am Paul and I decided to go for the 'big bang' across the Moray Firth all the way to Fraserburgh and save two days on the coast-hugging route. It was a windy day, the remnants of last night's gale still in evidence but with a forecast maximum of force 7 for Cromarty, we thought it safe to have a go. The lifeboat honorary secretary appeared looking more cheerful than yesterday and confirmed that we ought to be blown across pretty quickly. Dashing ashore to make a quick phone call I was nearly knocked into the harbour by a vicious gust of wind that swept onto me across the roofs of the harbour buildings.

The phone call was to arrange a live interview with Radio 2's John Dunn Show. The latest they could manage that day was 7.15pm, which gave me just seven hours to cover some sixty miles across the Moray Firth. Looking out of the call-box window at the wind-lashed harbour I decided that the crossing would either be possible in seven hours or not at all and, sprinting back to the boat, the adrenalin began to flow.

We nosed out of the harbour into a breathtaking seascape: the blue water was flecked with wind-blown spray glittering in the sunlight as it frothed down the wave fronts. I looked at Paul and met his smile – prospects seemed good. My exhilaration soured rather on the way to our starting point as I began to feel sick. Once again it was an enormous relief to flounder off *Morningtown* onto the board. The beginning of the run was shaky while the feeling of sickness wore off and the wind made up its mind what force it was going to blow. I was using *Pytheas II*, the speed board, expecting a good fast reaching slant, but I lurched uncomfortably for the first hour and tried three different sails before settling on the 6m. Everyone, including myself, was beginning to wonder if this dream run would materialise when suddenly the breeze came just right and I was away down the waves.

It was indeed a perfect reach. *Morningtown* was quickly left behind and I followed my own course, trusting to the wind for direction until I could make out the land ahead. Puffy, cumulo-nimbus clouds scudded across the blue sky, the sun dappling the water and my board became a magic carpet, skimming down one heaving wall of water after another. At times we barely seemed to touch the sea and I

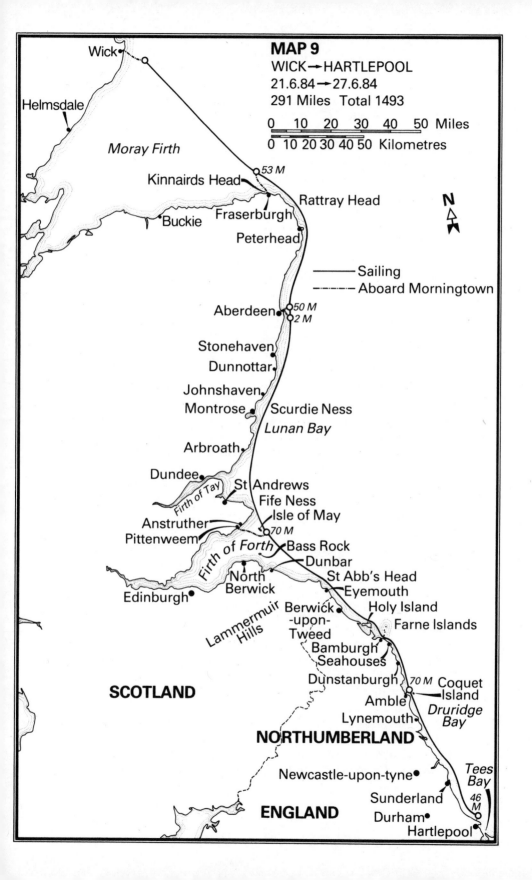

MAP 9
WICK → HARTLEPOOL
21.6.84 → 27.6.84
291 Miles Total 1493

0 10 20 30 40 50 Miles
0 10 20 30 40 50 Kilometres

Wick

Helmsdale

Moray Firth

Kinnairds Head ○ 53 M
Rattray Head
Fraserburgh
Buckie
Peterhead

———— Sailing
—·—·— Aboard Morningtown

Aberdeen ○ 50 M
○ 2 M

Stonehaven
Dunnottar
Johnshaven
Montrose Scurdie Ness
Lunan Bay
Arbroath
Dundee
St Andrews
Firth of Tay Fife Ness
Isle of May
Anstruther ○ 70 M
Pittenweem
Firth of Forth Bass Rock
Dunbar
North St Abb's Head
Berwick Eyemouth
Edinburgh Holy Island
Berwick Farne Islands
-upon-
Tweed
Lammermuir Bamburgh
Hills Seahouses
Dunstanburgh 70 M Coquet
SCOTLAND Amble Island
Druridge
Lynemouth *Bay*

NORTHUMBERLAND

Tees
Newcastle-upon-tyne *Bay*
Sunderland 46
Durham M
ENGLAND Hartlepool

found myself singing at the top of my voice. I would make perhaps a small tweak of the sail to keep the board on the plane at the top of the wave and then down we went. It was the thrill of a roller-coaster combined with the freedom of the ocean.

Time and miles flashed by in this effortless way and soon I could make out blue humps on the horizon that were the high ground on the southern shore of the Moray Firth. I bore away 20° or more, aiming a course for the eastern tip of land where Fraserburgh lay, and on this line stormed on until land was a clear unbroken line ahead. Muscles were now demanding rest; I had been sailing for five hours and I stopped for a cup of coffee and a chocolate biscuit in *Bumble*. Behind us *Morningtown* looked like a paper boat on a saucer. We watched her grow and grow until she was almost upon us and then I set off again.

To clear Fraserburgh to the east, I had to bear away several degrees more until I was almost on a run and unable to maintain planing speed. The sailing lost its magic and I began to grow tired; I even changed to the *Log* for the last hour. There was one more treat in store for us. Way off east I spotted an orange-brown smoke haze and beneath it the glint of metal. In what seemed like seconds, three naval frigates passed right in front of us, travelling at a good twenty-five knots. It was magnificent to watch the contemptuous way these iron sharks punched into the waves at such high speeds, spray flying up from the nose and dancing almost the full length of the ship. Five minutes later three more appeared like lightning from the horizon and *Morningtown* had to about-turn rapidly to avoid them. We all waved and shouted and tried to raise a response on the radio as they passed, but they seemed less than communicative – not even flashing a Morse message of *bon voyage*. We found out the probable reason later: they were German ships on a NATO exercise and had no doubt been forbidden to fraternise with ocean-going windsurfers.

We were some five miles short of Fraserburgh when I stopped for the day, leaving myself half an hour to reach land and a phone box. I had covered fifty-three miles in six and a half hours at an overall average speed of seven knots, my best to date. *Bumble* ferried me to *Morningtown* and I jumped on board to gather some extra ten-pence pieces. Expecting smiling faces after the day's excellent progress, I was surprised to find instead a fed-up-looking crew. In contrast to mine, their ride today had been one of the most uncomfortable of the trip – bludgeoned continuously by the waves. Furthermore, they seemed displeased that I was rushing ashore for a media commitment, temporarily forgetting that my sponsors had made the whole thing possible in return for these small media favours. With no time to explain, I grabbed the money and was back in *Bumble* in a second.

Charlie made good time to Fraserburgh and, locating a quayside phone box with a few minutes to spare, I crossed the road to the nearest pub for some Dutch courage. The sight of a man clad in black rubber dripping water must have been a rare one in this part of Scotland, because all heads turned to look at me, mouths open and eyes staring. Such was my ebullient mood that I could not resist the challenge, 'A pint for anyone who can guess what I've just been doing', addressed quite loudly to the bar. Suggestions ranged from deep-sea diving to cleaning drains to a rubber-only party. My pint was safe.

The John Dunn interview went smoothly enough. After that I was interviewed by Moray radio (Scottish local) who surprised me by asking how I responded to allegations by a Wick fisherman that my crossing of the Firth had been foolhardy considering the dangerously strong winds. I was quite indignant but left feeling rather puzzled as to the identity of this fisherman since we had not spoken to any in Wick. It later emerged that our old friend Jim Henderson had put some fellow up to it, staging the whole incident for the sake of some media controversy. In similar vein he later complimented me on having travelled from Wick to Fraserburgh faster than he could have done in his Honda Civic!

Spirits improved considerably back on *Morningtown* and we entertained first the harbour master and then Tommy, the friendly lifeboat mechanic. Fraserburgh is a large fishing port with several dock compartments, bristling with trawlers and other fishing craft, including huge factory boats complete with their own freezing chambers. Doubtless attracted by the abundance of fish scraps, there were literally thousands of seagulls swooping and flying everywhere and the quayside was carpeted with a thick layer of guano.

After supper Alice and I repaired to a nearby pub for a quiet drink. Wearing our Henri-Lloyd expedition jackets, we were recognised by the barman who plied us with interested questions and saved us from the attentions of a rowdy drunk. When we came to leave, the barman offered us some herring. We then had to choose between this and some salmon which we were suddenly offered by a neighbour at the bar who worked on an oil rig and poached part-time. In the end we decided against the 'hot' salmon for a price in favour of free herring. The barman called a friend of his who led us off to the docks.

Herring were being sucked up from the bowels of a trawler, salted and packed into large bins for loading onto a lorry and export to the Continent. A dozen men muffled against the cold wind were working through the night on this efficient production line. Our friend said something to one of the workers, stepped forward and held a large carrier bag under the stream of glistening fish. A few seconds later he turned round, the bag groaning with breakfast, and presented it to Alice with a smile. We were delighted with the present, made all the more significant by the fact that we were eating one of the first herring catches after seven years of prohibition due to overfishing. Alice had got fish on the brain and was up early the next morning to visit the fish market where she was amazed by the variety on sale. She was almost persuaded to go off on a trawling trip with a Grimsby fisherman, but came back instead pulling faces to imitate the fish she had taken a fancy to.

We did not need to sail till 3pm to catch the tide so it was a morning for washing, shopping and taking on water. I had a quiet cup of coffee and a sandwich in town and then walked back to the boat in a freezing wind and heavy rain. A journalist was waiting on board to interview me and a raven-haired, high-heeled photographer persuaded us all out on deck into the wind and rain for a picture.

Once again on our own, we held a council of war. The forecast for Viking, Forties, Cromarty was north-westerly 6–7 and rain, exactly what we had now. It was one of those days when no one seemed very keen to do battle, but we poked our heads out all the same. As soon as we rounded Kinnairds Head and started heading north into the weather we all wished we were back in the shelter of Fraserburgh harbour. A big sea was running and the wind was not only gusting savagely but bitingly cold so that hands and face were white and numb in seconds. 22 June, almost Midsummer Day, was certainly the coldest day of the trip! The decision of whether or not to sail was soon taken out of our hands: a particularly fierce barrage of wind was followed by a crunch on the foredeck. Haydn and I rushed forward to rescue the *Log* which was trying to escape over the stanchion rail. Examining it, we found a four-inch tear in the tail and a square hole through the board where it had smashed on the anchor.

Paul and I both blamed ourselves for having forgotten to lash the board down. It would not happen again. There being no chance of continuing with the *Log* out of use, back we went to Fraserburgh. Entering the basin we nearly ran down a smaller yacht; it really was not our day and a good thing we were not out at sea. The decision to return was vindicated by the course of the weather which deteriorated and by late afternoon a full gale was blowing.

I changed mental gear from psyching myself up for a tough forty miles on the board to wondering how best to get the *Log* repaired speedily. The obvious place for surgery was the lifeboat shed, as in Oban, and Tommy was only too willing to help, providing us with full use of the facilities including a key to the shed, tots of whisky and a heater to speed up the repair. All the lifeboat men we met were such great people. Paul and Charlie arrived to help and while we dried, sanded, filled and glassed the holes, we chatted to Tommy. Fraserburgh RNLI were in the process of running their own appeal to raise £435,000 for a new Tyne Class lifeboat. In recent years, two new boats had been lost in the terrible winter storms that are a feature of the north-east coast.

I stayed in the shed till midnight nursing my board and returned the next day to give it a coat of white paint. I was sure a bright finish would pep up the board's morale and make it go faster! Charlie and Chris met up that night with some garrulous fishermen in the pub and fell into hot water when they offered to light one of their fellow drinkers' cigarettes. The fisherman looked grave: ever since a local trawler called *The Swan* went down with all hands, none of them will have anything to do with Swan Vestas matches! Charlie then became involved in a drinking competition and did not come back till the next day – with a headache.

After lunch, Paul and I took a walk to the lighthouse to look at the sea. The wind had quietened down to about force 4 and the sea was flattening. We said goodbye to Tommy with yet another bottle of 'giggle water', and carried the board – still tacky with paint – back to *Morningtown*. We motored the five miles north into the Moray Firth and at 4.45pm I began sailing, now heading for Aberdeen. Expecting the wind to slacken further, I took the 8m sail and the *Log* and was pleasantly overpowered at first. I surged along with the wind behind me, reaching Fraserburgh again in less than an hour. It was a crisp, sunny afternoon. The beach to the east of the town was sandy and inviting, probably excellent for surf, but there was not a soul about. I looked towards Fraserburgh and wondered whether Tommy would be watching as we sailed by.

A few miles beyond Fraserburgh I came across Cairnbulg lighthouse jutting out of the sea ahead and surfed down the breaking waves between it and the shore. All around me gannets were diving and showing off. I guessed they were picking off salmon in the shallows as they migrated north towards the breeding grounds in the River Spey. Right on the shore was a links golf course: I was so close that I could surely have watched the rhythmic swing of the players' clubs had anyone been there, but for some reason on this lovely June evening the fairways were as empty as the ocean ahead. Now I was opposite a glorious sandy beach that stretched for miles and miles, interrupted only by Rattray Head all the way to Peterhead. The Fraserburgh harbour master had told us that in World War II forty allied ships were driven onto this shore by German fighters. You can still see some of the wrecks at times, but today the bay was putting up an innocent front and nothing was visible.

I had been windsurfing non-stop for over two hours and began to exercise my neck to soothe away some stiffness. Craning my head round I caught sight of what looked like a vast office block steaming along behind me. I whisked round for a longer look and identified my 'tail' as an oil rig rather than a skyscraper, though the size was much the same. 'Welcome to North Sea oil country,' I thought, feeling incredibly small. The rig gave up the chase at Peterhead, probably, I thought, to refuel – a clear victory for wind power over fossil fuels.

After Peterhead the coast curves south-west and, with the wind still north-west, I was able to harden up onto more of a broad reach which stepped up my speed nicely. Three hours later at 10pm my body told me to pause for a rest and I made my first pit stop after a record stint of over five continuous hours. This was to be my steadiest session of the whole journey: 6½ hours at 6½ knots making a total of 50 miles and all accomplished in these gentlest of conditions by just keeping going.

Beginning my final hour's sailing, a huge orange glow soon began to dominate the darkness ahead. Gradually, the features of a large city could be distinguished and clumps of glittering skyscrapers stood silhouetted against the black sky. This was Aberdeen, oil capital of Britain and often dubbed the Dallas of Scotland.

Wary of being run down in the dark by one of the multitude of ships plying in and out of the harbour, I came to a halt level with the lighthouse on the north pier just short of a promontory called Girdle Ness. Tired but happy I climbed onto *Morningtown* and hungrily ate a delicious supper of liver and bacon followed by rice pudding, and then watched in fascination as we entered the complex port on the mouth of the Dee. It was like a marine Spaghetti Junction choked with a collection of ships that would not have disgraced a James Bond or science fiction movie. We found a berth in one of the rear basins, thinking we were out of reach of these predatory oil-support vessels. In the morning, however, we had to move in a hurry to avoid being crushed like a ripe watermelon by a dinosaur of a ship that manoeuvred in next to us. Its principal feature was a great steel mesh helicopter pad that hung dizzily above the height of *Morningtown*'s mast.

24 June, day fifty-four of our voyage, dawned hot and muggy. It was a Sunday and we were not sailing till 5pm, so the day began with kippers and a leisurely read of the Sunday papers. Reading Sunday papers reminds me of eating Chinese food, filling at the time but an hour later you feel hungry again. Soon after breakfast we were treated to the uplifting sight of the camper, newly risen from the grave, rolling onto the quay beside us. We all clambered ashore to ogle at the damage and meet our new team member, Chris

Longman, who had kindly volunteered to act as chauffeur and assistant to Mark. It was ironic that Chris had missed his bus the night before and Mark, the crazy plastered fool, had driven forty miles to pick him up.

The rest of the morning and early afternoon was spent in cleaning up the truck, manufacturing new numberplates (the originals had stayed in the ditch) and rebuilding the trailer. At 4.45pm as we prepared to leave harbour, a broadcast came over the radio: 'Attention all vessels. A windsurfer on his way round Britain will be passing Aberdeen later today. Please keep on the lookout.' Something about the way the harbour master issued the message convinced me that he was referring to someone else. 'There must be another guy right behind,' I thought with a fright. My misapprehension, however, lasted only a few moments. Common sense soon told me that it was too much of a coincidence to be true; it was absurd to imagine that someone would have staged an attempt in secrecy and crept up behind me like this.

Chris, however, was not so easily shifted from the view that we were indeed being raced, and some ingenious propaganda from Haydn prolonged this illusion for several days. The game climaxed when Haydn kidded Chris that a board and sail floating unattended a few hundred yards off *Morningtown*'s stern belonged to our pursuer (though it was in fact my own). Chris was sent over to investigate and reported back that the brave windsurfer had vanished without trace, the effort of catching us up evidently being too much for him. My rival was thus pronounced missing, presumed drowned, and I, of course, claimed salvage of his equipment.

Competition or not, we were passing Aberdeen for some considerable time on that June day. Beginning by the lighthouse at 5pm I had made it just past Greg Ness, a mere two miles further on, by seven o'clock. An oil rig stood impassively as I beat painfully backwards and forwards into a fitful southerly breeze. It was cold and after a time my hands began to ache from gripping the boom. I did not feel like carrying on with this uphill struggle. Try as I might, I was unable to break through my impatience and discomfort; it just became worse, mainly because the pitiful reward for my efforts was measured so clearly on the land next to me. Eventually, I laid down my rig in disgust and, having told Chris and Charlie at great length how much I had hated the last two hours, I drank a cup of coffee and ate some chocolate. This warmed me up and I began to feel better. *Morningtown* was stooging up and down looking bored so I radioed Paul. To my relief, he was as keen as I on abandoning for the day and, our intention to anchor thirty miles away in Lunan Bay unfulfilled, we motored back to Aberdeen.

A superb dinner compensated for any disappointment. Charlie's girlfriend, Cheryl, had joined the boat bringing with her a mighty chunk of fillet steak which was made into delicious *boeuf en croûte*. Mark and Chris, who had raced off many miles down the coast, arrived back late and tried to make us feel guilty about not leaving them any supper. The tables were turned when some judicious detection work from Haydn produced evidence from the truck of the consumption of a substantial take-away.

The forecast for sea area Forth on 25 June was perfect – sunny with a strong offshore wind, north-westerly 5–6, which should mean flat water and a fast reach down the straight north-eastern coast. At 7.45am we left Aberdeen harbour for the second time, kissed goodbye to the 'sea of black gold' and started off on an astonishingly successful day.

The day's beginning was peculiarly unpleasant. Taking the 6m sail and *Pytheas II* I shot off southward at high speed in the powerful, gusty breeze. During the first half-hour of a session, while my body had still to adjust once more to the day's sailing and to the particular rhythm of the wind, I was prone to mistakes particularly in testing conditions. On this occasion I had not gone a mile before a malicious blast of wind flattened me. My sheet hand was torn from the boom and the sail collapsed on top of me. I was in a position that used to give me nightmares before the trip began and that I had been careful to avoid – until now. With the harness line snagged on my chest hook I was trapped under the sail in the water and unable to breathe.

With most harness jackets one would simply unclip the quick-release buckle and swim out. For reasons – and vital ones – of comfort over long distances, my jacket had leg-straps and four clips requiring release. Jettisoning the harness was impractical and the only way out was to unjam the harness line itself – with fingers made clumsy by rubber gloves. I managed in the end and spluttered to the surface feeling distinctly fragile. I now wanted a smaller sail and there followed a half-hour of unsteady sailing before I finally took hold of the situation, once again with the 6m sail.

I sped down towards Stonehaven, keeping a few hundred yards from the shore for the cleanest wind and making a steady eighteen knots, drawing away from *Morningtown*. The coastline here, enhanced, no doubt, by the speed and crisp conditions, was stunning: a lush patchwork of fields sloping back from the low cliffs. I could not disagree more strongly with those who had warned me that the east coast was dull.

I reached Stonehaven at 9.30, one hour after starting from Aberdeen – seven miles an hour despite the stops. Then I was passing Dunnottar Castle, a sprawling ruin perched about 150 feet above the

(*above*) Chris Longman finds a sponsor while Mark alerts the media to our arrival in Lowestoft; (*below*) Passing Felixstowe with the 10m sail

(*above left*) Southend pier, 1800 miles up; (*above right*) Time for champagne;
(*below*) Celebrating with local constabulary and lifeboatmen

waves on a plateau detached from the cliffs. After this unique sight my eyes faced ahead once more and focussed on a fishing boat trawling along in front of me, its brightly painted blue hull glinting in the sun. Overhauling it fast, I realised that with all this ocean to choose from the fishing boat was going to be directly obstructing my path. At the same time I was wrestling with some particularly wicked gusts of wind and was loath to get too close to the boat at this speed for fear of running right into it by mistake. By a combination of luck and skill, with a quickening pulse and a fair amount of swearing, I scraped past the little trawler, muttering under my breath, 'Won't see you again in a hurry, mate!' as I zoomed on south.

But things did not go quite according to plan: the wind strengthened dramatically, sweeping down on me in great waves like attacking cavalry. I held out for as long as I could, straining with every ounce. In the end sheer cowardice got the better of me. I knew that if I carried on some part of board or body would be bound to snap, probably the latter. Laying down the rig to wait for my support to catch up, I looked upwind with awe at the turmoil of froth that had temporarily beaten me.

The first boat to catch up with me was the blue fishing boat, steaming blithely past at what I would describe as a recklessly close distance. A fawning flock of seagulls, seemingly oblivious to the wind, wheeled above the boat shrieking with delight. I bounced up and down in the wake of the receding vessel and saw that her stern-plate bore the name *Perseverance*.

Soon I was armed with the 4m sail. Cutting inshore for reduced wind and even flatter water, I began to move with unprecedented speed, skimming along at over twenty knots and relishing all that the wind could throw at me. In conditions like these, thoughts about anything but the physical concerns of sailing were at most fleeting. The concentration, the exhilaration and the sensation of miles passing under the board were what occupied me and were more than enough to satisfy the conscious mind.

In a wind lull off Johnshaven I changed back up to the 6m sail and, extended to my limits once again, continued across Montrose Bay towards Scurdie Ness. I drew well ahead of *Morningtown*, and even *Bumble* could not keep up with the speed at which I was 'making palm trees'! We had adopted this term, first coined by Paul during his sailing days in the Caribbean; a good pace meant passing quickly down the line of palm trees fringing the beach, hence 'making palm trees'.

Eventually, the remorseless pace set by the near-perfect wind began to expose a few chinks in the armour: my eyes were stinging painfully from the constant spray which was burnt quickly to salt by the hot sun; my knees and thighs developed cramp from being continually bent in the same rigid position. I was being worn down and moved my feet around, looking for relief from the discomfort.

Another ruin slid by, Red Castle, once owned by Robert the Bruce, which dominates the golden sweep of Lunan Bay. Just as I was thinking what a superb place it would be to have a house, let alone a castle, a coincidence of wrong footing and a strong gust of wind caught me out. Unable to bear away in time to absorb the blast, the board slewed upwind and stopped dead, while I carried on, flying forward onto the mast and boom and landing with a crunch. I rolled onto my back in the water and lay there nursing a deeply bruised elbow and a throbbing shin. Not wanting to waste time I waterstarted and carried on, but a pause for rest was soon forced on me when I unwittingly sailed into the lee of Red Head Cliffs, a 250ft bluff of red sandstone, and out of the wind almost completely. After drifting aimlessly for a while I decided to eat lunch. Gazing towards the blue land on the horizon ahead, I could see the tops of the Lammermuir Hills in East Lothian, south of the Firth of Forth. It was unbelievable how far I had come – nearly fifty miles – and it was still only one o'clock. There were many more miles in me yet.

After lunch I scrambled my way past the obstruction of the cliffs and sailed back into a firm breeze that carried me once again at a gallop all the way to Fife Ness. On the way I passed Arbroath – home of the 'smokie', Dundee and another golfing town, St Andrews. To seaward I left the Bell Rock lighthouse that protects mariners from the fatal touch of the Inchcape Reef, once the haunt of a legendary wrecker with the deceptively jolly name of Ralph the Rover. It was the sail of my life: a scenic tour of Kincardine, Angus and Fife at a speed that the most whistle-stop of American tour operators would have envied.

Off Fife Ness at about 4pm I took another break while waiting for the wind to regroup its forces. Paul chose this moment to shin up the mizzen mast and rescue the VHF DF aerial which seemed to be reliving Lundy and had had another attempt at braining one of the crew. From Fife Ness I forged on into the Firth of Forth heading for an isolated island in the middle called the Isle of May. Approaching the island, I could see a seething confusion of white-capped, disorientated waves ahead that I knew meant a tide-race with overfalls. Considering myself something of a connoisseur of such things by now, I charged into the fray with complete abandon – and got a nasty shock.

The standing waves were unusually tall and steep and in a moment I had hit a monster wave, the unnatural union of perhaps three of its outsize fellows. Travelling stupidly fast for the conditions, I exploded up the sheer face of this wall of water and, on reaching the top, just kept going. Some ten feet off the water, though it felt like more, my instinct for self-preservation yelled at me to jump and, slipping my toes out of the footstraps, I let go of the rig and fell back to earth, landing in a welter of spray just behind my board, and glad for once to feel solid water around me.

Once reunited with the board, I proceeded with more caution till I was level with the island and had left the smoking waves behind. A squadron of puffins swept out from their cliff-top home and a solitary gannet looked on imperiously from above as I made my erratic way south. Seventy miles had been chalked up and I was in the mood to sail on across the Firth of Forth and beyond to England; but it was not to be. This was one of the very few occasions during the trip when we were held back by *Bumble*: the boys had underestimated our petrol needs for the day (forgivable, considering the exceptional mileage) and with all reserves on *Morningtown* exhausted, we were now critically short of fuel and would have to stop. It was very disappointing and, huddled in *Morningtown*'s cockpit on our way to port, I stared at the sea contemplating what might have been. It was only 5pm; by ten o'clock I could have covered the magic one hundred miles. But I knew that 'might-have-beens' would not get me round Britain. Seventy miles was still a magnificent day's run, and England could wait till the morning.

We motored due north-west to the Fife coast and, finding ourselves still very much exposed to the fresh west-north-westerly wind, anchoring was out of the question. We arrived first outside the lifeboat town of Anstruther, but the harbour master told us that the harbour was too shallow for *Morningtown* at low tide and suggested Pittenweem, a few miles west, as a safer bet. Knowing from the *Cruising Manual* that Pittenweem is not recommended for yachts because of its narrow entrance, we asked the Anstruther harbour master if he would be prepared to pilot us in there – and were very glad we did.

Bumble was despatched to bring back our pilot. He turned out to be the lifeboat coxswain as well as harbour master and fitted exactly my image of an old sea salt – of enormous build, with a huge bushy beard, a steely gaze and alarmingly long eye-teeth that were revealed in all their fearsome glory when he grinned!

Our first pass at the entrance had to be aborted at binocular distance when the coxswain realised that the tide was not yet high enough for us to get over the entrance mud bar. We rocked around outside in the swell while the tide rose. No sooner had we established that it was now safe to motor in than a fishing boat popped out, followed by a dozen or so more, heading for the night's crab catching.

We made radio contact with the camper parked on Pittenweem quay and Mark now informed us that we were in the clear, no more boats coming out. Duly on our way in and almost at the point of no return where the channel becomes too narrow to turn around, a large white fishing boat squeezed round the corner. 'Sorry about this,' came Mark's plaintive voice over the radio. 'I couldn't get through to warn you.' Paul went white, swung the wheel hard to starboard and we retreated hastily. The fishing boat, however, motored straight after us and began to overhaul *Morningtown* swiftly. Paul did his best to shake off the pursuer but the fisherman soon wrongfooted us and came steaming forward, as if to hit us amidships.

Paul had gone from white to deep red, the coxswain was shaking his head in disbelief and the rest of us were preparing to abandon ship, but at the last second the fisherman threw his engines into reverse and swung hard to port. The vessel slewed sideways suddenly and lay rocking a yard or two off our beam. We eyed the skipper warily as he came up on deck, half expecting him to throw down some bizarre marine gauntlet, a challenge of sorts. He merely said quietly, 'There are four more boats yet to come out.'

It was a relief at last to be out of the wind and swell in the cosy little harbour, built like a fortress with high walls ten feet thick. Mark drove the coxswain back to Anstruther. We loaded up with petrol and spent a comfortable night in a harbour deserted of fishing boats while the wind whistled through the top of the rigging. The strong north-westerly wind was still very much in evidence in the morning as we left Pittenweem at 11am for an hour's motoring to the Isle of May. The Firth of Forth was rough and *Morningtown* actually surfed down the larger waves, feeling like a lumbering whale in comparison to my sailboard.

My sailing began in familiar fashion. The wind played its favourite deception and began to blow like blazes as soon as I had started, forcing an immediate sail change from 6m to 5m. Even the 5m did not seem small enough as the wind funnelled furiously down the Firth, trying to sweep all before it. My arms were wrenched by every gust and the muscles soon became taut and burning with pain; I found myself unable to keep the board on course at all. The speed of a broad reach in the massive waves was too hair-raising for more than short bursts and I was continually hardening up to the wind and slowing down onto a close reach. This gruelling, patchy sailing typified the day and could not have been more different from the day before, although, by an extraordinary coincidence, I covered exactly the same distance – seventy miles.

It was a sharp sunny day and to the west I could distinguish the cone-shaped lump of basalt known as Bass Rock, a remarkable volcanic island rising 350 feet sheer out of the ocean. Once a few miles south of the rock I came under the relative shelter of the land masses behind North Berwick and Dunbar and, in the easier conditions, I was able to bear away back onto course for St Abb's Head and beyond to the north-east coast – of England.

At the head itself, whose light-red cliffs are home to thousands of seabirds, I felt drained of energy and eager for the chance to catch my breath. I stopped for an interview with BBC Radio North East who had just called up. It was 2pm and in the last two hours I had logged fifteen miles, surprising in view of the blustery conditions. The next three hours, however, were less profitable down past Eyemouth and Berwick-upon-Tweed to Lindisfarne. I struggled to sail *Pytheas II* in an inconsistent wind which came sometimes weakly from the north-west and sometimes strongly from the west. I fell in frequently, counting eighteen times during the day, which was certainly a record.

Something positive came from these regular dowsings: I developed a more efficient waterstart. Uphauling the slim unstable *Pytheas II* was never enjoyable and whenever possible I would waterstart. My efforts to waterstart in lighter winds often left me submerged in the sea with the sail hanging precariously above my head, praying for a gust powerful enough to pluck me out. This position is cold as well as tiring and was made more unpleasant by the loose neck-seal on my drysuit which allowed water to seep in and down my back. In my eagerness to escape from the water I discovered that by sliding first feet, then legs and finally thighs onto the board I could ease much of my weight out of the sea in advance, making it easier for the wind to lever out the rest of me. This useful development brought me some satisfaction among all the slog.

At around 5pm, after five hours of sailing, I came in sight of the famous Holy Island. The wind reached its peak of annoyance. It dropped right away for a time and, as the clear sky did not seem to be hiding any more, I changed from *Pytheas II* and 6m to the *Log* and 7m. No sooner did I have the fresh equipment in my hands than the breeze picked up; I was quickly overpowered and forced to change back again. As well as wasting time, the equipment changes caused problems with both *Bumble* and *Morningtown*. *Bumble* was towing the *Log* at speed in the rough sea when the nose dug into the water and the board disappeared below the surface. The *Log*'s descent to the sea bed ended abruptly when the towing eye pulled out and buoyancy took over, forcing the board back to the surface with such energy that it leapt clear into the air like a monstrous flying fish. Shortly afterwards, *Morningtown* also lost a board and there was a prolonged chase through the turbulent water before Haydn managed to spear it through a footstrap with the boat-hook. Meanwhile, I had a board but no sail; I decided to improvise and stood up on the board so that my body would act as a form of sail. In the strong breeze I made reasonable progress and even discovered that primitive steering was possible by judicious angling of the body, particularly arms. Then I was toppled in by a wave and woke up to the danger of getting separated from the board while playing this game.

Holy Island is shaped rather like an electric guitar, the body of which forms the main island while the narrow neck leads to the mainland. From the neck stretches a causeway, covered by the sea except at low tide – the moon firmly controlling the freedom of the island's few inhabitants. As I passed the tide was out, the drawbridge down and acres of sand around the causeway drying in the afternoon sun and wind. I had hoped for a good look at Lindisfarne Abbey but, by the time I had passed Emmanuel Head, the north-east corner of the island, the wind was so fresh that my hands were too full to allow more than a fleeting glance behind me as I flew by.

None the less, a like treat was in store. I rocketed a few miles along from Holy Island across Skate Road and a magnificent great castle came into view, crowning the golden shore ahead. The wind by now was nearly gale force and the 6m sail became dangerously large, so I laid down the rig and waited for my support to catch up. I was now almost opposite Bamburgh Castle. With its immaculately preserved keep and pink-stoned surrounding walls, it looks the part of a medieval fortress. I half expected a couple of monks, having observed my arrival from some lofty tower, to row out with bread and soup to sustain me on the journey!

Instead, *Morningtown* arrived and I had a squabble with Paul about whether we should continue in the rising winds. Paul, with one thing and another, had evidently had his fill of the day and tried to persuade me that there was little hope of further progress now and that I should be satisfied with the fifty miles covered. I, on the other hand, thought that many more miles were possible. It was only 7pm and, aside from the fierce wind, a glorious evening which at that moment I had no wish to spend on *Morningtown*. Finally, the dispute settled, I was allowed the *Log* and 4m sail for a trial period!

While awaiting the fresh equipment I sat and drank in some of the atmosphere of this unique place. West of me lay Bamburgh Castle and beyond it the little village of Bamburgh from where the first lifeboat was launched in the early 1780s. To the east were the Farne Islands, the best known – certainly in lifeboat circles – being Longstone, the island furthest east. It was from here that Grace Darling and her father, the lighthouse keeper, made that celebrated rescue rowing out to a stricken coaster in a storm in 1838 and saving nine men. I looked back up the coast. The wind must now be full gale, the surface of the sea alive with foam and spray. In a short time the waves would grow to match the wind; I hoped I could handle it.

Any thoughts of standing up and sailing my board conventionally were soon dismissed; it was much too windy. First I was sitting and then lying on my back, an identical position to when I rounded Cape Wrath, but this time the waves were closer together and harder to navigate. It was the oddest sensation to be lying down, surrounded on all sides by great, green walls. I could see nothing ahead but tumbling water and steered through the tunnels and clefts in the sea, trusting to the wind that I was moving in the right general direction.

Falling in took on a new meaning as there was considerably less far to fall and involved simply rolling over and into the sea. There was one unforgettable and painful exception. I had hooked myself into the harness while on my back and delighted in what must be the ultimate in lazy windsurfing, having the sail anchored to a supine body. This complacency vanished when a wandering blast of wind caught the underside of my sail and, before I could unhook myself, lifted me off the board and threw me forward like a rag doll to land 180° later with a sickening thud against the rig.

In the Inner Sound between the Farne Islands and the mainland, the sea, aggravated by the rushing tide, doubled in height and confusion. I kept falling in and was struggling to keep going at all when Paul, able to see more than I could from my sea-level vantage point, suggested I head a few hundred yards west into the shallows off Monks House where the water looked comparatively calm. This I did and, sure enough, emerged from the jungle of waves into flattish water fringing a long sandy beach. It was here that I made a refinement to my windsurfing technique that made waterstarting temporarily obsolete. I found that in the phenomenally strong wind I could flick the small rig up and out of the water and sail off, all from a sitting position on the back of the board!

We were approaching the village of Seahouses and the buzz of a strange motor heralded the arrival of the Seahouses 'D' Class, a smart new lifeboat, that ran rings round a bemused *Bumble*, twenty years the senior of the two inflatables. When they approached for a chat I was shocked to hear not Scottish but Sunderland accents from the cheery lifeboatmen. It took a few moments for the implication to sink in: we were now in England for the first time in six weeks. We were really on the way home. It was 8pm and five miles had been covered in the hour since Bamburgh. There were fifteen miles remaining to Amble, our next harbour. After Seahouses the coast bends east a few degrees and, threading my way through some reefs called the Snook, I came more under the shelter of the land. From here I had a two-and-a-half-hour reach until it grew dark, sitting or lying down when the wind blew hardest and standing when I could.

The sunset towards late evening matched the mixed mood of the day: the western sky was all streaks of bright red sandwiched between dark banks of cloud. It was the backdrop for another castle (it should be called the castle coast), Dunstanburgh, a lonely ruin once the stronghold of John of Gaunt. Then 10.40pm found me sailing the last few hundred yards in the dark towards the red pinpoint of light marking the channel between Coquet Island and the town of Amble. We had made it; after ten and a half hours on the water, another seventy miles. I was immensely pleased and proud, particularly after sailing through all the fierce wind. Feeling thoroughly seasoned, in my confidence that evening I believed I could handle anything the wind could throw at me.

Morningtown moored against the old dock in the mouth of the meandering River Coquet. We ate a nostalgic supper of haggis washed down with whisky and afterwards several lifeboat men came aboard for a glass of beer. We got to talking about salmon fishing and the Amble coxswain told us an interesting story about the Duke of Northumberland. He is said to have rights to all salmon caught off the coast as far out as he can ride on horseback at the lowest tide of the year (though how this could be enforced?) – one presumes he chooses the biggest shire horse in the county for the job!

I was woken in the night to an almighty crash against *Morningtown*'s bow. Charlie leapt out of his bed in the forepeak and shortly afterwards I heard him muttering on deck to somebody; apparently, a fishing boat had rammed us trying to get into the diesel bay where we were lying alongside, but fortunately there was no damage. I dropped off to sleep, again with the familiar sound of the wind shrieking in the rigging; tomorrow looked like being another windy, profitable day.

In the morning, 27 June, I went ashore early to make a phone call from the coastguard office and was surprised to see that the office windows were all protected by steel mesh. 'We've had two break-ins here recently,' the coastguard told me rather sadly. 'Maybe it's the unemployment rate, but it's a deal different from the island of Skye where I lived for seventeen years before coming here.' This was a reminder that sleepy Scotland was firmly behind us now. Our conversation drifted on in the English fashion to the weather and specifically fog. The coastguard warned me that we were passing through the peak area for fog, or 'sea-fret' as it is called locally, which stretches from Aberdeen to the Humber. So far the fresh west and north-west winds had kept the air clear as a bell and I prayed that our luck would continue.

Back at the boat a Tyne Tees TV crew were waiting to film a news piece on the trip; we all became rather over-excited, busying round and trying to squeeze into camera. There were a lot more smiling faces around that morning than on most! Later, a party of primary school children arrived on the quay to join in the fun and, still followed by cameras, we made ready and sailed off down the river to head on south.

The forecast for sea area Tyne was north-westerly 6–7, possibly gale 8 at times – a strong following wind, ideal for fast miles. When we began at 11.45am the wind was about force 4 and, wanting to conserve my strength, I took a small sail from the start. In fact, the wind remained at around force 4 all day but I did not mind, being content to plod steadily southwards and rest my arms from the previous day's exertions. We had only gone a few miles, perhaps half-way across Druridge Bay, when *Morningtown* developed a potentially disastrous problem: the bilge pump began to recycle rather than pump out the sea water leaking in from the stern gland. There was half an hour of panic while Haydn and Paul took turns plunging into the steadily rising bilges to try to reverse the process. With a lot of blood, sweat and tears, the pump was mended just before the water level reached the battery boxes and shorted out the whole boat.

The rest of the day was spent sailing down the industrial north-east coast of England. Passing Lynemouth we were sailing over the mineshafts of the Lynemouth and Ellington collieries which extend several miles under the sea. There would be nobody toiling at the faces today – the miners' strike had been in progress for some months – but the area's beaches were still blackened by coal dust washed down from nearby tips. A few hours later we passed the huge industrial area of Newcastle upon Tyne and had to dodge one or two ships plying in and out of Sunderland, Britain's largest shipyard after the Clyde. My primitive sailboard seemed somewhat at odds with this place of smoke and steel.

Our lifeboat friends in Amble had warned us about the salmon nets that proliferate along this coast, each net stretching often for several miles across the main path of coastal traffic. The fishermen patrol their nets in little boats, darting out to head off approaching ships and steering them round the obstacle. It must be a nightmarish job in bad weather or fog, especially when there are several boats coming from different directions. Our little convoy threaded its way through several nets without mishap until some way south of Sunderland.

Morningtown, two hundred yards to my left, was shepherded through a gap in the nets by a fisherman while I was waved on. 'No problem your end' the man shouted across the water. In the foam-flecked sea I did not notice the tell-tale white floats until it was too late and I steamed straight into a net. I was travelling at a good pace and when the fin snagged on the heavy nylon of the net, the board jerked to a halt and I was thrown forward, landing flat on my face on the deck. The accident could not be wholly blamed on the fisherman but I shook my fist at him all the same, hoping that I might get a couple of salmon by way of apology. None was forthcoming, however, the guardian of the nets turning his attention to out-manoeuvring the next vessel that strayed into his territory. I continued rather sulkily, nursing my back and checking for signs of serious damage. Chris and Charlie took the incident very personally and *Bumble* subsequently rode ahead in a vigilant fashion. For the rest of the afternoon raucous cries of 'Nets!' would periodically pierce the warm sunny air.

About half an hour later at 4.30pm I made another, this time scheduled, stop for a live interview with Radio Cleveland. The interview itself was great fun as the disc jockey was both interested and well informed; later I regretted his playing 'Sailing' by Rod Stewart to phase me off the air as the theme lodged in my head for some time.

Initially, I had set my sights on the hat-trick of three seventy-mile days and this meant sailing all the way to Whitby today. As afternoon turned to evening it became clear that we did not quite have the legs to reach Whitby and decided instead to stop at Hartlepool. This made forty-six miles for the day – still respectable in nine and a half hours.

My new sails had at last arrived that morning and included was the 10.5m which would enable me to keep up a good speed even if the wind dropped right off, as it surely must eventually. For the last stretch into Hartlepool, I tried the new fully battened cut in a smaller sail, the 6.5m. The only snag was the window which had been cut out of an opaque material; sailing on a run I was unable to see where I was going. I had to keep peeking round the side of the sail to make sure I was not about to run into something. At the end of the day I was most disconcerted when laying down the sail, thinking *Morningtown* was steaming ahead, to find that she had turned round and was in fact coming straight at me!

We tied up in the rough-and-ready Victoria yacht basin in Hartlepool that is shortly to have a million-pound facelift. I pounded ashore to the nearest pub to ring home and quaffed a most welcome pint of Vaux bitter. My family were taken completely by surprise. 'No, I'm not in Aberdeen,' I said excitedly, 'I'm in Hartlepool!' What a phenomenal week it had been.

11 TEES BAY TO SOUTHEND

The next day dawned very cold and windy, a violent contrast to the muggy weather of the previous day that had even induced me to strip off under my drysuit. While *Morningtown* rocked and swayed under the wind's attack in the harbour, Paul and I debated whether or not to set off on the sixty-five-mile leg to Bridlington. The forecast for Humber/Tyne was north-westerly 6–7 and a friendly tanker in the bay reported thirty-five knots at present and a good 4m swell. We were anxious to keep up the pressure, but these conditions made it dubious. Whitby and Scarborough, our only ports on the way, would probably be closed and there was the hurdle of Flamborough Head to consider, testing in almost any conditions and sure to be horrendous today.

The decision was taken out of our hands by the arrival of Mark. He had just been on the telephone to Charles Heidsieck in London, who were concerned at our rapid progress. 'At this rate you'll arrive back round about Wimbledon Finals [which would mean very little press coverage]. Could you possibly slow down a bit?' It was ironic that after eight weeks of instinctively going as fast as possible, we were now being asked to do the opposite! After all Charles Heidsieck had done for us, and not forgetting the importance of media coverage to the appeal, there was no choice but to lose a day or two, so we immediately declared a rest day. Though I knew that to finish was the important thing, that it was not a race, I could not help feeling disappointed. The time and miles till now had been so hard won.

News of our staying in Hartlepool did not please the grouchy occupant of the next door boat. 'Shove off some place else. You're trespassing on private property!' he growled. Mark was sent over clutching sponsorship forms in a plastered hand and soon we were all the best of friends (there's professional PR for you!). Later, we went ashore and watched a video of the Tyne Tees news piece which had everyone amused, especially the closing shot of me sailing rather diffidently out of Amble to the accompaniment of Wagner's 'Ride of the Valkyries'! Alice was piqued that the camera had faithfully recorded her trying to hide some dirty dishes in the galley, while I came away thinking that I resembled the wild man of Borneo and headed off to down-town Hartlepool for a haircut and shave.

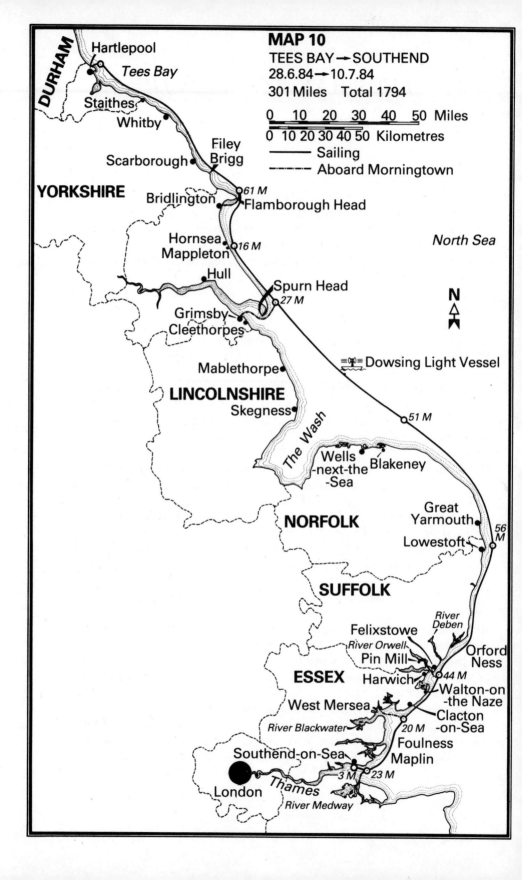

In the evening Mark and Chris Longman drove everyone off to Durham for a 'night on the tiles' and Alice and I stayed behind for a peaceful evening on board. Unexpectedly we were joined by Ian, a disc jockey from Radio Tees and himself a keen windsurfer, claiming to sail in Hartlepool Bay every day of the year that there is wind.

After an interview with Ian, we migrated to an Indian restaurant for hot curry washed down with plenty of beer. We were joined there by several more windsurfing enthusiasts who, among other things, told us something of Hartlepool's dark past! Some time in the sixteenth century a French ship was wrecked off the coast, the sole survivor being a little proboscis monkey. There was great hostility and suspicion between England and France at the time and this fuelled suggestions that the monkey was in fact a Frenchman and a spy! No one, of course, would have ever been to France – this swarthy, small, hairy creature could conceivably have been a Frenchman – and the monkey was tried and hung as a spy. The memory of this absurd barbaric incident has by no means died and the monkey-hanging scaffold is still a popular symbol in present-day Hartlepool.

At 7.25am on 29 June the sixty-five-mile haul to Bridlington began. The wind was north-westerly 4 and I set off across Tees Bay on a run with the *Log* and the 6m sail. The sea was still churned up from the day before, the anchored tankers in the bay rolling rhythmically in a sizeable eight-foot swell. This made the sailing tricky – in the valleys there was no wind, while on the crests of the swells there was a frisky blow – and prompted an early mistake which earned me a ducking and the unwelcome trickle of cold water down my neck.

I was not cold for long; the sun came up and soon the character of the day was established – hot and gruelling. The grind was dictated by commitments we had made to the media to be at Whitby at about midday and Bridlington by early evening. This meant an early start and sailing for the first five hours against the tide. It was galling whenever I passed an anchored lobster pot to see the water bubbling past the wrong way, and to keep up the necessary average I took few stops during the day.

By coincidence, this day was the one on which I fell most in love with the coastline. Being of Yorkshire extraction I had a strong identity with this part of the country but, bias aside, the view of the Yorkshire Moors from the sea takes a lot of beating. The first treat was Boulby Cliffs, just beyond Tees Bay, shelving 660 feet to the sea in great chalk terraces awash with the greenery of bushes and trees. From there the coast stretched warm, varied and inviting for sixty miles – rolling cliffs punctuated with wide bays or valleys hiding

remote, unspoilt villages – and climaxed in the white battlement of
Flamborough Head.

The first village after Boulby Cliffs is Staithes, once home of
Captain Cook. As I slogged past at about 10am we were joined by
the local Atlantic 21 lifeboat which approached with the roaring of
highly tuned twin 60hp engines and the crashing of spray as it
bounded across the swells. The coxswain delighted everyone by
taking each of the crew in turn for a bone-crunching ride in the boat.
He joked with the boys and flirted with the girls, exulting in his
machine like some Marlon Brando of the Yorkshire coast.

Two hours later we were opposite Whitby, also having a Captain
Cook connection, being the birthplace of his three ships – *Endeavour*,
Resolution and *Adventure*. We were greeted as planned by Whitby's
lifeboat, bristling with Yorkshire Television personnel. There was
no time to stop and we conducted an interview on the move with the
lifeboat motoring along beside me. The interviewer took me by
surprise, recalling an early press release of David's which had
described my diet as consisting entirely of 'baked beans and
champagne'. 'What's the reason behind that?' he asked innocently. I
was racking my brains for a suitable reply when a friendly gust of
wind suddenly blew along and I surged ahead. 'I've been waiting for
that gust all day!' I called back, relieved at not having to answer.

When the TV interview had finished, the lifeboat was offered a
thank-you bottle of champagne (no beans) and manoeuvred in to
Morningtown's stern quarter where the bottle was being held out. The
coxswain must have misjudged the swell as the two boats came
briefly together and the lifeboat caught its prow under *Morningtown*'s
mizzen shrouds. There was a wrench before the lifeboat broke free
but the mizzen mast held firm and there was no real damage.
Everyone was tickled pink that our first prang at sea had been caused
by a lifeboat – everyone, that is, except the coxswain, who went
extremely silent on the radio until Paul teased him gently with, 'Is it
all right if I send the bill care of Whitby lifeboat, then?' There was a
muffled, 'Oh,' followed by a pause and then, 'Yeah, sorry about that
mate – she's still afloat is she?'

Once we were on our own again I began to feel rather unwell,
nauseous, and put it down to the curry and beer the night before.
Three hours later off Scarborough I was sufficiently tired to make
my first major stop of the day. It was 3pm and we had covered about
forty of the sixty-five-mile target. I picked at a lunch of Soyabean
Feast and looked across to Scarborough, famed as England's first
seaside resort since 1660 when a Dr Wiltie persuaded the public that
swimming naked in the sea was a healthy pursuit. There was no
evidence of any going on today.

To speed up the miles from Scarborough I exchanged my 6m for the 8m sail and hurried on, somewhat overpowered now, and struggling to control my sail. By 5.30pm I had passed Filey Brigg and was off the long white cliffs running up to Flamborough Head. I looked towards the lighthouse, so tired now that the head would have to be kind for me to have a chance of rounding it. It was not. In fact, everything went wrong: the wind slackened, reducing my speed and stability, and the large swell rebounding off the cliffs made the sea horribly confused. Within a short time I was no longer making real headway and merely slopping about in the chop, at the mercy of the tide. Coming at the end of a hard ten hours' sailing, it was, frankly, a nightmare, ranking alongside the Mull of Galloway as one of the worst experiences of the journey. I fell in once, swore, started again and promptly fell in once more. I sprawled on my board feeling rotten and sorry for myself. *Bumble* came up with a message from Paul: 'Do you want to stop?' 'No way,' I shouted back angry and defensive. 'I'm just resting.' 'Flamborough Head isn't going to go away,' I kept thinking. 'I've got to do it some time.'

But it was not going to be that day. Though I struggled to my feet to try again, I was only upright for a short time before being toppled afresh. Two duckings more and I was finished. Fed up and dispirited I clambered onto *Morningtown* and collapsed onto the aft deck. I found that I was terribly thirsty and it was not until I had drunk three pints of water that I realised I had been seriously dehydrated and suffering from heat exhaustion.

Off my board the world no longer seemed like such a hellish place. I had made sixty-one of the sixty-five-mile target, not a total failure, and Flamborough Head itself would wait till another day. We motored round the headland towards Bridlington and came across half a dozen windsurfers who had sailed out to meet me. I did not want to disappoint them after they had made all this effort and decided to rejoin my board for the last three miles into Bridlington. The breeze was perfect for the 10.5m sail and for the first time and with great excitement Paul and Haydn rigged the acre of yellow cloth on the foredeck. By a combination of luck and skill we managed to transfer the sail from *Morningtown* to the *Log* without it touching the water and I was spared the back-breaking task of up-hauling such a giant. The *Log* stalled for a second while I found the position for my hands on the extra long boom and then I felt the sail's incredible power as it filled in the light breeze and lifted the board effortlessly onto the plane. I hooked into my harness, leant back and purred towards Bridlington, overtaking half a dozen astonished windsurfers on the way. 'We thought you were a yacht,' they said later.

I aimed, as instructed, for the church tower in Bridlington and, when I got closer, for a knot of people on the beach at North Sands. This was the first time I had actually sailed into a welcome and I was excited. In moments the nose of the *Log* ground up the sand and I laid my new ghoster proudly beside it. There were many friendly faces on the beach, among them my parents and grandparents, who live not far away near Hull. The president of the Yorkshire Tourist Board greeted me and a journalist's microphone was thrust forward. 'Apparently you are not well after a bad curry in Hartlepool?' said the voice. I remonstrated that it was probably less the curry and more the result of ten hours in the sun in a black rubber suit. The next day the *Sunday People* carried a little piece entitled 'Surfer encounters ill wind', concentrating on the curry. I had to admit it made a better story!

Mark and Chris had done a great job. Our reception in Bridlington was quite the best of the voyage. The local windsurfing club laid on a superb celebration dinner and, what's more, hotel accommodation for all of us, so that night it was comfortable beds and hot baths (Paul and Liz will be upset if I forget to say that they were martyrs and spent a rocky night keeping ship-watch in the bay!). In the morning Paul and I conferred on the radio and agreed to take a rest day as I was still feeling run-down after the previous day. Perhaps it was for the best that Charles Heidsieck had asked me to take it a bit easy.

While the others filtered off onto the moors, Alice and I spent a relaxing day at my grandparents'. I was reminded of the history that my mother's family has with the sea: my great-grandfather was a Hull trawlerman for sixty years, forty of them as a skipper, and others of the family were in the Merchant Navy and Royal Navy. Maybe there is something in genes after all!

The following day, Sunday 1 July, was warm and sunny and a light sea breeze rolled in as the morning wore on. The tide did not begin to run south from Flamborough Head till mid-afternoon, so we spent the morning reading the papers and entertaining our hosts of yesterday from the Yorkshire Windsurfing Association. It seemed at one stage that half the population of Bridlington were on board. As the breeze hardened I grew impatient, knowing that if only I had rounded the headland during the previous session I could now be gliding comfortably south towards Spurn Point in the fair wind, instead of sitting and waiting for the fierce tide round the head to turn in my favour.

After loading up with petrol and making the ship ready for sea again after the invasion, we said our goodbyes and motored off to the headland, arriving at the spot opposite the lighthouse at 4pm. My apprehension at returning to the scene of former agonies was unfounded as conditions had improved out of all recognition – a steady breeze, a calmish sea and a strong following tide. Beginning with the 8m sail I soon changed up to the ghoster for a fast reach across Bridlington Bay and was staggered by the speed of the 10.5m, even in this lightest of breezes. The outline of Flamborough Head soon faded in the sunny haze and I approached the Yorkshire coast, south of Bridlington. We were hoping that the sea breeze would bend north with the contours of the land and enable me to stay on a reach, but unfortunately this was not to be. The wind stayed locked in the south-east and, though I hardened up as much as possible, I hit the coast at Hornsea and then began an awkward beat south to Spurn. The day's fun was over: I changed to the 8m sail, finding the 10.5m a handful for tacking, and, as the sun went down, began to shiver with cold. I changed out of my wetsuit, which I was using for the first time on the voyage, and back into my drysuit which, despite holes in the knees, was much warmer.

As the tide in our favour diminished, progress on the beat slowed. I did not feel one hundred per cent today and it was a relief when the wind dropped sufficiently so that I could stop with a clear conscience about not wasting miles. It had not been a very profitable day, with sixteen miles to show for four hours' work. The last hour, which was worth just one and a quarter of these miles, was only livened up by a radio call from the *Daily Express*, which made me feel important, and by an outbreak of further hostilities between *Bumble* and *Morningtown*. Haydn began the fun by raiding the hen-house and hanging articles of Chris's clothing over the stern. Chris and Charlie won the day, however, first catching Haydn with an egg as he stood at the wheel and later washing it off with an ingenious water-cannon, made by attaching a rubber tube to the cooling pipe on *Bumble*'s engine. At eight o'clock we prepared to anchor for the night. Mappleton, our finishing point, was an unsuitable spot because of the swell rebounding off some low cliffs on the shore – we could hear the thud as the waves in a cloud of pink spray crashed against the red mud wall. Accordingly we back-tracked a few miles to Hornsea.

The trade-off for a short day and stopping early was that it was to be a creasingly early start in the morning to catch the tide. Alice cooked spaghetti bolognese and we drank some red wine, a rare treat designed to help us sleep. It cannot have helped much because I did not seem to get more than thirty minutes' sleep in the entire night. The anchorage was exposed to the weather and the rising wind produced a nasty swell that rolled the boat and dragged the anchor across the rocky sea bottom. At one point I became convinced –

nightmares reminiscent of Lundy – that we were dragging fast towards the shore; I went on deck for a look where I found Paul relaying out more chain. A short time later it was 4.30am and time to get up. While the anchor was hauled up and we motored back to Mappleton I drank a cup of tea and tried to wake myself up. I felt appalling but was actually glad to be on the move; lying in the tossing boat had been purgatory.

Within twenty minutes I was on the board and sailing. Feeling rustier than ever and so unlike windsurfing I wondered how I would keep going till we reached Spurn. It was only twenty-five miles but the journey could take five hours or more. We were planning to anchor round the corner of Spurn Head in the River Humber where the Humber lifeboat is stationed. The coxswain of the boat is Brian Bevan who must be the best known of any coxswain in the country. He holds the gold medal for bravery, the lifeboat equivalent of the VC and featured in the BBC-TV series on the Humber lifeboat. I was very much looking forward to meeting him and the thought of perhaps spending the afternoon watching Wimbledon on television in one of the lifeboatmen's houses was an encouragement to keep going.

The wind direction was north-westerly force 3 so I was on a run and using the *Log* and the 7m sail. Within minutes of starting the wind rose to force 4 and I changed down to the 6m. To my frustration the wind quickly rose further to force 5 or more and I could hold on no longer with the 6m sail, or what I thought was the 6m. My request to change to the 5m was greeted with howls of laughter from Paul and Haydn. 'You've already got the 5m,' they said, much thrilled. They had anticipated the growing wind and given me the 5 on the first sail change; it says something about my tiredness that I did not spot the difference. Revising my request I now changed to a 4m sail and was happy at last – well in control of the wind and able to thrust steadily down the coast.

Two hours later I nodded off momentarily on my board and came round to find my knees crumpling as I slid towards the deck. I stopped for a reviving cup of coffee and watched a huge black cloud formation approach us from the north. The wind began to gust viciously and then came a tremendously heavy rainstorm. There was no chance of sleeping now and I just counted the yards as I approached the agreed stopping place, the Spurn light vessel. The last hour seemed to go on forever but finally I was there, looking up at the lightship like a huge red bathtub in the middle of the ocean. The four people who comprised the crew and looked as if they had just woken up appeared on deck. They peered incredulously at us through the drizzle as if to say, 'We know why we're here – we're paid for it – but what the hell are you lot doing?'

Morningtown gathered up my 'tools', sailboard and rig. We should have given the lightship crew a quick explanation but left them instead to puzzle it out in the rising storm and headed towards the mouth of the Humber and shelter. There was eggy bread and tomatoes for breakfast which I ate with great gusto, jubilant that my day's work was already over.

A number of big ships were sleeping at anchor in the mouth of the Humber. Approaching Spurn, Paul trained the binoculars on our anticipated mooring spot and found it alive with the crests of surging waves. The Humber lifeboat came briefly alongside and, echoing our thoughts, someone shouted, 'You won't get much peace there!' We would have to seek shelter up the river at Grimsby and all hopes of tea and telly with Brian Bevan were washed overboard. I went down below and crawled into a bunk with a book while *Morningtown* began the long battle up to Grimsby against the tide. The Humber, brown and frothy, was bubbling past us towards the sea at more than five knots and it took an hour and a half to reach Grimsby, as opposed to twenty minutes next day on the way down.

The first thing you notice about Grimsby is the Dock Tower, a three-hundred-foot Victorian finger of brick by the entrance to the Royal Docks. Our entry into the harbour was not smooth: while waiting outside for the dock gates to open we went aground briefly on a spit of mud and once the gates opened we narrowly missed being crushed by a wayward trawler, nearly losing *Bumble* as well when the great wooden gates swung shut behind us. Inside we found the harbour authorities the least sympathetic to our venture of any around the coast and all this prompted Paul to describe Grimsby as fulfilling his worst expectations. We discovered that the name, whatever one may think, originates not from the adjective but from a Danish fisherman called Grim.

The rain continued to batter us throughout the afternoon and Alice and I got thoroughly soaked while being photographed on deck for the *Daily Express*. When another group of journalists appeared, this time from the *Grimsby Evening Telegraph*, I persuaded them to let me accompany them back to town to watch some tennis on their office television, and spent a couple of hours watching Jo Durie win through to the last eight. That evening I spoke to Oliver Moore of Charles Heidsieck on the telephone and it was agreed that I would try to arrive back at Southend on the morning of Tuesday 10 July. This gave us a week to cover the last two hundred miles of the trip – just under thirty miles a day – which was a reasonable target. We were all glad that the uncertainty over our estimated time of arrival at Southend was now resolved.

By midday the following day we had left Grimsby and moored up by Spurn Head where we tucked into a hearty meal. The tide did not run south till past four o'clock, so there was time after all for a chat with Brian Bevan. A soft-spoken Yorkshireman with a strong, confident gaze, he asked many questions about our trip so far, and was keen to hear of our experiences in Scotland. We looked round the Spurn boat, a 54ft Arun, built like a tank but looking inside almost like a dentist's surgery, spotless and organised with high-tech swivel chairs surrounded by banks of equipment.

Going ashore briefly, we took a walk round the end of Spurn Head, the extraordinary five-mile hook of sand that juts out across the Humber estuary. The spit is made of the same sand that we saw being eroded from the coast at Mappleton a few miles north and, in a process of continual change, it is supposed to dissolve and re-form itself over a 250-year cycle. Walking round, the spit felt fairly solid to us; there were even several old gun emplacements there dating from World War II when the Humber was thought a possible invasion target for the Germans. On the end of the spit stands a collection of small buildings, mostly housing lifeboat crew and Humber pilots (the Humber is reputed to be one of the most dangerous rivers in the world). Almost all the buildings are single storey because they are, after all, built on sand. One, however, is a conspicuous exception, the coastguard observation building which is four storeys high and commands excellent views out over the North Sea and back up the Humber. Here at last was fulfilment for my expectation of coastguards looking out over an angry sea.

Haydn and I went to investigate, climbing to the top of the tower and poking our heads round the operations-room door. We were immediately recognised and welcomed. Haydn was intrigued that the Radio 4 Test Match commentary seemed to be playing such a major role in the coastguards' afternoon. We discussed the forecast with them. For Humber they were predicting flat calm for later in the evening. This was not promising as to reach our next port, we faced the longest crossing so far – a hundred-odd miles. I left the coastguards thinking in terms of several days at sea – what a turn of events, then, that in fact we covered the distance in just twenty-four hours!

We set off from Spurn light vessel at 4.30pm, this time without an audience on deck, and headed south-east to Lowestoft, 107 miles away on the hump of Norfolk, well to the other side of The Wash. At first I thought I could just make out land to my right to the south of the Humber and Cleethorpes, but soon there was not even a hint and we passed both Mablethorpe and Skegness on the Lincolnshire coast well buried in the haze over the horizon. When I began sailing the breeze was about ten knots from the north-east and I reached comfortably in my harness using the 7m sail and the *Log*. After two hours, Haydn's clew knot played the same trick on me as it had off Port Quin in Cornwall and the sail collapsed, dunking me in the silty ocean. Altogether, it was an amusing day for Haydn, as later the Humber coastguard came over the radio and gave the cricket score before the forecast.

An hour and a half later at about 8pm we approached the Inner Dowsing light vessel, a large, manned cabin sitting above the ocean on stilts; it must be weird and exciting looking down from there when the North Sea is raging below. Chris suggested that we drop in for tea, but since this involved a long climb up a slippery metal ladder we decided against it. The wind was fading fast and I began to worry about the distance ahead. A short time later a huge cargo ship steamed up when I was flapping helplessly without any wind and nonchalantly ripped at eighteen knots through the gap between *Morningtown* and me. Seeing the ship so close it looked bizarre, a long rectangle of steel with the superstructure like a square white block of flats perched on the end. I watched it disappear into the glowing sunset. It was the most spectacular evening and the pink sky surely indicated a fine day tomorrow and, hopefully, some wind.

Half an hour later I was poised to lay down my sail and stop for the evening when I felt the first stirrings of a breeze on my face and within a few minutes a steady wind was blowing from the north-west. This point of the compass had become a real ally. It was 8.30pm when the wind came. We had been intending to stop at 9.30, but the breeze being so solid and the tide unexpectedly favourable, we carried on for over three hours until midnight, only stopping when it became too risky to continue. It was my first real night sailing of the trip. As it grew dark the lights of the lighthouses and lightships began to appear around me and in the far distance I could see the glimmer of lights from the towns on the north Norfolk coast, probably Blakeney and Winterton. I was pleased because it meant that I had made good distance across The Wash and there would be less to do the next day.

Above me I could see hundreds of stars between the broken cloud and, for the hundredth time in my life, I was staggered by the enormity of the universe. At school my physics teacher once said that the universe is so large that the chances are there's another solar system out there with another earth on which Tim Batstone is sitting in class discussing the nature of the universe. Ever since then I had pictured myself doing such improbable things that not even the most mind-boggling universe could exactly duplicate. Windsurfing across The Wash at night on one's way round Britain surely had to come close, except – and I realised I was missing the point – the universe really is infinite and there is no beating that for possibilities.

When it became too dark to distinguish any contours of the sea, the sailing changed totally in feel. I could no longer see the waves coming and instead bent my knees ready to absorb the impact. I could no longer see the gusts of wind approaching and instead cocked my head and listened for them. This said, balancing was easier than I had expected and any minor impairment of sailing efficiency was far outweighed by the sheer thrill and uniqueness of moving through the inky blackness.

The bad side emerged before long. I fell in and found that the experience took on a whole new and frightening meaning. While I might feel secure on my board and cocky enough to think I could survive a night out on my own in The Wash, as soon as I fell in, it was a different matter. I clung to any part of my gear that I could grab, thinking I was doomed once parted from it. Then, when sailing ahead of *Morningtown* and looking back at the bulk outlined by her navigation lights, the thought struck me that if I fell in now she might run me over, perhaps not even noticing, thinking I was a piece of driftwood. After that I tucked in behind *Morningtown*, and *Bumble* motored along beside me, Chris shining a searchlight on my sail at ten-second intervals which, though dazzling, undoubtedly made things safer.

Towards midnight the numbers and size of passing lights began to increase as we entered a major shipping lane across The Wash. Before long, *Morningtown*'s radar indicated that a ship was heading straight for us and it was time to stop. My excitement at the unique sailing and the achievement of having covered almost half the distance to Lowestoft was soon dampened by the usual onset of queasiness on getting back on board *Morningtown* when the sea was rough. I bolted down my supper and dived into an aft bunk before the feeling of sickness could get any worse.

We spent the night drifting with the tide, hove to under yankee and mizzen. Sleep I found hard to come by as a fresh wind tore mercilessly through the rigging and the waves rocked the boat, sometimes smashing alarmingly against the hull. Lying there I thought about the coastguard solemnly telling me it would be flat calm – I wondered what he thought about it now. He was doubtless asleep, dreaming about cricket. After a particularly hefty crash that seemed to shake the whole boat, I clambered out of my bunk and went up on deck. Liz was on watch at the wheel, cradling a mug of tea. 'It always sounds much worse down below,' she said, smiling.

Though hating myself for it, I still could not seem to get off to sleep and when 8am came and time to get up, I felt predictably dreadful. I cheered up somewhat over tea and toast and by nine o'clock I was back on the board to let the morning sun complete the rejuvenation. The wind was force 5–6 and for once I had the humility or good sense to begin with a small sail (4m) that was no real effort to handle yet kept me licking along steadily enough. *Bumble* was bouncing along beside me, Chris up in front, only his long legs visible as he burrowed beneath an acre of plastic sheet to change films in his camera. Earlier, at the start of the session, he had a scrap with Paul after Paul had dropped Chris's camera bag into *Bumble* to get him moving, Chris yelling, 'If you ever do that again . . .!' He took great pains with his photography that day.

By eleven o'clock I had closed the Norfolk coast and was heading unerringly towards Lowestoft; I would undoubtedly get there today and felt a glow of pleasure that we had broken the back of the last long stretch of the journey. The wind died gradually throughout the morning and I kept changing up sails (ending up with the 7m), managing, with the staunch help of the tide, to maintain a consistent and excellent average speed of nearly seven knots. On the way to Great Yarmouth we came across miles and miles of fine sandy beach, ironically a dangerous place to swim because of the strong tide I was finding so invaluable. Then we passed the town itself, its harbour entrance bristling with gas-drilling rigs and ancillary vessels, and finally reached Lowestoft. It was almost exactly seven hours since breakfast. Catching a sudden powerful thrust of wind, I sailed through the harbour entrance and, dismounting, was greeted by a great cloud of kittiwakes flying up from the eaves of surrounding buildings. Just for fun I stood on my board and let *Bumble* tow me in to the inner harbour, pretending to anyone who was watching that this was the normal method of travel. All went well until Charlie revved the throttle and bowled me backwards into the harbour!

It was 4.20pm when we tied up at the quayside. We had left Spurn Head only twenty-four hours earlier and had covered 107 miles since then. It was incredible. Two weeks into the trip, for example in Cornwall when we were sometimes covering under fifteen miles in the same number of hours, over a hundred miles in a day would have been inconceivable and at best a remote dream. Somehow we had improved and toughened over the weeks. Feeling wonderfully contented I went below and slept till suppertime.

Lowestoft is a popular yachting harbour and we were made very welcome by the Royal Norfolk and Suffolk Yacht Club, quickly establishing a rapport with the club barman, Jim Hawkins, a rosy-faced man with smiling eyes and a former Chief Warrant Officer in the Navy. The following day, 5 July, was a lay day and we took on board a final load of diesel and water. Reminding us how close we were to home, Haydn took a train back to West Mersea to see his wife. The rest of us fanned out into the Norfolk countryside or went into town to send off cards we had intended to post since the Isle of Man.

While reading the *Daily Mail* over a coffee and sandwich, my eye caught a centre-page article on windsurfing entitled 'Captain Courage'. Described was an army captain's attempt to windsurf the three hundred miles from Tewkesbury, Gloucestershire, to Land's End. It was a very worthy effort raising money for cancer research – the captain had recently recovered from cancer – but my indignation was aroused by the words, 'Nothing like this has ever been attempted before.' Here I was with 1,700 miles already behind me, also trying to raise money for charity and equally dependent on publicity in order to do that. I went straight to the nearest phone box and rang the *Daily Mail*, who had previously published a good-sized article on my attempt and should have known all about it (one tiny line of acknowledgement in today's article would have been enough). But there was no satisfaction to be had. I was put through to an anonymous voice on the sports desk. 'What did you say you were doing? Sounds interesting. Tell us about it. When do you start?'!

On the next day, 6 July, I woke to find Martin, my old flatmate, in our cabin. He and Alice's brother, Jamie, had come to join us for several days. We had two other passengers on board, Simon Ollington, who was making a video of a day at sea for us and a freelance photographer. With all the extra people and the closeness to home there was a carnival atmosphere to the day. For me this wore off quickly when I discovered that the windsurfing had not become any easier. I had an eight-hour slog into the wind to cover the forty-four miles to Harwich.

At 10.45 Paul and I slipped outside the harbour in *Bumble* to check on the wind (which turned out to be south-easterly 3) and discovered that the tide was early and slackening already. We made ready to leave and found that Haydn was not yet back. 'We told him to be back by 10.30am,' Paul said, 'but we'd better give him a bit longer. It would be such a shame for him to miss this last bit after coming so far.' My relief when Haydn appeared, smiling, on the quay two minutes later brought home to me what a close team we had become over these nine weeks. It was hard to imagine it all ending.

At 11.20am precisely I pulled my 8m sail out of the muddy brown sea at the entrance of the harbour and was off on port tack along the sea front. There were few people on the beach this early, but it made a nice change to be sailing close even if only to beach huts and deck chairs. For the first mile we were accompanied by a BBC *Look East* TV crew in the yacht club launch; much to their delight I misjudged my first tack and fell in.

I soon settled in for a long hard beat south, my port tack taking me along the shore, my starboard tack almost directly out to sea. The wind was south-easterly 3 plus and it was hot and hazy, the sun glinting off the scum that littered the surface of the brown sea (it looks like soap suds but is apparently a harmless phenomenon of the Suffolk mud). At 1.20pm we stopped for a pizza lunch near the massive bulk of Sizewell power station, noticing several fishing boats close in to the shore. Shoals of fish are attracted by the warm water, which is pumped out at half a million gallons a minute after cooling the reactors.

After lunch things went badly for a time. The tide was well in my favour down the coast, but I mistakenly sailed out of the main surge – by straying in too close to the shore – and made only eight miles in nearly three hours, one of the worst stretches of the whole trip. I was shocked and headed offshore and worked harder to sail close to the wind: tilting the board to leeward, leaning my body out to mirror the curve of the sail, and urging the yellow expanse of the 8m to suck me forward.

I made better ground and at 4.40pm at last reached the end of my beat, Orford Ness, the extraordinary spit of gravel where the Suffolk coast bends south-west. Strong tides give the Ness a reputation for bad seas, but today there were barely any waves and it was difficult to imagine it ever being rough. I still had my problems as the fair tide was petering out and I was slowing down with it. Crossing Hollesley Bay my progress with the 8m became too slow for us to reach Harwich before the tide turned heavily against us and so I changed up to the 10.5m sail, immediately putting on several knots of speed.

Stopping later for a coffee and a rest I found Martin balancing on *Bumble*'s sponson to pee over the side and could not resist nudging him on the shoulder. In he went head-first and I laughed so much that Charlie had no problem in tipping me in after him. It was certainly a hot enough afternoon for a swim and when I continued sailing I donned sunglasses and hat to rest my eyes and head from the sun.

Despite the need to rig the ghoster, the day had not been a particularly challenging one for the support and rescue services. Towards late afternoon they began to work off their excess energies with a battle. *Bumble* roared back and forth round *Morningtown* loosing off volleys of water. Those on *Morningtown* retaliated with a variety of missiles which included left-over dough from the pizza. The fight climaxed with Chris boarding *Morningtown*, pirate-style, and exploding a bag of flour over the occupants of the cockpit. A few hundred yards behind I watched the proceedings, miffed at not being able to join in and that for once I did not seem to be the centre of attention!

At last we passed the River Deben and reached Felixstowe. We decided against going any further as the shipping traffic seemed particularly heavy tonight, Harwich being one of the busiest harbours in the country. We stopped off Landguard Point at 7.20pm and I clambered gratefully onto *Morningtown*. As we motored up the River Orwell to Pin Mill I sat on deck with a beer and, watching the sunset, reflected that after today the hard work was really over. All that remained were two twenty-mile stretches which should present no problem. I would finish in three days.

At Pin Mill, apart from Mark and Chris, we were meeting up with my parents and sister Rose, Henry Farrer, and two other friends, one of them Neville Wakefield from the Scillies. The rendezvous was at the Buck and Oyster pub where you can get a drink 'without stepping off your boat'. This evening, however, the tide was not co-operating and we squelched ashore through several hundred yards of mud. Seeing the numbers of people sipping their drinks on the river bank enjoying the balmy evening, it struck me that summer had arrived without our realising it.

Eventually, we tied up at Woolverstone marina and Alice cooked a magnificent meal for a record sixteen people, while Henry delved deep into his *petit sac* to keep everyone's glasses full of wine. We were tethered next to a Thames barge, all ready for the annual races which, by a lucky coincidence, began the following morning. Thames barges are huge wooden sailing vessels that in Victorian times used to carry grain, coal and hay to and from London. They are flat-bottomed to allow them to dry out on the mud for unloading and instead of a keel employ great lee boards, like wings, that are lowered down from the sides into the water. After supper I went across to have a look at our large neighbour.

It seems that the only cargo barges now carry are people; companies use them for entertaining clients on weekends. One of these lucky fellows emerged from the bowels of the boat as I arrived and I asked if I might have a quick look round. To my surprise, the man gave a categorical, 'No – not convenient,' and then embarrassed my curiosity by tottering drunkenly to the side of the barge and throwing up into the river!

The barges were an unforgettable sight under sail. In the morning, eating breakfast on deck, we threaded our way down the river between the lumbering beasts with their splendid brown wings. There was time to kill before the tide ran fair for the passage south and we anchored in Dovercourt Bay in Harwich harbour and made the most of the sun and light breeze with some gentle windsurfing.

We moved on at 1.45pm. The decks were crowded and the end-of-term atmosphere still prevailed, but this time I was able to enjoy it too, having the easiest sail of the trip. I made the twenty miles past Walton-on-the-Naze and Clacton-on-Sea to West Mersea in under three hours, purring along with the ghoster at eight knots on smooth water and I could not help wondering if my family would think it had all been this easy.

We stopped at 4.30pm in the Wallet Spitway, a narrow channel between Gunfleet and Buxey Sands. Paul's father met us in his yacht *Tramp* and we motored on to Mersea and all the memories. Entering the mouth of the Blackwater I looked round at the familiar landmarks, the placidly anchored ships; Mersea seemed like a much smaller place.

In the evening Jill Hill entertained our entire party to a delicious buffet supper and the celebrations really began. The next day was our last lay day, 8 July, Wimbledon Finals. We played football next to the village cricket ground. Returning to *Morningtown* we were astonished by the bright green phosphorescence in *Bumble*'s wake. It was like the Caribbean – the sparkling little creatures must have multiplied after all the warm weather. Chris became so involved with the phenomenon that he went for a violently thrashing swim in the darkness, first setting up his camera on a tripod with an exposure of a minute to record his antics.

Of the twenty-five miles remaining we planned to cover twenty the next day, leaving us only five miles to do on the following morning; the arrival at Southend had to be accurately timed for 11.30am to suit the PR arrangements. The last full day of the trip, 19 July, dawned hot and muggy and promised a violent act from the heavens before very long. The downpour came at midday and, delaying our departure till the last moment consistent with the tide, we sat in the yacht club bar watching the driving rain and talking about the weather (this trip really had been a chance to indulge an English obsession to the maximum!). It was disappointing that the fine spell appeared to have broken just before I finished – still, tomorrow was the important day.

Morningtown finally left for the Spitway at 2.45pm and as we motored away from Mersea I thought what a different bunch we were from that which had left two and a half months earlier, nervous and wondering what lay ahead. I started sailing at 3.45pm. Not only was it pouring with rain but the wind was blowing from exactly where I wanted to go. Stoically, I began the final beat round the corner of Foulness to Maplin and Southend, eyes narrowed against the rain, armed with the 7m sail in the gusty conditions. After an hour or so the rain eased and there was brief excitement when I ran myself aground on what turned out to be Barrow Sands. *Morningtown* was a few hundred yards off safely in deep water but *Bumble* was behind me and well within signalling range. I kicked my daggerboard up and stood back on the board in the shallow water beckoning energetically to *Bumble.* It worked like a dream. They came zooming over and straight onto the mud.

The afternoon wore on: I was not going as quickly as I had hoped, but there was plenty of tide left and I would get there eventually even if it meant sailing after dark. I knew I was nearing the finish when Red Sands Towers appeared on the horizon, where I had lost my watch and had such a bad time on the first day of the trip; the wartime Daleks looked more friendly now. Passing through The Swin I fulfilled an ambition of the trip, before it was too late, and clambered onto one of the large navigation buoys, S-W Swin. With my board tethered nearby, I sat on the side of the iron bell and drank a leisurely cup of coffee.

By 8.30pm I was off the Maplin Sands and passing along an avenue of ships that seemed to be guiding me up the estuary to Southend. Inclined to dally now that the prize was so nearly in my grasp, I stopped at the small man-made island on Maplin Sands. The little handkerchief of gravel and grass was crowded with birds, some dead or dying and many skeletons. It appeared to be a favourite final resting-place.

Half an hour later I had swung a little further round the corner and, the wind on my beam for the first time that day, I flew along this last stretch of the coast. Southend Pier came into view and in the heat of the moment I kept going beyond the appointed stopping place opposite Shoeburyness power station. I was so intoxicated that I would probably have finished there and then if Chris and Charlie had not roared up in *Bumble* and reminded me to stop. It was 9.30 and I had been on the water nearly six hours. There were three miles now remaining.

Morningtown motored across the Thames and up the River Medway to the West Swale for the night. I ate and then went quickly to bed, tired and wanting to be alone with my thoughts of the morrow. I had known that I was going to make it when things had started going so very well on the way down the east coast. That was when I had privately celebrated. But tomorrow was the finish, the seal on it. It would all be over. No more *Morningtown*, no more team spirit, no more soaking feet. I would miss the sense of purpose, the simple certainty of what I had to do each day, but at the same time the absence of pressure to climb onto my board every day and balance on it for maybe ten hours or more would be a great release – almost, I imagined, like coming out of prison.

On the seventieth day of the voyage we left our anchorage at 9am and were on station off Shoeburyness by 10am. The wind was ideal, force 3 from the south-sou'west. I would be close-reaching or close-hauled all the way to the pier. It should not take more than half an hour and we had to wait to avoid arriving too early. There was a great buzz in the air and constant radio chatter with Mark and all the shore party. Luckily, the sun was out, flitting among the ragged clouds. I began to fidget, looking anxiously towards the pier; at 10.45 I could wait no longer and was away like a greyhound after a hare.

I had said farewell to the *Log* and *Pytheas II* and sailed a new Klepper board (204) for the final stretch. I made excellent ground with the 6m sail and was soon little more than a mile from the pier. Nothing could stop me now. I really was going to make it. Charles Heidsieck would be delighted; the RNLI would be delighted. *Guinness Book of Records* here I come!

In the last mile I was joined by a flotilla of several lifeboats, a police launch, TV launches, dozens of windsurfers, other small boats and even a canoe. What a welcome! I recognised smiling faces on many of the boats. I had not dreamt the whole thing. At last I neared the lifeboat slipway and could read FINISH in big letters. It was official. In the final hundred yards I met the last disturbed wind of the trip, faltered, tacked twice and crossed the line slap in the middle – it was 11.21, Tuesday 10 July 1984.

The BBC news announcer described the last yards thus: 'After 1,800 miles Tim Batstone fell off his board with exhaustion.' I alone knew that at that moment I felt infinitely fresher than when I had set out. Wallowing in the warm Thames, I could have been floating on air. I savoured the feeling for several glorious seconds then climbed back onto my board to a shower of champagne from *Bumble*. *Morningtown* came alongside – all the team were waving and shouting; I toasted them with the half-empty bottle.

Acknowledgements

My grateful thanks to the following:

Alice for her invaluable help with this book.

CHAMPAGNE CHARLES HEIDSIECK without whom the Round Britain Windsurf could not have happened.

The support team: Liz Bindon, Haydn Cook, Chris Darwin, Paul Harrison, Rodney Hill, Mark Hubbard, Chris Longman, Alice Lumsden, Charlie Williamson.

The RNLI; Her Majesty's Coastguard for so diligently monitoring our progress.

And: Klepper for the excellent range of sailboards, masts and booms, and Nigel Fawkes and all at the London Windsurfing Centre; Tris Cokes and Limited Edition for building three good boards at such short notice; Willem Blaauw and Neil Pryde Sails for a superb range of sails; Ron Clarke and Cannon's Gymnasium for providing me with a place to train; John McFadyen and Southampton University PE Unit for monitoring and encouraging my training; Phil Hadler and Thanet Electronics for waterproof radios; Spartan for drysuits and drygloves; Typhoon for drysuits; Gul for wetsuits; Interwind for harnesses; Henri-Lloyd for foul-weather clothing; Pergamon/BPCC for printing; Michael Pettifer of Douglas, Cox, Tyrie and National Employers Mutual for insurance; Imray Charts; Ordnance Survey; Woody Blagg and Blagg Boats; Mariner; Firdell Multiflectors; Yamaha; the Meteorological Office; J. Sainsbury; Silva Compasses; Sky Photographic; Nikon; Fuji; Ilford; Simon Ollington Video; Aquaman; Sony; Jeremy Evans for permission to base the points of sailing diagram on page 10 on his illustration in *The Complete Guide to Windsurfing* (Bell & Hyman).

And my family and friends for their support and understanding.

Appendix I

Liz is back in New Zealand but returning to England soon.
Haydn is out of retirement and working as chief administrator on a hospital project.
Chris Darwin is working as a 'runner' for a film production company.
Paul is training to be an accountant.
Rodney is back running his marine engineering business in West Mersea.
Mark is working as a porter in Harrods while looking for a job in the media.
Chris Longman is finishing his studies at Sheffield University.
Alice is looking for a job in publishing.
Charlie is decorating houses.
I am wondering what to do next.

Statistics

Distance: 1,794 miles
Time: 70 days altogether
      54 days' sailing (average 33 miles a day)
      340 hours' sailing
Speed: average 5.2mph or 4.6 knots
Best stretch: 70 miles
Longest distance in 24 hours: 107 miles

Some approximations:
Points of sailing: 40% of time close to wind or beating
                33% of time running
                27% of time reaching
Boards and sails: 65% of time on the *Log*
                24% of time on *Pytheas II*
                 6% of time on Klepper Division II
                 5% of time on Klepper 103, 204 and 205
                8m sail most popular – 30% of time
                Over 100 sail changes
Average wind speed: 8–9 knots
180 duckings!
The truck, though off the road for a week, managed to clock up 6,000 miles.

'Bloody Cornish wreckers!'
(Merrily Harpur *Punch*, May 1984)

Appendix II

At the time of going to press the lifeboat appeal has raised £40,500. Further contributions to: Windsurf Appeal, RNLI HQ, Poole, Dorset.
We are launching a 'Round Britain Windsurf' Atlantic 21 lifeboat in 1986.

My warmest thanks to all those who supported the appeal, and particularly to **CHAMPAGNE CHARLES HEIDSIECK**.

And to: Bass; Bis Mercers Sailboard Club; Blundell Permoglaze Holdings; *Boards* magazine; Donald Macpherson Group; Douglas, Cox, Tyrie; Gul; Hawker Engineering; Horizon; J. Hepworth & Son; Klepper; John Laing; Neil Pryde Sails; *On Board* magazine; Pergamon/BPCC; Pritchard Services Group; Regent Hotel, Bridlington; Securicor; Spartan; Typhoon; Ultramar; Vinta Sailboards; West Country Windsurfing; Whitbread & Co.; *Windsurf* magazine.

And: Alan Griffin, G. W. Cadbury, Ian Russell, Kevin Maxwell, Mark Hubbard, Ray Healey, William Batstone.

And: Chris Bonington, Sir Ranulph Fiennes and Sir Alec Rose – my patrons.